When Sacred and Secular Mix

Religious Forces in the Modern Political World
General Editor Allen D. Hertzke, The Carl Albert Center,
University of Oklahoma at Norman

Religious Forces in the Modern Political World features books on religious
forces in politics, both in the United States and abroad. The authors examine
the complex interplay between religious faith and politics in the modern
world, emphasizing its impact on contemporary political developments.
This new series spans a diverse range of methodological interpretations,
philosophical approaches, and substantive concerns. Titles include:

God at the Grass Roots: The Christian Right in the 1994 Elections (1995)
   edited by Mark J. Rozell, University of Virginia, and Clyde Wilcox,
   Georgetown University
Let Justice Roll: Prophetic Challenges in Religion, Politics, and Society (1996)
   edited by Neal Riemer, Drew University
*When Sacred and Secular Mix: Religious Nonprofit Organizations and Public
   Money* (1996) Stephen V. Monsma
*The Right and the Righteous: The Christian Right Confronts the Republican
   Party* (1996) by Duane Oldfield, Knox College
Religion and the Culture Wars: Dispatches from the Front (1996) by John C.
   Green, Bliss Institute of Applied Politics, University of Akron; James L.
   Guth, Furman University; Corwin E. Smidt, Calvin College; and Lyman
   A. Kellstedt, Wheaton College
*Beyond Missionaries: Toward an Understanding of the Protestant Movement
   in Central America* (1996) by Anne Motley Hallum, Stetson University
The Christian Democrat International (1996) by Roberto Papini, Trieste
   University, translated and with a foreword by Robert Royal, Ethics and
   Public Policy Center
*A Conscience as Large as the World: Yves Simon Versus the Catholic
   Neoconservatives* (1996) Thomas R. Rourke, Florida International
   University

When Sacred and Secular Mix

*Religious Nonprofit Organizations
and Public Money*

Stephen V. Monsma

ROWMAN & LITTLEFIELD PUBLISHERS, INC.

Published in the United States of America
by Rowman & Littlefield Publishers, Inc.
4720 Boston Way, Lanham, Maryland 20706

3 Henrietta Street
London WC2E 8LU, England

Copyright © 1996 by Rowman & Littlefield Publishers, Inc.

British Cataloging in Publication Information Available

Library of Congress Cataloging-in-Publication Data

Monsma, Stephen V.
When sacred and secular mix : religious nonprofit organizations and public money /
Stephen V. Monsma.
p.   cm.—(Religious forces in the modern political world; 5)
1. Church and state—United States.   2. Freedom of religion—United States.
2. Nonprofit organizations—Law and legislation—United States.   4. Federal aid
to nonprofit organization—United States.   5. Religious institutions—United
States.   I. Title.   II. Series.
KF4865.M664   1996   346.73'064—dc20   95–52003 [347.30664]   CIP

ISBN 0–8476–8182–3 (cloth : alk. paper)

Printed in the United States of America

○∞ ™ The paper used in this publication meets the minimum requirements of
American National Standard for Information Sciences—Permanence of
Paper for Printed Library Materials, ANSI Z39.48–1984.

To Paul B. Henry (1942–1993),
Member of Congress, teacher, friend,
model of integrity

Contents

Tables

Preface

The partnership between government and nonprofit organizations—which has long been in existence—is receiving renewed attention and emphasis. This partnership is most commonly marked by government providing a portion of the funding, with nonprofit organizations providing much of what is considered an important public service in such fields as education and social services. This sort of a partnership has been present in the United States since the seventeenth century and the colonial Massachusetts government's support of Harvard College. In recent years, both scholarly and journalistic awareness of this partnership has been growing. Both the "reinventing government" initiative of the Clinton administration and the conservative revolution in Congress have called for a greater use of nonprofit organizations in a variety of public service programs.

What is almost always missing from the discussion of the nonprofit-government partnership, however, is a consideration of the fact that many nonprofit service organizations are deeply religious in their character and practice. Given American church-state theories, which often emphasize strict church-state separation and no governmental aid to religion, the picture of thousands of religiously based nonprofit organizations receiving millions of dollars in tax dollars raises many profound questions. Yet those questions have gone largely unexplored.

It is these questions that this book addresses. It analyzes Supreme Court legal principles and public attitudes related to religious nonprofit organizations' receipt of public funds, and reports on the results of a nationwide questionnaire survey of over 760 nonprofit organizations from the educational and social service fields. It concludes that religious nonprofit organizations in fact receive much public funding and that they are nevertheless surprisingly free to engage in religiously based practices, but that they are in a legally unprotected, vulnerable situation. It therefore also recommends important modifications in the existing legal principles used to interpret the First Amendment's religious freedom clauses.

My hope is that this study will help religious nonprofit organizations as they seek to navigate the uncertain waters of public funding, the legal community as it seeks to interpret and apply the First Amendment to religious nonprofit organizations' receipt of public money, students of public policy as they seek to understand the nature of the government-nonprofit partnership, and policy makers as they seek to form public policies that make full use of religious nonprofit organizations in delivering vital services without violating the ideal of full freedom for Americans of all faiths and of none.

In writing a work of this scope, one incurs many debts. At the risk of leaving out some whose help I should acknowledge, I want to be certain to express my appreciation to Pepperdine University for a sabbatical leave for the 1993–94 academic year during which I conducted the research for this book and for Calvin College's Center for Christian Scholarship for providing me with office space, administrative support, and an intellectually stimulating atmosphere in which to pursue my research. I owe a special debt to Ronald Wells, its director, and to Kathleen Miller and Donna Romanowski, its able administrative assistants. I would also like to thank Pepperdine University for a University Research Grant that helped with expenses involved in the questionnaire study reported here. Also very helpful in this aspect of the study was the Calvin College Social Research Center, which provided technical advice and assistance. Both its director, Rodger Rice, and its assistant director, Ann Annis, provided invaluable assistance. I also wish to thank the many persons associated with the nonprofit sector who agreed to be interviewed and who shared with me many valuable insights and perspectives. I also surely need to pay tribute to the heads of hundreds of nonprofit organizations that took the time to respond to what for them was yet another questionnaire with many intrusive questions.

I also owe thanks to several scholars who read all or parts of the manuscript and offered many helpful corrections and improvements: Carl Esbeck of the University of Missouri School of Law, Paul Weber of the University of Louisville, Corwin Smidt of Calvin College, my colleague Christopher Soper, and several reviewers who must remain anonymous. Their comments, criticisms, and suggestions have greatly improved this work. I also wish to thank Stephen Wrinn of Rowman and Littlefield for his editorial guidance and supervision. I must, however, emphasize the traditional disclaimer that all errors of fact or judgment are properly to be laid at my feet, not theirs.

Finally, I wish to pay tribute to Paul B. Henry, to whose memory I dedicate this book. He was a public servant in the truest sense of that term, an effective scholar and teacher, a friend it was always a delight to be with, and a person of unwavering integrity. The world is an emptier place since his untimely death.

Chapter One

Nonprofit Organizations in a Pluralistic Society

The Supreme Court has periodically declared in ringing words that no public tax dollars may go to support religion. In one of its most famous church-state decisions, for example, it proclaimed: "No tax in any amount, large or small, can be levied to support any religious activities or institutions, whatever they may be called, or whatever form they may adopt to teach or practice religion." It then went on to insist there is to be "a wall of separation between church and state. That wall must be kept high and impregnable."[1]

This "impregnable wall," however, does not stop a host of religiously based nonprofit organizations—Catholic, Jewish, and Protestant—from receiving millions of public tax dollars. In 1993, 65 percent of Catholic Charities' revenues came from government sources, as did 75 percent of the Jewish Board of Family and Children's Services' revenues, and 92 percent of Lutheran Social Ministries' revenues.[2] The Supreme Court's ringing declarations that no public funds may go to support religion, taken in conjuncion with millions of tax dollars going to a host of religious organizations, ranks among the world's great anomalies. One of the best kept-secrets in the United States is that when it comes to public money and religious nonprofit organizations, sacred and secular mix.

This book explores the world of religiously based, private, nonprofit organizations and their receipt of public funds. More specifically, it considers the church-state constitutional principles and public attitudes under which public funding of religious nonprofit organizations occurs, and utilizes the results of a nationwide questionnaire survey of 766 nonprofit organizations to document the extent and nature of government funds flowing to religiously based nonprofit organizations and the impact those funds have upon their nature and practices. My basic thesis is that the practice of funding most types

1

of religious nonprofit organizations and the Constitutional-legal principles justifying that practice do not mesh, and, as a result, religious nonprofit organizations—although still largely possessing religious autonomy—have been put in a legally uncertain, vulnerable position. This book, therefore, suggests a new principle to guide the public funding of religiously based nonprofit organizations.

This chapter lays the groundwork for the book by developing the key issues mentioned in the previous paragraph and putting them into the needed context. It does so in three basic sections. Since the flow of public money to religious nonprofit organizations is part of a broader pattern of state support for nonprofit organizations, this chapter first explores the nature of the American nonprofit sector and the roles played by public funds and religiously based nonprofit organizations within it. Next, it specifies how the patterns highlighted in the first section help bring into focus certain key questions concerning religious nonprofit organizations and public money. The third section suggests a conceptual framework within which to view religiously based nonprofit organizations and their role in society.

The Nonprofit Sector

Some 160 years ago, the astute French observer of American life and politics, Alexis de Tocqueville, was struck by the rich proliferation of independent associations he found in the United States.

> Americans of all ages, all conditions, and all dispositions constantly form associations. They have not only commercial and manufacturing companies, in which all take part, but associations of a thousand other kinds, religious, moral, serious, futile, general or restricted, enormous or diminutive. The Americans make associations to give entertainments, to found seminaries, to build inns, to construct churches, to diffuse books, to send missionaries to the antipodes; in this manner they found hospitals, prisons, and schools. If it is proposed to inculcate some truth or to foster some feeling by the encouragement of a great example, they form a society.[3]

If Tocqueville could make a return visit today much that he observed in early nineteenth century America would be changed: the size, diversity, and urban nature of the nation have increased enormously; and modern technological devices undreamed of in the 1830s are everywhere. But the rich associational life of the United States has not changed. There continues to be a profusion of voluntary nonprofit associations, that is, formally organized associations that "are private in structure yet not profit seeking."[4]

It seems there is no disease without an association offering support for its victims and raising money to find a cure, no addiction without an association offering help in overcoming it, no form of recreation without a club composed of fellow enthusiasts, or no social problem without a community group working to solve it. Lester Salamon of Johns Hopkins University is correct when he writes that "without a clear understanding of the nonprofit sector, it is as impossible to comprehend American society and American public policy today as it was in the time of Tocqueville."[5]

There were approximately 1.4 million nonprofit associations in the United States in 1992, up 27 percent from 1977, when there were 1.1 million of them.[6] Their total income was estimated in 1990 to be $316 billion—a 336 percent increase from their total income of $94 billion in 1977.[7] Over 11 percent of the American work force, or 16 million persons, work in the nonprofit sector.[8] In health care, 51 percent of all hospitals, with 56 percent of all beds and 65 percent of all expenditures, are private, nonprofit institutions.[9] Among nursing homes, 20 percent are nonprofit.[10] In education, 24 percent of all elementary and secondary schools are private, nonprofit schools, with 11 percent of all students. This is an area that is growing rapidly, with a 46 percent increase in expenditures in the 1980s, compared to a 29 percent increase in public school expenditures.[11] In higher education, 49 percent of all colleges and universities are private, nonprofit institutions, with 20 percent of all higher education students and conferring a majority of the doctorates and professional degrees in the nation.[12]

The social service field is dominated by nonprofit agencies. Some 74 percent of all social service revenues go to nonprofit agencies, and nonprofits employ 58 percent of the workers in the social service field.[13] Over 200 private, voluntary agencies, with revenues of over $4 billion a year, are active in the area of international aid.[14] In the field of arts and culture, 40 percent of the theatrical companies, 95 percent of the orchestras, and 71 percent of the museums and art galleries are nonprofit organizations.[15] Michael O'Neill has noted, "Nonprofits employ more civilians than the federal government and the fifty state governments combined. The yearly budget of the American nonprofit sector exceeds the budgets of all but seven nations in the world."[16]

In short, the American nonprofit sector is alive, growing, and plays a vital role in many key areas of American life. Tocqueville would feel right at home. As Peter Hall has observed, "No other nation [except England] has depended so heavily as has the United States on private nonprofit organizations for performing so many public activities."[17]

This book is largely concerned, however, not with all nonprofit organizations, but with those that have primarily public service or public benefit purposes.[18] Included in this category are a wide variety of organizations that exist for health, education, and social welfare purposes, the advancement of the arts and culture, and community or neighborhood improvement. It excludes nonprofit organizations that exist primarily to serve or benefit their own members (for example, Chambers of Commerce, labor unions, and recreation clubs), to meet essentially sacramental or worship purposes (for example, religious congregations), to fund other charitable or service projects (for example, the United Way or grant making foundations), or to achieve political goals (for example, political interest groups). Approximately 220,000 out of the more than one million nonprofit organizations fall into this category.[19] When this book refers to nonprofit organizations, it is referring to these 220,000 service-providing nonprofit organizations, unless otherwise specified.

Nonprofit Organizations and Public Money

Two characteristics of service-oriented, nonprofit organizations are important for the purposes of this study. One is that the various governments of the United States—national, state, and local—often accomplish their public policy objectives by funding programs and activities of these nonprofit organizations, rather than creating their own agencies to provide services directly; on the other side of the coin, these nonprofit organizations often look to government as a source of funds. Salamon has concluded that "government has tended to turn to nonprofit providers to help deliver publicly funded services—in health, education, and social services. . . . Although government provides most of the funds in many of the key social welfare fields, private institutions deliver most of the services."[20]

Nonprofit organizations as a whole receive approximately 31 percent of their income from government sources (another 51 percent comes from fees and charges and 18 percent from private giving).[21] Even these figures do not tell the entire story of the importance of government funds for nonprofits and the importance of nonprofits for government services. Government funds are especially important for nonprofit organizations that provide social welfare and legal services, with 42 percent of all their funds coming from government.[22] Political scientists Steven Smith and Michael Lipsky have concluded that "most nonprofit service organizations depend on government support for over half of their revenues: for many, government support comprises their entire budget."[23] Even in private higher education, where the major source of funds is tuition payments, 20 percent of funding for private, nonprofit colleges and universities comes from the government.[24] In the area of international aid and relief, 28 percent of the income of private, nonprofit international aid agencies comes from the government.[25]

Government funds flowing to nonprofit organizations are generally of three types. One is purchase of service contracts, in which the government contracts with a private, nonprofit organization to provide a service instead of providing it directly through a government agency. Examples include payments to a child and family service agency for providing foster care to abused or neglected children and payments to a private hospital for care provided to Medicaid recipients. A second way in which public funds flow to nonprofit organizations is through direct government assistance in the form of grants, in-kind contributions, and low-interest loans or loan guarantees. Construction grants to hospitals under the Hill-Burton Act and surplus foods given to homeless shelters are two examples. The final type of program providing government funds to nonprofit organizations consists of grants to individuals who may then choose to spend them in nonprofit institutions or agencies. Pell grants for college students is a familiar example of such a program. Here, the federal government makes grants available to college students with demonstrated financial need, and they can then use their grants at a private for-profit, private nonprofit, or public institution.

This pattern of government achieving public policy objectives by funding private, nonprofit organizations and of private, nonprofit organizations looking to government as a major source of funds is so common that various observers have coined terms such as the "third sector," the "third America," and "third-party government" to refer to the nonprofit sector.[26] All these terms pick up on the idea that there is a third phenomenon not accounted for by the public-private bifurcation with which most Americans are familiar. The nonprofit sector is neither wholly private nor wholly public, but is instead marked by nongovernmental institutions and agencies receiving large amounts of government funding in support of certain public services they provide.

The third sector is thereby marked by a mutual dependence between government and nonprofit organizations. Neither can get along without the other. Without government funds, many private, nonprofit associations would collapse or have to cut back their programs drastically; without private, nonprofit associations, government would have to expand dramatically to meet public needs in such areas as health, education, social services, and overseas relief. In the end, as Smith and Lipsky have put it, "Mutual dependence blurs the lines between public and private."[27]

This pattern of mutual dependence is not a recent phenomenon, but has been present throughout American history. Salamon has noted, "Government support of voluntary organizations has roots deep in American history. Well before the American Revolution, for example, colonial governments had established a tradition of assistance to private educational institutions, and this tradition persisted into the nineteenth century."[28] In colonial America, care for the poor and sick was typically handled by individuals, but with financial subsidy from government. The town records of Fairfield, Connecticut, for April 16, 1673, for example, read: "The Towne desires and orders Seriant Squire and Sam moorhouse to Take care of Roger Knaps family in this time of their great weakness: and to procure for them such nezssesary comforts . . . as they stand in need of and it shall be satisfied out of the Town treasurie:"[29] Similarly, an entry marked March 4, 1699/1700, reads: "The Towne this day grants to Robert Turney ten Pounds to be paid out of the Towne Treasurie in Consideration of maintaineing his Brother Benjemin who is blinde."[30]

The New York Orphan Asylum Society opened a home for orphans in 1806, and within a few years it was housing 200 orphans—with the help of a state subsidy.[31] Ralph Kramer reports that "the use of subsidies [to voluntary institutions] accelerated from the mid-nineteenth century on. In the last quarter of the century, subsidies became the prevailing method of financing most voluntary institutions."[32] In 1898 New York City funneled 57 percent of its money for relief of the poor through private agencies.[33] In the District of Columbia "about half of the public funds allocated for aid to the poor went to private charities as of 1892."[34] An 1889 survey of seventeen major private hospitals revealed that 13 percent of their collective income came from the government.[35] In 1901 Frank Fetter of Cornell University concluded that "except [for] possibly two territories and four western states, there is probably not a state in the union where some aid [to private charities] is not given either by the state or by counties and cities."[36]

One of the clearest historical examples of government's use of private agencies to accomplish public policy goals was during the nineteenth century, when various church agencies were used to educate, train, and work with Native Americans, and—many today would add—in the process to subvert their culture. As J. Bruce Nichols has reported,

> The government's use of church workers to help build diplomatic, cultural, and religious ties with the Indian Nations continued unbroken from before the Revolution at least through 1912. . . . Baptists, Jesuits, Presbyterians, Moravians, Congregationalists, and others combined their private resources with resources of the [government's] Civilization Fund. By 1826 there were thirty-eight such government-subsidized schools.[37]

During and following the two world wars, the United States government depended heavily upon private agencies for relief of refugees and others whose lives were disrupted by war.[38]

Although there is abundant historical precedent for government funds flowing to private, nonprofit agencies and institutions, it is equally clear that this pattern has broadened and deepened since the 1960s. Smith and Lipsky report that "government contracting with nonprofits has expanded to meet a wider variety of needs."[39] They cite as an example the movement from large public institutions caring for the mentally ill to community based programs, often run by nonprofit agencies with government funding. They then note:

> Also, government contracting of nonprofit agencies rose sharply in services previously limited to a relatively small number of agencies dependent on private funds, including daycare, homeless shelters, child protection, counseling, home health, legal aid, family planning, respite care, and community living.[40]

The Republicans' winning control of Congress in 1994 led to many proposals for relying on private, nonprofit organizations as replacements for large, centralized government bureaucracies in meeting human needs.[41]

Paradoxically, both the war on poverty initiated by liberal Democrats in the 1960s and the retrenchment in government involvement in social welfare initiated by conservative Republicans in the 1990s looked to nonprofit organizations to play major roles. Cooperative relationships between the government and the nonprofit sector—long a feature of American public policy—have, in recent years, gained renewed vigor.

It would be easy to assume that when government becomes involved in providing education, health, and social services the private sector is gradually squeezed out. After all, these and others fields were historically dominated by private institutions and agencies, and now government has moved into these areas. However, since government's involvement in what previously had been a private sector activity is typically accomplished by working through and financing the private, nonprofit sector, the net result is that the expansion of government activity has usually worked to expand the private, nonprofit sector, not curtail it. Salamon has made the needed point:

> Government has tended to turn to nonprofit providers to help deliver publicly funded services—in health, education, and social services. As a consequence, the growth of government has helped to expand the nonprofit role, not limit or eliminate it. As a result, nonprofit organizations retain a significant foothold in virtually every sphere of human service, and in many cases have been able to expand their activities as a direct by-product of government involvement.[42]

The Religious Nature of Many Nonprofit Organizations

A second characteristic of the nonprofit sector of importance to this study is the extent to which many nonprofit institutions and agencies have a strong religious character. This is a feature researchers often miss, yet an understanding of the nonprofit sector is incomplete without an understanding of the large role played by religiously based nonprofit organizations.

Religiously motivated and religiously based organizations have historically played a vital role in one area of public service after another. Religiously based nonprofits have typically led the way in seeking to meet societal needs, with secularly based nonprofits and government entering later. Virginia Hodgkinson of the Independent Sector has expressed it well:

> One of the primary meeting grounds of this nation is not city hall but the local congregation. . . . Actions on issues relating to soup kitchens, shelters for the homeless, care of battered women and children, counseling for families under siege, child care, international efforts to curb hunger and provide disaster relief were not initiated by government but to a large extent by people in congregations. . . .[43]

A recent study by the Child Welfare League began by noting, "Most of the earliest institutions that cared for children in the United States were established by churches and religious orders."[44] O'Neill, in a chapter revealingly entitled, "Religion: Godmother of the Nonprofit Sector," concluded the following:

> Religion is a large and important part of the nonprofit sector and has given birth to many other nonprofit institutions: health, education, social service, international assistance, advocacy, mutual assistance, and even some cultural and grantmaking organizations. Directly and indirectly, religion has been the major formative influence on America's independent sector.[45]

It was the Puritans in New England who founded Harvard and Yale. In fact, 180 of the 207 permanent colleges founded prior to 1860 had a religious affiliation.[46] In 1813 the Quakers in Pennsylvania founded the nation's first mental hospital. Following the Civil War, various religious groups, and especially Roman Catholics, founded a series of hospitals, and Jews have founded such renowned hospitals at Mount Sinai in New York and Cedars of Lebanon in Los Angeles. Nichols has convincingly demonstrated that overseas refugee and relief work was initially dominated by religiously rooted groups.[47] Peter Hall reports that in the nineteenth century, "Wherever an orphanage, a library, a college, a hospital, an academy, or a professional society operated, it was almost invariably the work of a migrant New Englander with evangelical connections."[48] Typically, religiously motivated persons have been the first into areas of societal need. Secular agencies and government have followed.

The importance of religiously based institutions and agencies in the nonprofit sector can still be seen today. Some 55 percent to 65 percent of all charitable giving by individuals in the United States goes to congregations and other religious organizations.[49] If one adds individual giving to religiously rooted service agencies, clearly two-thirds of all voluntary, charitable giving goes to nonprofit organizations with a religious base. Eighty-six percent of all students enrolled in private elementary and secondary schools are in religiously based schools. There are 9,000 Catholic schools, with an enrollment of over 2.5 million students, and 11,000 other religiously based schools with an enrollment of 1.5 million students.[50] Of the 1,300 accredited private colleges and universities, over 1,000, or 78 percent, have a religious affiliation.[51] There are, for example, 240 Catholic colleges and universities, 100 Methodist schools, and 80 Baptist schools.[52] There are 88 colleges in the Coalition of Christian Colleges and Universities (an association of conservative Protestant colleges), and one should also note well-known Jewish institutions such as Yeshiva University and Mormon institutions such as Brigham Young University. Although many religiously affiliated institutions have left their original traditions, one study concluded that 54 percent of the religiously affiliated colleges and universities continue to have a strong religious orientation.[53]

Among all child care providers, one-third are church-based.[54] In New York City, private agencies under contract to the city provide most of the foster care for children and most of these agencies are religiously based.[55] Among the agencies belonging to the National Association of Homes and Services to Children, roughly one-half have a clear religious base.[56] A 1965 study reported there were 889 Catholic hospitals, 662 Protestant hospitals, and 57 Jewish ones.[57] A perusal of the membership list of InterAction, an association of international aid and relief agencies, reveals that roughly one-third to one-half have a religious base.[58] Of the 13 international aid and relief agencies registered with the United States Agency for International Development that in 1991 had total revenues of over $80 million, seven were religiously based.[59]

Public Money and Religious Nonprofit Organizations

These two characteristics of nonprofit service organizations—their receipt of large amounts of government funds and the religious nature of many of them—overlap, sometimes with surprising results. As seen at the beginning of the chapter, many religiously based organizations receive large amounts of government funds, just as their secular counterparts do. Bernard Coughlin has observed, "For over a hundred years there has existed in the United

States a partnership between local governments and sectarian welfare."[60] Thus a surprising 75 percent of the annual budget of the New York Roman Catholic archdiocese—some $1.75 billion—comes from government sources. Roughly one billion of this amount derives from federal health care programs in the form of Medicaid and Medicare payments to Catholic hospitals, nursing homes, and other health care agencies. In addition, the archdiocese had in 1992 city contracts for providing foster care for children ($121 million), day care, ($19 million), mental health services ($10 million), and other such social welfare services.[61]

According to the United States Agency for International Development, in 1991 the American Jewish Joint Distribution Committee received three-fourths of a million dollars in government contracts, grants, and other assistance, Catholic Relief Services received $187 million, the mainline Protestant Church World Services received $6.5 million, and the conservative Protestant World Vision Relief and Development received $19.3 million.[62] The president of one conservative Protestant college estimated that in a recent year 20 percent of the total operating revenue of his college originated in government aid to students.[63] And two scholars have reported, "What we have found is that a large amount of federal funding goes to church-affiliated colleges and universities under a variety of direct and indirect aid programs."[64] The major exception to this pattern of public funds for religious nonprofit organizations consists of religiously based elementary and secondary schools. Due to Supreme Court decisions holding that such aid violates the First Amendment establishment clause, only very limited amounts and forms of public funds go to religious K–12 schools.

Nevertheless, whether it was a matter of government funds going to Harvard in colonial Massachusetts, or financial aid to mission societies and schools for Native Americans in the early nineteenth century, or aid to religiously based hospitals in the late nineteenth century, or government funds going to religiously based international relief agencies in the twentieth century, government has sent tax dollars to a host of religious, private organizations in its efforts to accomplish its public policy goals, and religious, private organizations have looked to government as a source of funds.

Nonprofit Organizations and Public Money: Issues

The conjunction of a large, vital nonprofit sector—many of whose organizations are religious in nature—and the infusion of large amounts of government funds raises crucial issues with regard to organizational autonomy generally and the religious autonomy of religiously based nonprofits more specifically. In addition, it raises a whole phalanx of questions concerning the relevant constitutional principles and theories in light of American church-state traditions.[65] Americans profess to believe in the separation of church and state, often even embracing the Jeffersonian metaphor of a wall of separation. Yet in the case of religiously based nonprofits and public money, sacred and secular—church and state—clearly mix.

Taking the issue of organizational autonomy first, a presumed advantage of accomplishing public goals and meeting societal needs through private, voluntary associations lies in their claimed independence, flexibility, and creativity. Also, religiously based associations are often presumed to bring to their tasks a strong sense of caring and compassion, an idealism, and a sense of religious or ethnic solidarity. But if nonprofit organizations are dependent on government sources for much of their revenue, can they maintain their autonomy and the advantages presumed to flow from it? Is this perhaps a case where government funds work to destroy the very aspects of nonprofit associations that enable them to contribute to the common good of society? Smith and Lipsky, after a thorough study of government practices of contracting for services with nonprofit social service agencies, concluded the danger is great that this will be the precise result of government funds flowing to nonprofit organizations. They noted that government contracts have led to "a much more substantial private sector," but that this sector

> now depends upon government to sustain it, conforms to governmental expectations of service modes, standards, and client selection, and bends its internal structures toward ably performing as contracting partners. Critics who would see the private nonprofit sector as representing an important alternative to state action must recognize that the sector is significantly compromised in its ability to offer clear alternatives.[66]

This is a theme found at many points in their book, since they see government and private agencies as having different perspective and priorities, with government having the upper hand in the relationship and thus gradually moving the private agencies in directions they otherwise would not have gone. Without judging the outcome of the issue, there certainly is a clear danger that the old adage of "he who pays the piper calls the tune" will apply when it comes to governmental funds flowing to private, voluntary institutions and agencies.

This issue of institutional autonomy takes on crucial additional facets when religiously based organizations are the recipients of public funds. If agencies in general terms lose autonomy due to the receipt of government funds, do religiously based agencies lose religious autonomy when they receive government funds? Some researchers have answered yes. In regard to religiously based international relief agencies, Nichols concluded, "Financial cooperation between religious bodies and the government inevitably results in a loss of religious freedom . . . Religious institutions are allowed to expand through such funding arrangements but their specifically and distinctively religious functions are then restricted by law."[67] Thomas Jeavons has concluded, "But the fact remains that, in most cases, accepting government funds to support the work of Christian service organizations requires compromising the character of that work. . . ."[68] Sterling College, a small, conservative Presbyterian college in Kansas, was forced to abandon compulsory chapel services by the state of Kansas due to a tuition grant program it took part in. Soon after, the president, in a self-study document, struggled with the question of the possible loss of autonomy due to government funds:

> Being a college with a strong religious background we struggle with the questions of "How much farther can we go?" "Will we be able to garner enough support to go it alone?" Right now many of the very small colleges are playing both sides of the fence. The federal dollars are appealing and attractive, but how much of our soul do we sacrifice as a payoff? The fence sitting is becoming harder and harder. Maybe we have sat too long and now are faced with the decision whether we have the freedom any longer of an alternate choice.[69]

But the answer to the question of how much freedom religiously based nonprofit organizations give up by accepting government funds is far from answered. This issue has received little attention by researchers. This is part of a broader pattern I note in the next section: a surprising disinterest both in the government-nonprofit relationship in general and religiously based organizations within the nonprofit sector in particular. One purpose of this study is to explore in a more systematic fashion whether or not religiously based nonprofit institutions and agencies lose the right to maintain their distinctive religious missions and practices when they accept government funds.

A second basic issue raised by the specter of thousands of private, religiously based organizations receiving billions of tax dollars is that of church-state theory and practice. Practice seems to clash with theory. Those acquainted with Supreme Court jurisprudence in the area of church-state relations are accustomed to periodic ringing declarations by the Court against attempts to use tax dollars in support of religion, as in the quotation at the beginning of this chapter. Jefferson's wall of separation metaphor and James Madison's contention that not even "three pence" should go to support religion have been quoted more than once by Supreme Court justices in defense of their positions.

The Supreme Court, the lower courts, legal and public policy experts, journalists, and advocacy groups such as the American Civil Liberties Union and Americans United for Separation of Church and State appear to have given little time and thought to the constitutional theories and principles as they relate to government funds flowing to religiously based nonprofit agencies. One finds long-standing, pervasive practice largely unsupported by well-developed theories or principles. The Supreme Court has rarely even dealt with the issue. In 1899 a case concerning public support of a Catholic hospital came before the Supreme Court, in the 1970s three cases and in 1986 one case dealing with government funds for religious colleges and universities did so, and in the 1980s a case dealing with public money going to religiously based centers counseling teenagers on matters of sexuality did so. But that has been it. Down through the years the policy and legal communities have largely reacted to church-state issues implicit in granting tax dollars to religious nonprofit organizations with a collective yawn.

There is, however, a major exception to this general pattern. In the case of one type of nonprofit organization—religiously based elementary and secondary schools—legal and public policy experts, journalists, advocacy groups, and the courts have spent enormous amounts of time defending or attacking government funds going to private, often religiously based schools and developing principles in defense of or in opposition to such funding. That portion of the nonprofit-government landscape has been frequently and passionately explored. In the process, however, more confusion than clarity has been contributed to the answers to the twin questions of the freedom of action of religious nonprofits receiving public funds and of the permissibility of public funds for religious nonprofits under the First Amendment establishment clause. Much of the Supreme Court's sweeping language condemning public funding of religion comes from its decisions denying public funds to religious K–12 schools, yet, as I will argue later, it has failed to adequately distinguish public funding of K–12 schools from public funding of other types of religious nonprofit organizations.

Issues concerning church-state theory and practice are related to the issue of nonprofits' freedom or autonomy. The First Amendment religious freedom language reads: "Congress shall make no law respecting an establishment of religion, or prohibiting the free exercise thereof." One question to which this language gives rise is whether no-establishment limitations on governmental funds flowing to religiously based organizations can only be overcome if the religious characteristics of nonprofit associations—such as hiring practices, behavior standards, religious ceremonies, and religious symbols—are let go. In other words, does the receipt of governmental funds by religiously based nonprofits—given no-establishment limitations—inevitably result in explicit or implicit pressures to secularize and become more like secularly based nonprofits, or even like government agencies or institutions? A second key question, however, serves as a balance to the first one. Can the free-exercise language of the First Amendment be a defense that religiously based nonprofits use to protect their unique religious character and mission? If the institutional autonomy of religiously based nonprofits is being threatened by their receipt of public money—if they are being pressured to give up some of the practices rooted in their religious beliefs—can they defend themselves from such pressures on the basis of the First Amendment's free-exercise protections? Clearly the constitutional and public policy issues raised by public funding of religious nonprofits are neither simple nor easy to resolve.

The focus of this study is the realm of religiously based, public service, nonprofit organizations, their frequent receipt of public funds, and the Constitutional-legal interpretations and principles under which they receive those funds, or—in the case of K–12 schools—are not allowed to receive them. As I noted earlier, my thesis is that current practice and Constitutional-legal principles do not mesh, and as a result religiously based nonprofit organizations receiving public funds and their ability to help deliver public services have been placed in a vulnerable position.

I develop and document this thesis in the following chapters. First, the rest of this chapter seeks to construct a conceptual framework for the study by putting nonprofit associations—and especially religiously based, service-oriented ones—into the broader framework of society and public policies. Chapter 2 establishes the legal and societal setting within which religious nonprofit organizations receive immense amounts of public funds. It reports on Supreme Court decisions and the lines of reasoning underlying them that have permitted public funding of most religiously based nonprofit organizations while largely denying them to religiously based elementary and secondary schools. In addition, it explores the public's attitudes and societal and religious trends that also go towards making up the setting or context of this study. Chapter 3 reports the results of a nationwide questionnaire study of 766 nonprofit, public service organizations of three types: colleges and universities, family and child service agencies, and international aid and relief agencies. It reports on these organizations' existing patterns in terms of their religious nature and practices, their receipt of public funds, and the effects those funds are having on their freedom to pursue religiously based practices. Chapters 4 and 5 explore major tensions between the existing legal doctrines and public attitudes described in Chapter 2 and the actual practices being followed, as revealed by the findings of my survey of nonprofit organizations described in Chapter 3. Chapter 6 presents a principle for governing public money going to religiously based nonprofit associations that

I am convinced is a more defensible, more realistic principle than the ones now being followed. It outlines the permissible and impermissible forms of such funding and offers a rationale for it.

Private Associations, Society, and Government

Researchers usually pay little attention to the nonprofit sector and its role in providing public services. Salamon has commented, "Despite its scale and importance, however, this partnership between government and the voluntary sector has attracted little attention. . . . [A] blind spot has persisted with respect to the relationships between the voluntary sector and government."[70] In fact, scholarship has been afflicted by a double blind spot. Studies of the government-nonprofit relationship that have been done, have almost invariably ignored the fact that many of the nonprofit organizations are religiously based. Hall has commented on this omission,

> Quite clearly, the scholarship of philanthropy has given religion remarkably short shrift. This deficiency is particularly striking in view of the fact that churches and denominationally tied institutions command nearly two-thirds of all the contributions, 34 percent of all volunteer labor, 19 percent of all the wage earners, and 10 percent of all wages and salaries in the nonprofit sector.[71]

Jeavons has noted that even as scholarly interest in the nonprofit sector has increased in recent years, "attention on the part of scholars to the religious roots of the sector and to religious organizations has been almost nonexistent."[72]

Salamon has argued persuasively that the lack of attention given the nonprofit sector—and, I would add, the role of religiously based nonprofits within it—can be traced back to the lack of a theoretical framework with which to take note of the world of nonprofit organizations and relate it to concepts and categories with which most persons are accustomed to thinking. He has argued,

> The partnership between government and the nonprofit sector has been overlooked, in my view, not because of its novelty or a lack of research but because of a weakness in theory. . . . It is the role of theory, after all, to direct attention to the facts that are most relevant to a particular process. . . . Our failure to perceive the reality of extensive government-nonprofit ties is, I believe, a product in substantial part of the limitations of the conceptual equipment through which this reality is being perceived.[73]

Many would trace the problem with our existing framework of concepts and categories back to the eighteenth-century Enlightenment. It has bequeathed to the typical American student of society and politics a sensitivity to and respect for individuals and their personal freedoms. It also encourages a focus on governmental structures and actions but has left blind spots when it comes to religion and private, voluntary associations. Enlightenment liberalism tended to privatize religion and view it as inconsequential for the affairs of state, and, in its emphasis on freedom for individuals, it tended to downplay private associations. Peter Berger and Richard Neuhaus have noted that within Enlightenment liberalism "the great concern is for the individual ('the rights of man') and for a just public order, but anything 'in between' is viewed as irrelevant, or even an obstacle to the rational ordering of society."[74] Similarly, Mary Ann Glendon of Harvard University has noted that

> although we have a highly developed linguistic and conceptual apparatus for thinking about and dealing with individuals, market actors, and the state, we lack adequate concepts to enable us to consider the social dimensions of human personhood, and the social environments that individual men, women, and children require in order to flourish.[75]

These tendencies of liberalism to overlook the importance of intermediate structures between the individual and the government and to privatize religion and thereby see it as irrelevant and of little concern to the public realm combine to create a situation where religiously rooted associations—even when they exist in profusion—are simply not seen as features of society relevant to an understanding of it. Law professor Frederick Gedicks has correctly noted, "American liberalism, with its uncompromising focus on state and individual, often overlooks institutions like religious groups that are neither governmental nor individualistic."[76]

Before proceeding with this study, therefore, it is advisable to pause in order to develop a conceptual or theoretical framework that will prove helpful as a corrective to present-day tendencies to overlook religiously based nonprofit organizations and as a means for thinking about them and their role in society. The conceptual framework presented here has four stages or steps to it and is based on a structural pluralist view of society.[77]

The Importance of Associations and Communities

The first step in the framework of concepts developed here is the recognition of the importance of private associations and communities in society.[78] They grow out of the very nature of human beings as social beings who need each other. Recognition of the social nature of human beings is as old as Aristotle's description of human beings as political animals and the biblical Genesis account of Adam not being able to find a suitable companion for himself among the assortment of animals God brought before him. Only when God created woman—another human being—were Adam's social needs met.

Wherever human society has existed, associations such as families, clans, villages, and religious cults have also been found. Ancient human beings hunted, farmed, raised children, and sought to placate the gods in ongoing kinship and tribal groups. Modern, Western human beings also raise children, pursue economic activities, worship God, and recreate, not as isolated individuals, but as members of groups. The beginning sentences of the official platform of the communitarian journal, *The Responsive Community*, makes this point in especially clear terms:

> American men, women, and children are members of many communities—families; neighborhoods; innumerable social, religious, ethnic, workplace, and professional associations; and the body politic itself. Neither human existence nor individual liberty can be sustained for long outside the interdependent and overlapping communities to which all of us belong.[79]

In American society, religious communities and associations are especially important, as evidenced by the profusion of religiously based associations already noted as well as by polls that regularly find high levels of religious practices and deeply held religious beliefs.[80] The results of a 1994 poll of the American people, for example, demonstrated that "at the end of the 20th century, the wealthiest, most powerful and best educated country on Earth is still one of the most religious."[81]

In short, one should expect to find a plurality of religious, work, family, play, and problem-solving social structures in any society. It would be their absence—not their presence—that would be surprising and in need of explanation.

Social structures play especially crucial roles in meeting three societal needs. One is that they themselves meet many personal and social needs. Families nurture, support, and teach children. Churches, synagogues, and mosques meet the religious needs of their members and offer emotional and physical support in times of crisis, such as unemployment, divorce, sickness, and death. Neighborhood groups work to prevent crime, eliminate drug dealing, and stem deterioration.

Second, social structures give the sense of purpose and meaning all persons crave. Typically it is within families, religious congregations, and neighborhoods that persons find meaning and purpose in life. Third, persons learn a basic sense of morality in the groups within which they live. It is within communities and associations that one learns to respect the rights of others, to contribute to the needs of others, and to meet the other responsibilities that go to make up what has been termed civic or public virtue.[82] Amitai Etzioni has written:

> We gain our initial moral commitments as new members of a community into which we are born. Later, as we mature, we hone our individualized versions out of the social values that have been transmitted to us. As a rule, though, these are variations on community-formed themes. . . . Communities speak to us in moral voices. They lay claims on their members. Indeed, they are the most important sustaining source of moral voices other than the inner self.[83]

Simply put, it is hard to exaggerate the importance of associations and communities. Without them and the needs they meet, the sense of meaning they impart, and the moral standards they teach, society as we know it would collapse. Without them, either anarchy and the loss of order or totalitarianism and the loss of freedom are the remaining options.

The Autonomy of Communities and Associations

Communities and associations—whether religiously or secularly based—are best seen, not as creatures of government and subordinate to it, but as prior to and existing independently from government. Thus they possess an autonomy that is theirs by right and not at the sufferance of the state. This is the second step in the conceptual framework being presented here. John Figgis, an early-twentieth-century English pluralist, made this point especially clearly:

> Now the State did not create the family, nor did it create the Churches; nor even in any real sense can it be said to have created the club or the trade unions; nor in the Middle Ages the guild or the religious order, hardly even the universities or the colleges within the universities: they have all arisen out of the natural associative instincts of mankind, and should all be treated by the supreme authority [that is, government] as having a life original and guaranteed.[84]

Pluralism insists that human associations and communities are natural, necessary features of human society that exist independently of and have as much right to exist as does government.

Associations and communities—such as families, the news media, and trade unions—thereby possess a zone or sphere of autonomy that should not be violated, but recognized and respected by society and government. This is not to claim that social structures have an absolute autonomy, that they may do whatever they like, whenever they like. Their autonomy must be balanced by their responsibility to respect the rights of other persons, associations, and communities—and by government's responsibility to assure that those rights are respected and the public interest protected. Thus social structures have an autonomy that is real, but it is also limited. They are not to seek to do that which is not within their area of competence or responsibility.

This principle of autonomy flows from the very nature of communities and associations, but respecting their autonomy is also in the long-term, practical interests of society and government. If healthy, active associations and communities are essential to a healthy polity—a polity here defined as a society and its governing structures—then public policy surely should not limit or undercut them, but recognize, affirm, and accommodate them. Respecting their autonomy has practical as well as theoretical justifications.

Due to the crucial role religious structures play in American society and due to the focus of this study on religiously based nonprofit associations, it is important to be especially clear with regard to the nature and importance of the autonomy of religious associations and communities. Their autonomy is rooted in the concept of freedom of conscience, which is distinguishable from freedom of choice. The latter implies individual choice, rooted in personal preferences, reasoning, or even arbitrary decision. Freedom of conscience is the freedom to follow the dictates of a conscience that has been molded in a community or association. It implies being rooted in a social structure that compels a response to a given situation, not a freedom to make individual choices. Orthodox Jews do not choose whether or not to open their stores on the Sabbath; given the religious community of which they are a part, they have no choice. As Michael Sandel of Harvard University has written, "Where freedom of conscience is at stake, the relevant right is to exercise a duty, not make a choice."[85] The autonomy of religious groups means religious communities and associations and their members must be free to follow the dictates of conscience without penalty or hindrance, and they must be free to protect the group itself and its development.

Yale law professor Stephen Carter, in his best-selling 1993 book, *The Culture of Disbelief,* has rightly emphasized the importance of autonomy for religious groups:

> Autonomy is often the missing element in America's confused relationships with its religions. Our tendency is to speak not of autonomy but of freedom: we talk about the freedom of people to worship, which is not quite the same as the freedom of religions, of corporate worship, to be left alone. . . . [T]he autonomy

of the religions involves a recognition that what is most special about religious life is the melding of the individual and the faith community in which, for the devout, much of reality is defined. Religions are in effect independent centers of power, with bona fide claims on the allegiance of their members, claims that exist alongside, are not identical to, and will sometimes trump the claims to obedience that the state makes.[86]

More specifically, there are two fundamental aspects of religious group autonomy. The first is a religious group's right to self-definition. This right needs to be protected even if it sometimes means individuals who wish to be a part of the group are prevented from doing so or in other ways are disadvantaged by the group. If a group cannot control or define who is and who is not a member, the autonomy of that group has been severely—perhaps even fatally—compromised. Gedicks has stated it well:

> When the government coerces a group to accept or to retain as a member a person whom the group would otherwise reject or expel, it blindly enters the religious domain. It arrogates to itself the power to define the boundaries of group membership—the greatest intrusion that the government can perpetrate against a group. The group loses the authority to define and to control the terms of its own existence. In a very real sense, the group ceases to exist. The group's vision of itself, its ability freely to tell and retell its narrative story, is destroyed by the insistence on conformity to majoritarian values.[87]

Also fundamental to a religious group's autonomy is its right to define for itself its doctrines, practices, purposes, and goals. Being able to do so goes to the heart of what a group is, for doctrine, rituals, practices, and purpose are vital in defining a group. It is a serious violation of a religious group's autonomy for outside groups or the government to dictate belief and practice.

Various religious communities have attempted to articulate their conception of religious autonomy. Political scientist Richard Regan, writing from the Thomistic, Catholic tradition, has done so especially clearly in noting that voluntary associations

> that proceeded from the free initiative of individuals should enjoy as much autonomy as possible precisely because humans develop themselves by their free associations with one another. Thus, in the Thomistic theory, pluralism is inherent in every rightly ordered political society. The body politic and its chief agency, should not swallow up the parts, families and voluntary associations, but should function to order the parts into a whole, while preserving the maximum autonomy of the parts.[88]

The concept of autonomy developed in this section has been important in the thinking of the Christian Democratic parties of western Europe, and has been nicely summarized by Michael Foggerty in these words: "Every social unit or group has a sphere of work which it can do efficiently in the interests not only of its members but of society as a whole, and this sphere must be defined and reserved for it."[89]

As noted earlier, all this is not to suggest that associations and communities—whether religious or nonreligious in nature—possess an absolute autonomy. Their autonomy is circumscribed and limited by their responsibilities to other persons, associations, and communities. Also, sometimes the broader public interest will require that certain restrictions be placed on the autonomy of a group. The key point is that every community or association has a proper sphere of activity, and within that sphere its freedom of action should be respected by other social structures and the state. This is also true of religious groups. There will at times be practices of religious groups that are so inimical to overriding public interests or so contrary to the proper nature of religion that they may appropriately be suppressed. Religious associations or communities will sometimes seek to move beyond their proper spheres of activities and attempt to arrogate to themselves activities or functions that properly belong to government, family, or other societal groups. Imperialistic religious associations and communities—from the Catholic Church of the Spanish Inquisition to present-day cults that deny persons their own identity—stand as testimonies to this danger. When religious associations or communities go outside their proper sphere of activity and seek to arrogate to themselves powers they have no right to exercise or have interfered with the appropriate activities of other associations or communities, they may and should be limited by the government or other societal structures. Their autonomy should at that point be limited. But doing so is no small matter—it should only be done following a careful weighing of the rights and responsibilities of the relevant societal structures and a careful weighing of the demands of the broad public interest.

The Limits of Communities and Association

The third step in the conceptual framework presented here holds that one cannot assume that existing associations and communities are adequate to meet all societal needs. In a recent book, Salamon outlined four reasons why private associations sometimes fail in meeting needs and why intervention by government or higher associations is thereby needed.[90] The first is what he termed philanthropic insufficiency. Here he refered to situations where private nonprofit associations are unable to raise sufficient money, volunteers, or other resources needed to meet a problem from which society is suffering. Second, there is philanthropic particularism, the tendency of private associations "to focus on particular subgroups of the population,"[91] while others are left out or inadequately served. Third is philanthropic paternalism, that is, the tendency for those running voluntary associations themselves to be well off and thus not sufficiently sensitive to or knowledgeable about those in need. Finally, Salamon listed philanthropic amateurism, or a tendency in private associations for professional skills and perspectives to be undercut or watered down by the pet nostrums of nonprofessionals. One could add to or subtract from Salamon's list, but the key point for our purposes is to recognize the fact that, for whatever reasons, voluntary associations and communities, if left to themselves, are sometimes inadequate to meet existing human and societal needs. Government—whether national, state, or local—has a continuing important role to play.

Minimal Government Intrusion

The fourth and final step in the conceptual framework presented here grows out of the nature of the autonomy of associations and communities, which, as just noted, is real yet limited, and out of the recognition that one cannot expect associations and communities to met all societal needs. Sometimes government needs to intrude into areas of activity previously left to individuals or to private groups, but when it does it should do so in the least intrusive manner practicable. Both the autonomy of private structures and their ability to deal with societal needs are real and to be respected; they are also limited. Their limited nature means government sometimes needs to intrude into areas in which they also are active. But government shows a proper respect for both their autonomy and their ability to contribute to meeting societal needs by intruding as little as possible.

The ordering of the state and its voluntary associations so as to minimize the intrusion of the state is captured by the principle of subsidiarity, a helpful attempt by Catholic social teaching to give concrete expression to the concept of associational autonomy. Reagan has defined the principle of subsidiarity this way, "[T]he state should do for its citizens, families, and voluntary associations only what these individuals and groups cannot or will not do for themselves."[92]

This aspect of the framework of concepts is largely in keeping with existing traditions of the American polity. Salamon has made reference to "third party-government" to refer to the American tendency to avoid taking governmental action, but when such avoidance is no longer possible, to achieve public policy goals by the lowest level of government and by the least intrusive means available.[93] Local government action is preferred over state government action; state government action is preferred over national government action. Loan guarantees are preferred over loans; loans are preferred over grants. National government grant-in-aid programs to states or localities are preferred over directly run national government programs. The pattern noted throughout this chapter—of the government making use of private, nonprofit organizations by helping fund them instead of creating its own directly run programs—fits this pattern. Salamon has noted that this pattern "reflects . . . the conflict that has long existed in American political thinking between the desire for public services and hostility to the government apparatus that provides them."[94] Thus the already-existing American pattern of often using private associations in carrying out public policies should be seen as a part of a broader pattern of seeking a less intrusive government.

The conceptual framework put forward here affirms this pattern, highlights the appropriate role that both religiously and secularly based, voluntary, nonprofit organizations play in it, and emphasizes the importance of protecting the autonomy of nonprofit organizations taking part in a government-nonprofit partnership. That partnership ought to strengthen private social structures, not undercut or replace them. A totalitarian state is defined by its violation of all other societal spheres as it seeks to make loyalty to the state the overriding value. Both the totalitarian state and lesser, gentler interferences with the autonomy of other societal spheres must be guarded against. This study is especially concerned that both religion and government—church and state—not interfere with or violate the appropriate domain of the other.

Notes

1. *Everson v. Board of Education*, 330 U.S. at 16 and 18 (1947).
2. On the first two of these organizations, see Sean Mehegan, "The Federal Connection: Nonprofits are Looking More and More to Washington," *The Nonprofit Times*, 8 (November 1994): 43. On the third of these organizations see William Tucker, "The New Welfare State," *The American Spectator*, 28 (February 1995): 38.
3. Alexis de Tocqueville, *Democracy in America*, vol. 2, Phillips Bradley, ed. and trans. (New York: Vintage Books, 1990), 106.
4. Lester M. Salamon, "Nonprofit Organizations: The Lost Opportunity," in *The Reagan Record*, John L. Palmer and Isabel V. Sawhill, eds. (Cambridge, MA: Ballinger, 1984), 262.
5. Lester M. Salamon, *America's Nonprofit Sector* (New York: The Foundation Center, 1992), 3–4.
6. Virginia Ann Hodgkinson, Murray S. Weitzman, Christopher M. Toppe, and Stephen M. Noga, *Nonprofit Almanac, 1992–1993* (San Francisco: Jossey-Bass, 1992), 16, 23. On the size and significance of the nonprofit sector, also see Gabriel

Rudney, "The Scope and Dimensions of Nonprofit Activity," in *The Nonprofit Sector*, Walter W. Powell, ed. (New Haven: Yale University Press, 1987), 55–64.

7. Hodgkinson et al., *Nonprofit Almanac*, 26–27.

8. Hodgkinson et al., *Nonprofit Almanac*, 28–29.

9. Salamon, *America's Nonprofit Sector*, 60.

10. Salamon, *America's Nonprofit Sector*, 64.

11. Salamon, *America's Nonprofit Sector*, 76.

12. Salamon, *America's Nonprofit Sector*, 73.

13. Salamon, *America's Nonprofit Sector*, 83–84.

14. Salamon, *America's Nonprofit Sector*, 101.

15. Salamon, *America's Nonprofit Sector*, 93.

16. Michael O'Neill, *The Third America: The Emergence of the Nonprofit Sector in the United States* (San Francisco: Jossey-Bass, 1989), 1–2.

17. Peter Dobkin Hall, "A Historical Overview of the Private Nonprofit Sector," in *The Nonprofit Sector*, Powell, ed., 3.

18. Salamon has developed a four-fold categorization of nonprofit organizations. The service-oriented nonprofit organizations with which I am largely concerned in this book conform to the fourth of his categories: ". . . those that serve primarily a public or charitable purpose, direct their efforts to a broader public than only the immediate members of the organization, and provide actual services in such areas as health care, education, the arts, and others." Salamon, "Nonprofit Organizations," 263. Also see Salamon, *America's Nonprofit Sector*, 13–32. The distinction Salamon makes between public-serving and member-serving nonprofits "is far from perfect," as he himself has acknowledged (*America's Nonprofit Sector*, 14). Salamon falls back on the distinction made by the federal tax code and considers as public organizations those that qualify for Section 501(c)(3) tax-exempt status (Salamon, *America's Nonprofit Sector*, 14–15). I will do the same.

19. Salamon, *America's Nonprofit Sector*, 13.

20. Salamon, *America's Nonprofit Sector*, 105.

21. Salamon, *America's Nonprofit Sector*, 26.

22. Salamon, *America's Nonprofit Sector*, 27.

23. Steven Rathgeb Smith and Michael Lipsky, *Nonprofits for Hire: The Welfare State in the Age of Contracting* (Cambridge, MA: Harvard University Press, 1993), 4.

24. Salamon, *America's Nonprofit Sector*, 73.

25. Salamon, *America's Nonprofit Sector*, 101.

26. These terms are used, respectively, by David Osborne and Ted Gaebler, *Reinventing Government* (New York: Penguin Books, 1992), 43–47; O'Neill, *The Third America*; and Lester M Salamon, "Rethinking Public Management: Third-Party Government and the Changing Forms of Government Action," *Public Policy*, 29 (1981): 255–75.

27. Smith and Lipsky, *Nonprofits for Hire*, 4.

28. Lester M. Salamon, "Partners in Public Service: The Scope and Theory of Government Nonprofit Relations," in The *Nonprofit Sector*, Powell, ed., 100. The piece from which this quotation is taken has been reprinted in Lester M. Salamon,

Partners in Public Service (Baltimore, MD: The Johns Hopkins University Press, 1995). Smith and Lipsky have a somewhat contrary view. While recognizing the pattern of government working through nonprofits at various points in American history, they stress the wholly new situation in terms of the amount and prevalence of government working through nonprofits since mid-twentieth century. I personally believe Smith and Lipsky have underplayed the extent to which government funding of nonprofits has been a feature of the American experience throughout its history. Today's situation represents an expansion of a pattern present since colonial times, not a break in past practices. For a summary of their views see Smith and Lipsky, *Nonprofits for Hire*, 49.

29. "Fairfield, Connecticut, Town Records," in *The Heritage of American Social Work*, Ralph E. Pumphrey and Muriel W. Pumphrey, eds. (New York: Columbia University Press, 1961), 22.

30. "Fairfield, Connecticut, Town Records," 23–24.

31. See Marvin Olasky, *The Tragedy of American Compassion* (Washington, DC: Regnery Gateway, 1992), 14.

32. Ralph M. Kramer, *Voluntary Agencies in the Welfare State* (Berkeley, CA: University of California Press, 1981), 61.

33. Salamon, "Partners in Public Service," 101.

34. Salamon, "Partners in Public Service," 101.

35. Salamon, "Partners in Public Service," 100–101.

36. Frank A. Fetter, "Subsidizing of Private Charities," *American Journal of Sociology*, 7 (1901): 360. Also cited by Salamon, "Partners in Public Service," 101.

37. J. Bruce Nichols, *The Uneasy Alliance: Religion, Refugee Work, and U.S. Foreign Policy* (New York: Oxford University Press, 1988), 24–25. Another scholar writes: "There were two and a half centuries, from the beginning of the missionary work of the Mayhews and John Eliot about 1641 to about 1890, when there was a partnership between church and state in the maintenance of the Protestant mission to the American Indians." R. Pierce Beaver, *Church and State, and the American Indians* (Saint Louis, MO: Concordia, 1966), 4.

38. Nichols, *The Uneasy Alliance*, 29–36, 52–71.

39. Smith and Lipsky, *Nonprofits for Hire*, 9.

40. Smith and Lipsky, *Nonprofits for Hire*, 9.

41. As the *New York Times* reported: "What America needs, Speaker Newt Gingrich says, is a dismantling of the welfare state, with many of its functions turned over to private charities." *New York Times*, 4 June 1995, A1. Also see Newt Gingrich, *To Renew America* (New York: HarperCollins, 1995), 75–77.

42. Salamon, *America's Nonprofit Sector*, 105.

43. Virginia A. Hodgkinson, "The Future of Individual Giving and Volunteering: The Inseparable Link between Religious Community and Individual Generosity," in *Faith and Philanthropy in America: Exploring the Role of Religion in America's Voluntary Sector*, Robert Wuthnow and Virginia A. Hodgkinson, eds. (San Francisco: Jossey-Bass, 1990), 285.

44. Diana S. Richmond Garland, *Church Agencies: Caring for Children and Families in Crisis* (Washington, DC: Child Welfare League, 1994), 3.

45. O'Neill, *The Third America*, 20.

46. See Paul J. Weber and Dennis A. Gilbert, *Private Churches and Public Money: Church-Government Fiscal Relations* (Westport, CT: Greenwood, 1981), 126–28.

47. Nichols, *The Uneasy Alliance*, 23–83.

48. Hall, "A Historical Overview," 7.

49. Salamon, *America's Nonprofit Sector*, 15, and Christopher Jenks, "Who Gives What?" in *The Nonprofit Sector*, Powell, ed., 322.

50. U.S. Bureau of the Census, *Statistical Abstract of the United States: 1994*, 114th ed. (Washington, DC: GPO, 1994), 172.

51. "Institutional Identifying Characteristics," *HEPS Profile of Independent Higher Education*, 1 (April, 1991): 8.

52. "Institutional Identifying Characteristics," 8.

53. "Institutional Identifying Characteristics," 16.

54. *Congressional Quarterly Weekly Report*, 46 (July 2, 1988): 1834. Also see Charles Austin, "Churches Are Main Suppliers of Day Care," *New York Times* (November 6, 1982), A14.

55. See Dennis R. Young and Stephen J. Finch, *Foster Care and Nonprofit Agencies* (Lexington, MA: Lexington, 1977).

56. Interview with the executive director, Brenda Russell Nordlinger (September 1, 1993).

57. Bernard J. Coughlin, *Church and State in Social Welfare* (New York: Columbia University Press, 1965), 69.

58. See *InterAction Member Profiles, 1993* (Washington: American Council for Voluntary International Action, 1993).

59. *Voluntary Foreign Aid Programs, 1993* (Washington, DC: Agency for International Development, Bureau for Food and Humanitarian Aid, 1993), 60–87.

60. Coughlin, *Church and State in Social Welfare*, 44.

61. See Thomas Maier and Tom Curran, "Church Services: Public Funds Help O'Connor to Help Others," *Newsday* (May 17, 1993), 6 and 26.

62. *Voluntary Foreign Aid Programs, 1993*, 9–87.

63. David K. Winter, "Rendering unto Caesar: The Dilemma of College-Government Relations," in *Making Higher Education Christian*, Joel A. Carpenter and Kenneth W. Shipps, eds. (St. Paul, MN, and Grand Rapids, MI: Christian University Press and Eerdmans, 1987), 255.

64. Weber and Gilbert, *Private Churches and Public Money*, 103.

65. Throughout the book I follow the conventional practice of using the terms "church and state" to refer to religion in its various manifestations and traditions and to government in its various manifestations.

66. Smith and Lipsky, *Nonprofits for Hire*, 206–07.

67. Nichols, *The Uneasy Alliance*, 187.

68. Thomas H. Jeavons, *When the Bottom Line is Faithfulness* (Bloomington, IN: Indiana University Press, 1994), 129.

69. Quoted in Edward McGlynn Gaffney and Philip R. Moots, *Government and Campus* (Notre Dame, IN: University of Notre Dame Press, 1982), 29.

70. Salamon, *Partners in Public Service*, 34.

71. Peter Dobkin Hall, "The History of Religious Philanthropy in America," in *Faith and Philanthropy in America*, Wuthnow and Hodgkinson, eds., 38–39. As striking as Hall's figures are, by concentrating on actual churches and denominational agencies he probably understates the size of the religiously based nonprofit sector.

72. Jeavons, *When the Bottom Line Is Faithfulness*, xiv.

73. Salamon, *Partners in Public Service*, 35–36.

74. Peter L. Berger and Richard John Neuhaus, *To Empower People: The Role of Mediating Structures in Public Policy* (Washington, DC: American Enterprise Institute, 1977), 5.

75. Mary Ann Glendon, "Law, Communities, and the Religious Freedom Language of the Constitution," *George Washington Law Review*, 72 (1992): 674.

76. Frederick Mark Gedicks, "Toward a Constitutional Jurisprudence of Religious Group Rights," *Wisconsin Law Review*, 1989 (1989): 100.

77. On structural pluralism, see Carl H. Esbeck, "A Restatement of the Supreme Court's Law of Religious Freedom: Coherence, Conflict, or Chaos?" *Notre Dame Law Review*, 70 (1995): 641–43; Stephen V. Monsma, *Positive Neutrality* (Westport, CT: Greenwood, 1993), chap. 4; Richard J. Mouw and Sander Griffioen, *Pluralisms and Horizons* (Grand Rapids, MI: Eerdmans, 1993); and James W. Skillen, *Recharging the American Experiment* (Grand Rapids, MI: Baker, 1994).

78. Associations and communities can be distinguished in that communities rest upon informal, affective ties of shared traditions, experiences, and beliefs that have led their members to see or identify themselves as a distinct collectivity. Associations are formal organizations that have been intentionally formed in order to achieve certain specific purposes. I will use *group* or *structure* as inclusive terms that include both communities and associations, and I will use the term *organization* as synonymous with association. Some of the same distinctions I make here can be found in Jacques Maritain, *Man and the State* (Chicago: University of Chicago Press, 1951), 1–19.

79. "The Responsive Communitarian Platform," *The Responsive Community* 2 (Winter, 1991/92): 4. On the social nature of human beings also see James Q. Wilson, *The Moral Sense* (New York: Free Press, 1993), 121–40.

80. See, for example, George Gallup Jr. and Jim Castelli, *The People's Religion* (New York: Macmillan, 1989).

81. "Spiritual America" *U.S. News & World Report*, 116 (April 4, 1994), 48.

82. See Richard Sinopoli, *The Foundations of American Citizenship: Liberalism, the Constitution, and Civic Virtue* (Cambridge, MA: Oxford University Press, 1992), and Richard Vetterli and Gary Bryner, *In Search of the Republic: Public Virtue and the Roots of American Government* (Totowa, NJ: Rowman and Littlefield, 1987).

83. Amitai Etzioni, *The Spirit of Community* (New York, Crown, 1993), 30–31. On this point, also see Gedicks, "Toward a Constitutional Jurisprudence," 116.

84. John N. Figgis, *Churches in the Modern State*, 2nd ed. (New York: Russell and Russell, 1914), 47.

85. Michael J. Sandel, "Freedom of Conscience or Freedom of Choice?" in

Articles of Faith, Articles of Peace, James Davison Hunter and Os Guinness, eds. (Washington, DC: Brookings, 1990), 88. This essay is an excellent analysis of the difference between religious freedom as protecting the freedom of conscience and the lesser concept of religious freedom as the freedom of individual choice.

86. Stephen L. Carter, *The Culture of Disbelief* (New York: Basic Books, 1993), p. 35.

87. Gedicks, "Toward a Constitutional Jurisprudence," 114.

88. Richard J. Regan, *The Moral Dimensions of Politics* (New York: Oxford University Press, 1986), 41.

89. Michael P. Foggerty, *Christian Democracy in Western Europe, 1820–1953* (London: Routledge & Kegan Paul, 1957), 41.

90. See Salamon, *Partners in Public Service,* 45–48.

91. Salamon, *Partners in Public Service,* 45–46.

92. Regan, *The Moral Dimensions of Politics,* 42. On this point, also see Coughlin, *Church and State in Social Welfare,* 32.

93. See Salamon, "Rethinking Public Management," 255–75 and Salamon, "Partners in Public Service," 107–13.

94. Salamon, "Partners in Public Service," 110.

Chapter Two

The Setting: Legal Principles and Public Attitudes

Imagine two scenes. One, a teacher in a religiously based school is making use of a new wall map of Eastern Europe to explain to her seventh graders the sweeping changes that have occurred in recent years in that part of the world. The map was purchased with funds the state government made available for that purpose. The second scene involves a child who was removed from her home due to suspected sexual abuse by a live-in boyfriend of her mother. She has been placed by a religiously based agency in the home of a deeply religious couple where she is receiving temporary foster care while the whole tragic situation is sorted out. The state government is paying for her care. Before putting the child to bed at night the foster mother seeks to quiet the child's fears by assuring her that God is watching over her and leads her in a simple prayer. Under present legal principles—and, implicitly, under prevailing public attitudes—the teacher is violating church-state separation, while the foster mother is not.

These hypothetical examples help illustrate the fact that the subject of religious nonprofit organizations and public funds is not simple or unidimensional. It is marked by widely diverse concrete situations, cross-cutting theories, and clashing values. It is a difficult task this book has taken up.

In order to interpret and understand the significance of the results of the questionnaire study of nonprofit organizations reported in the next chapter, it is crucial at the outset to have a clear understanding of the setting, or context, of public funding for religious nonprofit organizations. This chapter explores three key aspects of this setting. First, it describes the Supreme Court's constitutional interpretations and legal doctrines that draw the line between permissible and impermissible forms of public funding. Next it

29

considers public and elite attitudes as they relate to governmental funding of religious nonprofit organizations. These first two sections of the chapter highlight the legal theories and the public and elite attitudes against which the current practices revealed in Chapter 3 can be compared. Third, this chapter considers four key, evolving characteristics of religion and government—church and state—in American society. These trends are powerful, pervasive, and highly consequential for religious nonprofit organizations and their relationship to government; they are also often ignored. Their existence and significance need to be taken into account in order to react thoughtfully to the legal theories and societal attitudes described in the first two sections of this chapter and the current practices presented in the following chapter.

Constitutional Interpretations and Legal Principles

There are two distinct strains in Supreme Court interpretations relevant to religious nonprofit organizations and their receipt of public funds. One grew out of Supreme Court decisions regarding public funds for religious elementary and secondary schools and is rooted in the no-aid-to-religion principle on which those decisions are based. The second strain has developed more recently and is based on the legal principle that no constitutional problems are raised when religious and nonreligious organizations are given equal access to public benefits. The no-aid-to-religion strain is directly relevant to the issue of public funds for religious nonprofit organizations, but the equal access or equal treatment strain has indirect implications and must also be taken into account in assessing the legal position of religious organizations that receive public funding. This section considers in turn both of these lines of reasoning in Supreme Court jurisprudence.

Public Funds and Religious K–12 Schools

Two of the church-state decisions of the Supreme Court that are widely considered landmark decisions in church-state jurisprudence dealt with public money and religiously based nonprofit organizations. The cases are *Everson v. Board of Education* (1947) and *Lemon v. Kurtzman* (1971), and the religiously based nonprofits were K–12 schools. The *Everson* case dealt with a New Jersey law that established a program of state aid for the transportation of children to religiously based schools and public schools alike. The Supreme Court's 5–4 decision established two legal principles crucial for our purposes. The first one is that the First Amendment's establishment clause ("Congress shall make no law respecting an establishment of religion . . .") means no government aid may be given in support of religion, even aid given not to any one religious group but in support of religion generally. In an often-quoted passage, Justice Hugo Black, writing for the Court majority, stated: "The 'establishment of religion' clause of the First Amendment means at least this: Neither a state nor the Federal Government can set up a church. Neither can pass laws which aid one religion, *aid all religions,* or prefer one religion over another."[1] A few sentences later Black added, "In the words of Jefferson, the clause against establishment of religion by law was intended to erect 'a wall of separation between church and State.' "[2] With those words, the Supreme Court adopted the legal doctrine of no aid to religion, either to specific religious groups or to religion generally.

Somewhat surprisingly the Supreme Court held, in spite of the no-aid doctrine it articulated, that New Jersey could pay for the transportation of children to religious schools. Black's opinion acknowledged: "It is undoubtedly true that children are helped to get to church schools. There is even a possibility that some of the children might not be sent to the church schools if the parents were compelled to pay their children's bus fares out of their own pockets."[3] This leads to an obvious question: How did Justice Black square the giving of aid for the transportation of children to religiously based schools with his own just-enunciated no-aid doctrine? He did so by distinguishing between programs that would contribute "money to the schools" or would "support them" and those, such as the one that was being challenged in that case, "indisputably marked off from the religious function" of schools.[4] He held that bus transportation was clearly separable from the religious mission of the schools and similar to general public services such as police and fire protection and sewage disposal. Thus it could be supported by public funds.

The Supreme Court thereby established a second crucial legal doctrine, namely, that while public money may not go to support religious programs or organizations, it may go to provide services not directly related to the religious mission of religious organizations. This was the beginning of the legal doctrine that separates the sacred and the secular aspects of a religiously based organization, and holds that public money may flow to its secular, but not its sacred aspects.

A second key case, *Lemon v. Kurtzman,* was decided by the Supreme Court in 1971. It dealt with Rhode Island and Pennsylvania programs that were built squarely on the secular-sacred distinction just mentioned. Both programs supplemented the salaries of teachers in religiously based, private schools for teaching secular subjects. The Supreme Court by a 7–1 vote found both states' programs in violation of the establishment clause.

The Court's opinion, written by Chief Justice Warren Burger, articulated a three-part test that became a foundation of most subsequent establishment clause decisions for twenty years. Burger describes the test in these words: "First, the statute must have a secular legislative purpose; second, its principal or primary effect must be one that neither advances nor inhibits religion; finally, the statute must not foster 'an excessive government entanglement with religion.' "[5] Deeply imbedded in Chief Justice Burger's reasoning was the sacred-secular distinction and the Supreme Court's evaluation of the state's attempts to separate out the two and subsidize only the latter. His opinion noted that at the trial-court level several teachers had testified "they did not inject religion into their secular classes. And the District Court found that religious values did not necessarily affect the content of secular instruction."[6] Burger agreed, but made the additional, crucial observation that "the potential for impermissible fostering of religion is present."[7] He then went on to conclude that under such circumstances state attempts to assure a strict separation of the sacred and the secular would require continuing state administrative supervision and surveillance, resulting in state entanglement with religion. The programs of both states were ruled unconstitutional.

The *Lemon* test was used by the Supreme Court in numerous establishment clause decisions for twenty years, but recently its usefulness has been questioned by a majority of the sitting justices, and key establishment clause cases have been decided without reference to it.[8] Nevertheless, it has not been formally overruled and the basic principles on which it rests—no-aid-to-religion and the sacred-secular distinction—still form the core of what is the dominant line of reasoning dealing with public funds going to religious nonprofit organizations.

Two further legal principles have emerged from Supreme Court decisions dealing with public money going to private, nonprofit, religiously based elementary and secondary schools. One is the principle—foreseen but not clearly articulated in the *Lemon* case—that if a school receiving public money is "pervasively sectarian," it is extremely difficult to separate the sacred from the secular and then aid only the secular. The Supreme Court has held that a state loan of secular instructional materials and equipment to religiously based schools (such as the map alluded to in the illustration at the beginning of the chapter) violated the First Amendment, largely because "the predominantly religious character of the schools" meant the sacred and the secular could not be neatly separated and only the secular aided. The sacred and secular were so intertwined, the Court ruled, that to aid one was to aid the other.

[I]t would simply ignore reality to attempt to separate secular educational functions from the predominantly religious role performed by many of Pennsylvania's church-related elementary and secondary schools and to then characterize Act 195 as channeling aid to the secular without providing direct aid to the sectarian.[9]

Similarly, in a 1985 decision the Supreme Court ruled against a program of the Grand Rapids, Michigan, school district that provided religiously based schools with public school teachers to conduct certain secular classes. The Court ruled against this program in large part because it judged religion was being advanced in violation of the second aspect of the *Lemon* test. This was true, the Court ruled, since the pervasively sectarian nature of the schools meant "students would be unlikely to discern the crucial difference between the religious school classes and the 'public school' classes, even if the latter were successfully kept free of religious indoctrination."[10] In these circumstances a "symbolic union of government and religion"[11] would be created that would have the effect of advancing religion in violation of the establishment provision of the First Amendment. In short, public money flowing to "pervasively sectarian" schools runs the danger both of excessive entanglement of government and religion and of impermissibly advancing or endorsing religion.

A final legal doctrine important to note in order to understand Supreme Court jurisprudence as it relates to aid to nonprofit, religiously based K–12 schools is the principle that public money given to schools indirectly through parents or students does not carry the same connotation of state support or endorsement of religion as does money given directly to schools. In 1983 the Court approved a Minnesota program of limited tax credits for all parents who had incurred expenses in the education of their children, whether in the form of tuition payments for children attending nonpublic schools or supplementary charges or incidental expenses for children attending public schools. Writing for the Court majority, Justice William Rehnquist stated that "by channeling whatever assistance it may provide to parochial schools through individual parents, Minnesota has reduced the Establishment Clause objections to which its action is subject. . . . [U]nder Minnesota's arrangement public funds become available only as a result of numerous, private choices of individual parents of school-age children.[12]

The Supreme Court has never ruled that a general program of indirect aid to nonprofit, religiously based schools would pass constitutional muster. Nevertheless, it is clear that a program of indirect aid to private, nonprofit schools—where the aid is channeled through parents or children—has a greater chance of withstanding Supreme Court scrutiny than does a program that grants money directly to the schools themselves.

This brief survey of basic legal doctrines the Supreme Court has invoked to judge the constitutionality of public money flowing to religiously based, nonprofit elementary and secondary schools reveals that they are all rooted in a secular-sacred distinction. This distinction is fundamental to the no-aid-to-religion strain in the Supreme Court's approach to the issue of permissible and impermissible aid to private schools. The principle established in *Everson* of no aid to religion has been accepted, with the result that the sacred-secular distinction becomes the only basis on which public money going to religiously based schools can be justified. The remaining three principles— the three-part *Lemon* test, no aid to pervasively sectarian institutions, and indirect aid being more acceptable than direct aid—are really guidelines created to help judge whether or not public money going to religiously based schools is violating the norm of no aid to religion.

Although rejected by the Supreme Court, an argument can be made in favor of public aid to religious K–12 schools based on the free exercise clause of the First Amendment ("Congress shall make no law . . . prohibiting the free exercise [of religion] . . ."). If parents whose religiously informed consciences require them to send their children to religiously based schools must first pay taxes to support the public schools that they do not use, and then must pay tuition charges so their children can attend religious schools, is not their ability to follow freely the dictates of their consciences being burdened? Some of the dissenting justices in cases in which the Supreme Court decided against the constitutionality of aid to religious K–12 schools have made this sort of a free-exercise argument. Justice White, in dissenting from the majority decision in the *Lemon* case, wrote:

> The Establishment Clause, however, coexists in the First Amendment with the Free Exercise Clause and the latter is surely relevant in cases such as these. Where a state program seeks to ensure the proper education of its young, in private as well as public schools, free exercise considerations at least counsel against refusing support for students attending parochial schools simply because in that setting they are also being instructed in the tenets of the faith they are constitutionally free to practice.[13]

Similarly, in another dissent White argued that leaving parents who send their children to religiously based schools without any financial relief "also makes[s] it more difficult, if not impossible, for parents to follow the dictates of their conscience and seek a religious as well as secular education for their children."[14] Chief Justice Burger—while dissenting in the same case—also made a free-exercise argument when he wrote that "the statutes . . . at issue here merely attempt to equalize that 'benefit' by giving to parents of private school children, in the form of dollars or tax deductions, what the parents of public school children receive in kind. It is no more than simple equity to grant partial relief to parents who support the public schools they do not use."[15]

The Supreme Court majority has, however, not bought such arguments. Its establishment clause interpretations that bar aid to religion trump, in its thinking, any disadvantages suffered by religious parents—and therefore any limitations on the free exercise of their religious beliefs—due to their having to assume the financial burden of financing both public schools and schools in keeping with their religious beliefs.

Public Funds and Religious Colleges and Universities

The Supreme Court's legal doctrines developed in response to the issue of government aid to religiously based elementary and secondary schools have served as a backdrop for its decisions in regard to government funds going to other types of religiously based nonprofit organizations. Private, independent colleges and universities constitute one type of nonprofit organization that has received substantial public funds. Many of them are religiously based. Four cases challenging programs sending public funds to religiously based colleges and universities have come before the Supreme Court; in all four cases the Court held the public funding programs did not violate the First Amendment religion provisions. At first glance, this is surprising given the very few and limited aid programs for religiously based K–12 schools that have passed Supreme Court scrutiny. A review of the four cases that have come before the Supreme Court reveals that the Court maintained its no-aid-to-religion line of reasoning, but nevertheless approved aid programs to religiously based colleges and universities due largely to its application of two of the legal doctrines the Supreme Court had developed in its decisions regarding aid to religiously based K–12 schools.

One of these legal principles is the sacred-secular distinction. The aid programs under challenge were approved, first, because the Supreme Court was willing to accept the separability of the secular and sacred aspects of education at religiously based colleges, and therefore it could accept the theory that public funds were supporting the secular mission, but not the religious mission of the colleges. By making a clear-cut distinction between the religious and the secular elements in a college education and then only funding the secular elements, one can have government financial aid to a religious college without giving aid to religion (at least in legal theory). In one of the cases, the Court observed that the challenged program of aid "was carefully drafted to ensure that the federally subsidized facilities would be devoted to the secular and not the religious function of the recipient institutions."[16] Another decision noted that "the secular and sectarian activities of the colleges were easily separated."[17] This decision also quotes approvingly the lower court's finding that "the colleges perform 'essentially secular educational functions' that are distinct and separable from religious activity."[18]

But this approach by itself does not distinguish the cases dealing with higher education from those dealing with elementary and secondary education. After all, this is the claim the Supreme Court has largely rejected when it comes to K–12 schools. The key distinction the Court has made is that in its view religiously based colleges and universities are not "pervasively sectarian" while religiously based K–12 schools are. The first of the four cases dealt with a federal government program of construction grants to colleges and universities. In upholding this program, Chief Justice Warren Burger noted the four institutions whose construction grants were at issue in that case were not clearly sectarian in nature, but "were characterized by an atmosphere of academic freedom rather than religious indoctrination."[19] In the next case considered by the Supreme Court, dealing with a South Carolina program of assisting in the construction of college and university buildings, Justice Lewis Powell, writing for a 6–3 majority, made the point concerning the importance of a pervasively religious nature even more clearly:

> Aid normally may be thought to have a primary effect of advancing religion [in violation of the *Lemon* test] when it flows to an institution in which religion is so pervasive that a substantial portion of its functions are subsumed in the religious mission or when it funds a specifically religious activity in an otherwise substantially secular setting.[20]

He then went on to make the point that the college whose receiving of government funds was under challenge was not marked by such a pervasively religious nature.

Less clear, however, are the exact characteristics that distinguish a pervasively sectarian from a nonpervasively sectarian institution. The plurality opinion by Justice Harry Blackmun in *Roemer v. Maryland Public Works Board* is the most complete, carefully crafted of the decisions reached by the Supreme court in the aid-to-religious-colleges cases. Blackmun includes an extended discussion of the meaning of "pervasively sectarian." He begins by citing the *Hunt* decision as holding "that no state aid at all [may] go to institutions that are so 'pervasively sectarian' that secular activities cannot be separated from sectarian ones. . . ."[21] He then goes on to outline six indications from the case then before the Court that indicated the four Catholic colleges whose receiving of public funds was under challenge were not pervasively sectarian. They are worth examining in some detail since they are the best indication the Court has given of what it means by pervasively sectarian.

The first indication was the institutional autonomy of the colleges. The fact that they neither were controlled by the Catholic Church nor received funds from the church was important. Second, Justice Blackmun noted that religious indoctrination was not "a substantial purpose or activity" of the four colleges. This in turn was demonstrated by the fact that participation in religious exercises was not required and "spiritual development" was not a primary objective of the colleges.[22]

Third, Blackmun noted the presence of academic freedom on the four campuses. Instructors were free to teach courses in an "atmosphere of intellectual freedom."[23] The existence of mandatory religion or theology courses did not indicate a pervasively sectarian situation, since such courses "only supplement a curriculum covering 'the spectrum of a liberal arts program.' "[24] Fourth, although prayers at the beginning of classes and religious symbols on campus were common, the courses were taught in such a manner as to meet normal academic standards. Given that fact, prayers and religious symbols were not enough to indicate a pervasively sectarian situation. Fifth, Blackmun noted that religion was not taken into account in the hiring of faculty members. "Hiring bias" or an effort "to stack its faculty with members of a particular religious group"[25] would point towards a pervasively sectarian situation, but that was not the case here. Sixth, the student bodies at the four colleges were "chosen without regard to religion."[26]

These six observations made by Justice Blackmun in the *Roemer* case ought not to be taken as essential criteria, all of which, or even a preponderance of which, must be present if an institution is to avoid the "pervasively sectarian" tag. As Blackmun himself wrote, "To answer the question whether an institution is so 'pervasively sectarian' that it may receive no direct state aid of any kind, it is necessary to paint a general picture of the institution, composed of many elements."[27] The six observations Blackmun cited were seen by him as important characteristics of the four colleges that to him painted a general picture of nonpervasive sectarianism. Which ones and how many could be missing (or substituted by others) and a college still not be "pervasively sectarian" is unknown.

Some additional light is cast on the pervasively sectarian concept by Justice William Brennan's opinions in two cases dealing with aid to religious K–12 schools that were decided on the same day in 1985. *Aguilar v. Felton* ruled against New York's policy of providing public school teachers to teach in a nonpublic school program of remedial education for children from low-income families on the basis that "the aid is provided in a pervasively sectarian environment."[28] In describing this ruling Brennan listed four characteristics of the religiously based K–12 schools that led the Court to conclude they were pervasively sectarian: "[M]any of the schools here receive funds and report back to their affiliated church, require attendance at church religious exercises, begin the schoolday or class period with prayer, and grant preference in admission to members of the sponsoring denominations."[29] In *Grand Rapids v. Ball*, which dealt with placing public school teachers in religious school classrooms to teach certain secular subjects, Justice Brennan listed—using slightly different language—the same four considerations he did in the *Aguilar* decisions and added a fifth: having "faculties . . . composed largely of adherents of the particular denomination [sponsoring the school]."[30]

A comparison of the four characteristics of pervasively sectarian schools in the *Aguilar* case, the five listed in the *Grand Rapids* case, and the six listed in the *Roemer* case reveals the failure of the Supreme Court to define clearly what it means by "pervasively sectarian." There are three characteristics on which the three cases are in agreement. All three mention institutional control by the sponsoring religious body, required religious exercises, and giving preference in admissions to students from one's own religious tradition as indicating a pervasively sectarian institution (and their absence as an indication of an institution that is not pervasively sectarian). But that is where the agreement ends. Religious conditions in hiring faculty is mentioned in *Roemer* and *Grand Rapids*, but is very conspicuous by its absence in *Aguilar*, especially when one recalls that *Grand Rapids* and *Aguilar* were decided the same day and both opinions were written by the same person—Justice Brennan, a justice known for his carefully crafted opinions. Should this be interpreted as an indication that faculty from the religious tradition of the school is less important that the other characteristics in signaling a pervasively sectarian nature? Justice Brennan specifically mentioned prayers at the start of the school day and at the beginning of classes as important factors indicating a pervasively sectarian nature in *Aguilar* and *Grand Rapids*, but in *Roemer* Justice Blackmun took note of the fact that classes were sometimes begun with prayer at the challenged institutions, but concluded this was not important since class prayers did not seem to subvert "the academic requirements intrinsic to the subject matter" and did not signal that "religion [was] entering into any elements of" the educational programs.[31] What was specifically cited as an indication of a pervasively sectarian nature in the K–12 schools was dismissed as unimportant in the higher education cases. Finally, Blackmun mentioned academic freedom and normal academic standards, but they were never raised in Brennan's *Aguilar* and *Grand Rapids* opinions. One can only guess what role they play in defining the absence or presence of a pervasively sectarian nature. It is hard to disagree with the conclusion Justice Blackmun himself reached in 1988 when he acknowledged that the "pervasively sectarian" standard is "a vaguely defined work of art."[32]

In addition to the two legal principles the Supreme Court has largely used to approve public funds for religious colleges and universities—the sacred-secular distinction and the pervasively sectarian standard—it has also made reference to two additional factors. One of these was also cited in some of the decisions regarding K–12 schools: the indirect nature of the funding. The most recent case dealing with public money going to a religiously based college was a 1986 case that concerned a blind student attending a Protestant college to study to be a pastor or other church leader. A unanimous Supreme Court overturned the Washington state Supreme Court, insisting that this program of aid to the student and, indirectly, to the college he was attending did not violate the establishment clause. Key to this decision was the indirect nature of the aid. As with the Minnesota tax credit program discussed earlier, the public money that ended up in the coffers of a religious institution was due to the individual student's decision. "Any aid provided under Washington's program that ultimately flows to religious institutions does so only as a result of the genuinely independent and private choices of aid recipients."[33] Nevertheless, the fact the public funds were supporting a student studying for a religious career at a religious college—and the unanimity of the decision— bear striking testimony to the Court's much greater willingness to approve public money flowing to colleges and universities than to K–12 schools.

A second additional factor that appears to have influenced Supreme Court thinking in distinguishing K–12 funding from higher education funding is the younger, more impressionable nature of the students at K–12 schools as compared to college and university students. In the *Tilton* decision the Court majority stated: "There is substance to the contention that college students are less impressionable and less susceptible to religious indoctrination. . . . The skepticism of the college student is not an inconsiderable barrier to any attempt or tendency to subvert the congressional objectives and limitations."[34] The Court's plurality opinion in *Roemer* also makes brief reference to this language from the *Tilton* decision, and later it briefly refers to the "impressionable age" of the students in elementary and secondary schools.[35] But having acknowledged this, a careful reading of these decisions indicates the nature of the institutions—that is, whether or not they were pervasively sectarian—was much more important than the nature or age of the students.[36] The impressionable-age argument never stands alone, but only appears in the context of the claim that religious secondary and elementary schools

engage in indoctrination, one of the marks of a pervasively sectarian institution.

Public Funds and Other Religious Nonprofit Organizations

As noted in Chapter 1, there is a plethora of programs sending public
funds to religiously based nonprofit organizations other than colleges and
universities. Yet only two cases have come before the Supreme Court
challenging this practice. One from the end of the nineteenth century dealt
with aid to a District of Columbia Catholic hospital, and one from the 1980s
dealt with funds going to some religiously based counseling programs dealing
with the issue of teenage sexuality and pregnancies. In each case the Supreme
Court upheld the program of financial cooperation between government and
the nonprofit organization within the context of its no-aid-to-religion strain
of judicial interpretation.

In the case dealing with government funds flowing to a Catholic hospital
the Supreme Court noted that the hospital, although it "is conducted
under the auspices of" the Catholic Church, was nevertheless separately
incorporated by an act of Congress. The Court saw it as ". . . simply the case
of a secular corporation being managed by people who hold to the doctrines
of the Roman Catholic Church."[37] Further, the constitutionality of the aid
was assured by the secular nature of the hospital's functions:

> The act of Congress, however, shows there is nothing sectarian in the corpora-
> tion, and "the specific and limited object of its creation" is the opening and
> keeping a hospital in the city of Washington for the care of such sick and
> invalid persons as may place themselves under the treatment and care of
> the corporation.[38]

The constitutional issues at stake were raised more clearly in the 1988 case
of *Bowen v. Kendrick*. In the Adolescent Family Life Act (AFLA) Congress
authorized federal grants for both public and private, nonprofit organizations
for the purpose of providing services relating to teenage sexuality and
pregnancies. By a close 5–4 vote, the Supreme Court ruled that on its face
the act did not violate the First Amendment establishment clause and
remanded the case to the lower courts to determine whether or not it did so
as actually administered. The majority opinion, written by Chief Justice
William Rehnquist, applied the three-part *Lemon* test and concluded, first,
that the act had a secular purpose: "As we see it, it is clear from the face of
the statute that the AFLA was motivated primarily, if not entirely, buy a
legitimate secular purpose."[39]

The key issue with which the Court struggled concerned the second part of the *Lemon* test, namely, whether or not the act's primary effect was to advance religion.

> In the District Court's view, the record clearly established that the AFLA, as it has been administered by the Secretary [of Health and Human Services], has in fact directly advanced religion, provided funding for institutions that were "pervasively sectarian," or allowed federal funds to be used for education and counseling that "amounts to the teaching of religion."[40]

One is back to the legal doctrines that government funds may not advance religion and that funds going even to secular aspects of an agency's program advance religion if the agency is pervasively sectarian.

The Supreme Court majority, while accepting the validity of these legal doctrines, reached quite different conclusions than did the District Court. It ruled that although there was no explicit statutory language in AFLA forbidding the use of funds provided under the act for religious purposes, such a prohibition was implied. In addition, it held that "the programs established under the authority of the AFLA can be monitored to determine whether the funds are, in effect, being used by the grantees in such a way as to advance religion."[41] The money could only go to support the secular aspects of the agencies' programs. Further, the Court majority ruled that the agencies receiving government funds were not pervasively sectarian, but seemed to be more like colleges and universities for whom public funds had previously been approved, than like K–12 schools for whom public funds had largely been rejected: "In this case, nothing on the face of the AFLA indicates that a significant proportion of the federal funds will be disbursed to 'pervasively sectarian' institutions."[42] Later Rehnquist's majority opinion made clear the importance of this pervasively sectarian concept, stating that when the case was remanded to the lower courts this issue would be crucial. "In particular, it will be open to appellees on remand to show that AFLA aid is flowing to grantees that can be considered 'pervasively sectarian' religious institutions, such as we have held parochial schools to be."[43]

It is noteworthy that the Supreme Court made its decision in this case totally on the nature of the programs and agencies under challenge, not on the basis of the age or level of maturity of the recipients of the services. In fact, it could not have done so and still approved the constitutionality of the program, since most of the recipients of the services were adolescents of secondary school age and thus of the same age as those attending schools that have been denied funding.

In summary, under the no-aid-to-religion strain in Supreme Court reasoning public money may flow to religiously based nonprofit organizations as long as the money goes to support secular services and programs and the nonprofit organizations to which the money goes are not pervasively sectarian. The chances of public funding programs being found constitutional is also enhanced when money is funneled to religious nonprofits indirectly through recipients of their services. That the decisions and interpretations of the Supreme Court in this area are highly controversial is revealed by the fact that of the six cases just discussed dealing with government funds and religiously based nonprofits (other than K–12 schools), three were decided by 5–4 votes, one by a 6–3 vote, and only the 1899 case of federal aid to a religiously based hospital and the 1986 case of a student aid program were decided unanimously.

The Equal Treatment Strain in Supreme Court Interpretations

There is a second strain in the Supreme Court's First Amendment interpretations and legal reasoning that also needs to be considered. Since the 1980s it has run parallel to the no-aid-to-religion line of reasoning, and in 1995 it received new, dramatic development by the Court. Establishment clause interpretation is presently in a state of flux on the Supreme Court. One senses that a majority of the justices are dissatisfied with no-aid-to-religion as the bed-rock principle on which to build the Court's no-establishment jurisprudence, but are undecided or in disagreement about what principle or principles with which to replace it. The equal treatment strain— also sometimes referred to as the equal access or religious liberty strain—is currently evolving, and whether it one day will replace the no-aid-to-religion strain, will partially replace it, or will simply peter out is unknown. It thus far has had only limited application, and none of the Supreme Court decisions based on it deal directly with nonprofit organizations and their receipt of public funds. Nonetheless the equal treatment line of reasoning is relevant to the issue of religious nonprofit organizations receiving public funds and needs to be taken into account.

This strain of jurisprudence was first clearly articulated in the 1981 case of *Widmar v. Vincent*, which ruled against a policy of the University of Missouri at Kansas City that excluded religious student groups from using university facilities for their meetings. Justice Lewis Powell, writing for an eight-person majority, argued excluding religious student groups from the use of university facilities all other groups could use violated their right to free speech and association. Then he used the *Lemon* test to conclude that allowing the religious group to use public facilities did not violate the establishment clause. He wrote that "an 'equal access' policy would [not] be incompatible with this Court's Establishment Clause cases."[44] Later he poured more content into this concept of "equal access" when he noted that the university had created an open forum "that is available to a broad class of nonreligious as well as religious speakers" and that "an open forum in a public university does not confer any imprimatur of state approval on religious sects or practices."[45] Both of these concepts—the availability of a public forum or benefit to a wide variety of religious and nonreligious groups and the absence of governmental endorsement or approval of religious groups or beliefs—were to prove crucial in the Court's subsequent development of the equal treatment line of reasoning. Three cases are especially helpful in seeing its development.[46]

Lamb's Chapel v. Center Moriches School District (1993) dealt with a school district's turning down the request of a church to rent its auditorium to show a series of religiously based films on child rearing. The Supreme Court's unanimous opinion held that since the school district's "property had repeatedly been used by a wide variety of private organizations,"[47] refusing to rent to a religious group violated that group's free speech rights. In addition, the Court held that renting a public school facility to a religious group would not violate the establishment clause, since "as in *Widmar*, there would have been no realistic danger that the community would think that the district was endorsing religion or any particular creed . . . ."[48] Only brief reference was made to the *Lemon* test. The concepts of nonendorsement of religion and governmental neutrality in treating religious and nonreligious groups alike were more important in the Court's thinking than a strict no-aid-to-religion standard and the "incidental" benefits being given religion.[49]

In 1995 the Supreme court handed down two decisions that significantly strengthened the equal-treatment line of reasoning. One dealt with the placing of a cross on the grounds of the Ohio state capitol by the Ku Klux Klan. In this case the Court held that there was no establishment clause violation by Ohio's permitting the display of the cross. Justice Scalia, writing for a plurality of the Court, relied on equal treatment reasoning:

> The State did not sponsor respondents' expression, the expression was made on government property that had been opened to the public for speech, and permission was requested . . . on the same terms required of other private groups. . . . We find it peculiar to say that government "promotes" or "favors" a religious display by giving it the same access to a public forum that all other displays enjoy. . . . [I]t is no violation for government to enact neutral policies that happen to benefit religion.[50]

Three of the justices would have given primary weight to whether or not the state's permitting the display of the cross implied the state's endorsement of the religious message conveyed by the Christian cross, while Justice Scalia's opinion downplayed this principle. (The three justices concluded that in this case it did not imply state endorsement.) But Scalia also argued one could not construe that government was favoring the religious display due to the equal access conditions under which it was displayed.

For the purposes of the present study the most important equal-treatment decision of the Supreme Court is its 1995 decision *Rosenberger v. Rector.* In this case the University of Virginia had refused to fund a Christian student publication, even though it had funded fifteen other student opinion publications. In a close 5–4 vote the Court held that the university's refusal to fund the publication violated the students' free speech rights, and that funding it would not violate the establishment clause. In his majority opinion, Justice Kennedy used the language of neutrality more than the language of equal access, yet the opinion is clearly rooted in the equal-treatment line of reasoning. He wrote:

> A central lesson of our decisions is that a significant factor in upholding governmental programs in the face of Establishment Clause attack is their neutrality towards religion. . . . We have held that the guarantee of neutrality is respected, not offended, when the government, following neutral criteria and evenhanded policies, extends benefits to recipients whose ideologies and viewpoints, including religious ones, are broad and diverse.[51]

A program funding a clearly—some would say pervasively—religious publication was saved from establishment clause violation because religion was not singled out for favored treatment and the funding was extended to "the whole spectrum of speech, whether it manifests a religious view, an antireligious view, or neither."[52]

In summary, there is a recent, developing strain within the Supreme Court's jurisprudence that runs parallel to the no-aid-to-religion line of reasoning. It would allow limited forms of governmental accommodation and assistance—even financial assistance—to religious groups and their activities as long as that assistance was offered equally to all religious groups and to religious and nonreligious groups on the same basis. This line of reasoning has thus far been used only in cases involving the question of the private expression of religious views and whether or not the establishment clause is violated when government in some way accommodates or assists in the expression of those views. Thus it has not directly challenged the no-aid-to-religion line of reasoning as it applies to nonprofit, public service organizations of the sort with which this study is concerned.

Nevertheless, the equal-treatment strain carries clear implications for religious organizations that receive public funds. When religious groups may not be excluded from participating in public programs or activities in which all other nonreligious groups are participating—even without giving up or segregating the deeply religious aspects of their programs—clearly the no-aid-to-religion principle and the sacred-secular and pervasively sectarian distinctions are being ignored, if not challenged. This can most clearly be seen in the *Rosenberger* case, which involved financial assistance to a Christian student publication by a state university. The four dissenting justices clearly saw that the no-aid-to-religion principle and the sacred-secular distinction under which religious groups have sometimes been permitted to receive public funds were being undermined by that decision. They wrote: "Even when the Court [in the past] has upheld aid to an institution performing both secular and sectarian functions, it has always made a searching enquiry to ensure that the institution kept the secular activities separate from its sectarian ones, with any direct aid flowing only to the former and never the latter."[53] They went on to advocate the continued reliance on "the no-direct-funding principle" over "the principle of even-handedness" of funding.[54]

Whether this new, equal-treatment line of reasoning on the Supreme Court will ever become the settled law of the land and be expanded to apply to public service nonprofit organizations receiving public funds is uncertain. Two strains of reasoning are today running parallel to each other on the Supreme Court and vying for dominance. One or the other may win out in the future, or an accommodation between the two may be found.

Nevertheless, the no-aid-to-religion line of reasoning is the longer, more fully established strain and only it has thus far been applied to the types of nonprofit service organizations with which this study is concerned. Thus I will largely assume it is the existing law, while also taking into account where appropriate the newer, parallel equal-treatment strain.

One final aspect of the legal situation nonprofits face as it relates to their receipt of public funds concerns civil rights law. The Supreme Court case of *Grove City College v. Bell* (1984) is relevant here. It established the principle that if a college receives government aid, even if it flows to the college indirectly by way of aid to students attending the college, the college is subject to certain federal civil rights regulations. The case dealt with Grove City College in Pennsylvania, a religiously based college that had accepted no government grants, but did have some students who had received grants under federal scholarship programs. The college claimed it did not have to comply with Title IX anti-sex discrimination provisions by filing an assurance of compliance. The Supreme Court ruled against the college, holding that although "federal funds are granted to Grove City's students rather than directly," the college was considered to be "receiving federal financial assistance,"[55] as defined by the act, and was subject to the act's reporting requirements. The Court went on to hold, however, that the requirements apply not to the college as a whole as the Department of Education had insisted, but only to the college's student financial assistance program.

In 1988 Congress overturned the aspect of this decision that held the anti-discrimination provisions of the civil rights law apply only to the office or program of the college receiving public funds.[56] The 1988 act made clear that if any financial aid is received by a college or university, all of its programs and offices are barred from practicing discrimination as defined by federal law. Thus, under existing law a college or university that receives any federal government money, either directly by way of grants or indirectly by way of student aid, is subject to federal anti-discrimination laws.

Public and Elite Attitudes

Parallel to and largely in support of the Supreme Court's decisions on public money and religious nonprofit organizations are opinions and attitudes prevalent in American society. This section examines the attitudes and opinions of the public and of societal elites towards tax dollars going to help fund religious nonprofit organizations. Attitudes towards public funds for religiously based K–12 schools, colleges and universities, and other nonprofit public service agencies are considered in turn. The factual information that is available is often sketchy, but what information is available is revealing.

A 1988 nationwide public opinion survey found the public sharply divided on the question of whether or not government should provide financial help to religiously based schools, with 41 percent favoring such aid and 50 percent opposing it.[57] Even more revealing is the fact that societal leaders in academia, the media, government, and business opposed financial aid to religiously based K–12 schools by 2:1 to 3:1 ratios. Among academicians 74 percent opposed it, among leaders in the media 67 percent did so, and among both high-ranking federal executive branch officials and business leaders 62 percent did so.[58] A similar reaction is observed among the media and other societal elites whenever a proposal to provide funds to religiously based schools finds its way onto a state's ballot. For example, in 1993 a proposal was on the California ballot that would have provided a $2,600-a-year voucher to the parents of every school-aged child in the state. These vouchers could then have been applied to children's educational expenses—either at a public school or a private school (including religiously based ones). This proposal was opposed editorially by virtually all the major newspapers in California, by the state's two senators (both Democrats), and by the governor and the mayor of Los Angeles (both Republicans). Mainstream opinion in both parties and in the media was nearly unanimous in opposing it. The proposal was rejected by the voters by a 2:1 ratio.[59] The Supreme Court, in rejecting most programs of financial aid to nonprofit, religiously based K–12 schools, is in the mainstream of public and elite opinion.

In regard to public and elite support for public aid to religiously based colleges and universities, it is difficult to say with confidence what level of support exists. What scattered pieces of evidence there are, however, indicate strong support for it. The simple lack of controversy attending such programs is one such piece of evidence. For example, in 1974 the Michigan legislature passed a program of direct state grants to all nonpublic colleges in the state (most of which are religious in nature), based on the number of their graduates who are Michigan residents. It passed both houses by overwhelming margins: 80–13 in the House of Representatives and 30–3 in the Senate.[60] On the national level, Basic Education Opportunity Grants and work-study grants regularly are given to private colleges and universities—religiously based and secularly based alike—without the great stirring of controversy that typically accompanies programs that would grant aid to religiously based K–12 schools. The same can be said of the earlier "G.I. Bill," which provided tuition grants to post–World War II veterans and could be used in either public or private (including religiously based) institutions. Similarly, the organized groups that raise the barricades against virtually any form of public money going to religious elementary and secondary schools are largely silent when it comes to aid to religious colleges and universities. One such organization is Americans United for the Separation of Church and State. An analysis of its monthly periodical, *Church and State*, published between January 1989 and December 1993, reveals there were 24 editorials related to the issue of aid to elementary and secondary schools and only four editorials related to the issue of aid to religious colleges and universities.[61] Similarly, there were a total of 175 news items or feature stories whose primary focus was some form of aid to K–12 schools, while only 25 dealt with public funding going to institutions of higher learning. The general rule is that among policy leaders, even those particularly concerned with church-state issues, aid to religiously based colleges and universities is largely a nonissue.

My wide reading in the area of public funds for K–12 religious schools versus public funds for religious colleges leads me to suspect that the differing ages and levels of maturity of the students in the two types of institutions plays a larger role in the thinking of the public and of policy elites than it plays in Supreme Court reasoning. I know of no systematic study of this question, but this distinction seems to come up frequently in discussions of aid to religious colleges and universities versus aid to religious K–12 schools.

As with colleges and universities, the attitudes of the public and of societal leaders towards public funds going to religiously based nonprofits other than K–12 schools have not been directly documented. What scattered evidence that is available indicates general agreement with public policies that provide public funds to religious nonprofit organizations. The best evidence is simply the lack of controversy attending such aid. In 1993 two *Newsday* reporters wrote a series of articles documenting the hundreds of millions of public dollars going to a variety of New York Catholic Archdiocesan social agencies. No great hue and cry—nor even a small hue and cry—followed their disclosures. One of the reporters stated he was "amazed at the nonreactions."[62] In Michigan, 75 percent of the children in foster care receive that care from private agencies, about half of which are religiously based.[63] The state, of course, pays for this care. From 1978 to 1982, I served in the Michigan Senate and chaired the Appropriations Social Services Subcommittee. Each year we appropriated the funds to pay for the care given by religiously based agencies. Not once in those four years was a single voice raised questioning the propriety under the First Amendment of sending millions of public dollars to religiously based agencies. The survey mentioned earlier of the periodical put out by Americans United for the Separation of Church and State, *Church and State*, found even fewer editorials dealing with religiously based nonprofit organizations and public funds than it did for colleges and universities. In terms of editorials, as seen earlier, 24 dealt with public funds and religiously based K–12 schools and four with public funds and religiously based colleges and universities, but only three with public funds and all other religiously based nonprofits. In terms of news items and feature stories, 175 dealt with public funds and religiously based K–12 schools, 25 with public funds and colleges and universities, and 34 with public funds and all other religiously based nonprofits (if it had not been for a series of stories on religiously based child care centers in 1989 and 1990 there would been even fewer stories than on colleges and universities).

In the following chapter, I report extensively on a questionnaire survey conducted of the heads of three types of nonprofit organizations: child and family service agencies, colleges and universities, and international aid and relief agencies. One question asked the respondents' opinion concerning public funds going to religiously based K–12 schools and another asked concerning public funds going to religious nonprofit organizations of the same type as that headed by the respondents.[64] Table 1 reveals the responses to these questions. As one would expect from previous studies, public aid to religiously based K–12 schools is highly controversial and largely rejected.

TABLE 1

Nonprofit Organization Heads' Opinions: Public Funds and Religious
K-12 Schools and Other Religious Nonprofit Organizations*

Heads of:	Percent who support-ed public funds to re-ligious K-12 schools	Percent who support-ed public funds to re-ligious organizations of type they head	Percent of those who opposed public funds to rel. K-12 that supported public funds to rel. orgs. of type they head
Colleges and universities	53% (N=384)	84% (N=383)	68% (N=124)
Child service agencies	33% (N=281)	81% (N=281)	72% (N=141)
International aid agencies	35% (N=81)	79% (N=81)	75% (N=44)

*See Appendix A for the wording of the questions on which this table is based.

Only one-third to one-half of the responding organization heads favored public funds for religious K–12 schools. But when asked about public funds going to religiously based nonprofit organizations of the same type as they headed, the responses were overwhelmingly positive. Four out of five said "yes" to public funds for religiously based nonprofits of the type they were heading (even though many, of course, were heading secularly based nonprofits). The third column of the table is especially revealing. It shows that even among the nonprofit heads that opposed public funds going to religious K–12 schools, strong majorities favored public funds going to religious nonprofits of the type they headed. Clearly—self-consciously or not—the leaders in the nonprofit sector who responded to the questionnaire were distinguishing between public funds going to religious K–12 schools and those going to other types of religious nonprofits.

For many of the religious nonprofit organizations receiving public funds, the distinction the public seems to make concerning the differing ages and levels of maturity of K–12 students versus college students cannot play a role. Many of them—such as family service and foster care agencies—deal with children of the same age as do K–12 schools. In addition, they often deal with children in at least as intensive or continuous a manner as do K–12 schools, as in the case of residential and drug intervention programs. In Chapter 4, I suggest an explanation for the sharply divergent public and elite attitudes towards public funds for religious K–12 schools and for other types of religious nonprofit organizations.

In short, whether tacitly or explicitly, majorities of the general public, societal leaders, and even church-state separation watchdog groups do not oppose public funds flowing to religiously based nonprofits, as long as they are not elementary and secondary schools. Whether the Supreme Court is leading public and elite opinion on this issue or vice versa can be debated, but one cannot deny that Supreme Court decisions are largely in keeping with public and elite opinion.

Religion and Government in American Society: Evolving Patterns

This section of the chapter presents four observations regarding religion and its changing role in American society today. Prevailing religious conditions in the United States, American society itself, and the role played by government in it are all clearly evolving. They are different today than they were at the start of the twentieth century—or even twenty-five years ago. In order properly to interpret and evaluate the legal principles and attitudes just presented and the data to be presented in the next chapter, it is essential that the four observations made in this section be fully understood and their significance appreciated. They form a crucial part of the setting for this study.

First, it is important to note that religion in the United States often has public as well as personal or private facets. There is a tendency in the United States to view religion as a purely individual, private affair. Religion—it is often assumed—deals only with an individual's personal, private relationship to the divine. This is the realm of personal belief and private devotion, a realm apart from those of business, technology, social problems, and public policy. That this image of religion is current among the United States policy elite is illustrated by a statement once made by former Speaker of the House of Representatives Thomas Foley: "Let me point out that I'm a Roman Catholic, and I've never—never—allowed my religion to affect my position on public policy."[65]

But a bifurcation that places religion in the purely private realm just does not square with reality. Religion often has public, social facets, in addition to private, personal ones. This is the case, first, because religion often has social or economic dimensions that compel its adherents to reach out to those in need. The pastor of a Presbyterian Church in Washington, D.C., for example, once said of his congregation's program of feeding the homeless: "The concept of feeding [the hungry] is rooted in Jesus' ministry itself. To prohibit us from feeding the homeless, they might as well close down our congregation."[66] The statement of identity of an interdenominational Christian nonprofit association working to provide low-income housing in Grand Rapids, Michigan, reads:

> The Inner City Christian Federation is a non-profit housing corporation whose leadership is motivated, and programs shaped by, our belief that all people deserve safe, clean, affordable housing, our response to God's desire that we seek justice in our communities, our grateful response to the saving love of Jesus Christ, and our desire to have others see His love in action.[67]

In reference to the host of social welfare agencies the Catholic church has established in the New York City area, Bishop Henry Mansell, the New York archdiocese's vicar for administration of Catholic Charities, has stated, "Look around the city at the variety of ways that people are taken care of. We do that because we believe in what we call the corporal works of mercy: feed the hungry, clothe the naked, shelter the homeless, visit the sick and imprisoned. It's classic, it's imbedded in the Gospel, and that's what we're called to do."[68] A sense of compulsion, of living out one's inner faith, of following the dictates of one's conscience is clearly present in all of these statements.

A second factor that results in religion having a public facet is the fact that religious beliefs often speak to issues of public policy. Robert Bellah and his associates took note of this fact:

> Yet religion, and certainly biblical religion, is concerned with the whole of life—with social, economic, and political matters as well as with private and personal ones. Not only has biblical language continued to be part of American public and political discourse, the churches have continuously exerted influence on public life right up to the present time.[69]

Whether it is a matter of hunger relief policy in Africa, abortion policy at home, nuclear deterrent policy during the Cold War, civil rights for African-Americans during the 1960s, or tax policies as they affect families today, religion and religious values speak continually to public policy issues. The bishops of Foley's own church have declared that ". . . love of neighbor impels us to work for laws, policies and social structures which foster human goods in the lives of all persons."[70] Many religious communities down through the centuries have believed that their religions speak to basic concepts of justice, order, morality, compassion, and freedom, and therefore that they speak to countless public policy issues.[71]

A third factor that frequently gives a public face to religion lies in the associations many religious faiths have formed in order to live out their faith in a wide variety of education, health, and social service enterprises. As

Chapter 1 has already noted, religion manifests itself in a host of associations dedicated to living out the tenets of faith by sponsoring a wide variety of social enterprises. As political scientist Kenneth Wald has written:

> In the United States, churches are not merely buildings that provide places for worship; rather, they have become multipurpose agencies providing an astonishing array of services, including formal education, social welfare, pastoral counseling, publishing, charitable fund-raising, recreational facilities, medical care, cemeteries, libraries, and summer camps. Several of the largest churches have become the hubs for worldwide operations, complete with the organizational complexity of a major corporation.[72]

The existence of a vast array of religiously based institutions and agencies leads to church-state interactions, since government is active in regulating such activities, is often involved in running similar or parallel programs, and, as noted earlier, often makes use of these religiously based agencies to achieve its public policy objectives.

This tendency of religious groups to establish a wide variety of associations is often a natural, and even necessary, outgrowth of their faith commitments, not something that is incidental or ancillary to their faith. It is no exaggeration to say their members are often compelled by conscience to establish and maintain certain service organizations. Religious nonprofit organizations are often concrete embodiments of certain beliefs of the religious faiths out of which they arise.

In short, the assumption that religion is a purely private affair is factually, demonstrably false, and efforts to develop church-state theories and concepts based on it are doomed to be misleading at best and destructive of religious freedom at worst. To interfere with or to disadvantage religious groups as they seek to meet the needs they perceive in society, to influence public policy, or to form their own organizations to live out their faith is to interfere with their religious autonomy, and possibly, with their free exercise of religion as guaranteed by the First Amendment.

Three major changes in American society and public policy that emerged in the twentieth century have made the consequences of ignoring the public, societal nature of religion particularly serious. These changes have worked to alter radically the context within which church-state relations must be worked out. Nevertheless, their significance for church-state relations and especially for religiously based nonprofits has largely gone unnoticed.

The first of these new conditions—and the second observation on religion in American society I wish to highlight—is that competition and debate among organized religious groups have largely been replaced by competition and debate between religionists and their allies on the one hand and secularists and their allies on the other. The early nineteenth century often saw sharp competition for adherents and community influence among various Protestant groups—Episcopalians versus Presbyterians, Baptists versus Methodists, and so forth. As the nineteenth century progressed, added into this competition was Protestant-Catholic competition, distrust, and often illwill and, to a lesser degree, Jewish-Christian competition and distrust. Today that situation has changed, as religionists from a wide variety of traditions band together to oppose an increasingly powerful secular movement. I am using the term *secular* here to refer to a view of the world, human relationships, and moral norms that makes no reference to a transcendent, supernatural world or being. The militantly secular periodical, *The Humanist*, describes itself in its masthead in words that virtually define secularism: "*The Humanist* presents a nontheistic, secular, and naturalistic approach to philosophy, science, and broad areas of personal and social concern." One can argue that the terms "nontheistic, secular, and naturalistic" are redundancies, but they help make the point that secularism denies any transcendent, supernatural realm that offers a guide to human morals and action.[73] As such it stands in stark contrast to religion, which, in its various manifestations, asserts God is there (or gods are there) and that he/she/they and his/her/their will for humankind are—to a greater or lesser degree— knowable by human beings.

Sociologist James Davison Hunter has concluded that "the secularists . . . represent the fastest growing community of 'moral conviction' in America."[74] He goes on to note that the proportion of the population without any religious commitment has increased from a mere 2 percent in the 1950s to about 11 percent at the start of the 1990s. If one looks behind persons' simple self-identification with a particular religious tradition (or the absence of any religious self-identification) and asks about more specific religious beliefs and practices, one finds that as much as 30 percent of the population can, for all intents and purposes, be considered secular.[75] Such figures represent only part of the story of secular strength in the United States, however, since secularists are disproportionately represented in positions of cultural leadership in American society. One study of key television writers and producers found that 93 percent reported they seldom or never attend religious services and 44 percent had no religious affiliation at all.[76] Another study of national media elite found 50 percent had no religious affiliation and 86 percent seldom or never attended religious services.[77] Much the same can be said for academic elites. Historian George Marsden has pointed out that early in the twentieth century one university after another, even those that were strongly rooted in a particular religious tradition, underwent a secularization process.[78]

Stephen Carter has described the net result of the power of secularism among the social elites of the United States:

> [O]ne sees a trend in our political and legal cultures toward treating religious beliefs as arbitrary and unimportant, a trend supported by a rhetoric that implies that there is something wrong with religious devotion. More and more, our culture seems to take the position that believing deeply in the tenets of one's faith represents a kind of mystical irrationality, something that thoughtful, public-spirited American citizens would do better to avoid.[79]

Meanwhile, religion continues to be a strong, vital force within the general American public. "The religious tapestry of America today shows a country that by external measures is at least as religious as it has always been. . . . [T]here are more churches per capita in the United states than in any other nation on Earth."[80] George Gallup Jr. and Jim Castelli, in summarizing fifty years of data collected by the Gallup organization, referred to "the enduring popularity of religion" in the United States, and went on to note: "There have been several periods of heightened interest in religion, but the baseline of religious belief is remarkably high—certainly, the highest of any developed nation in the world."[81] In addition, it is the more conservative, demanding religious groups, marked by the belief in a literal supernatural realm active in human affairs, that appear to have the most strength and vitality.[82]

The rise of secularism as a "community of moral conviction" in the United States alongside the continuing strength of conservative, literal religion has profound implications for church-state relations. Secularism and religion are engaged in an ongoing struggle for influence in American society. Hunter has given focus to the secular-religious struggle occurring in the United States today in his books *Culture Wars* and *Before the Shooting Begins*.[83] He persuasively argues that a struggle is going on in the United States between what he terms the orthodox and the progressives. At the heart of the differences between these two groups are "allegiances to different formulations and sources of moral authority."[84] The orthodox tend to accept a spiritual realm of existence, to believe in God's personal existence, and to accept the reality of divine revelation to humankind; the progressives emphasize the physical and material realms of existence to the *de facto* exclusion of the spiritual realm, reject the existence of a personal God or see him as removed from the daily affairs of this world, and emphasize empirical evidence and personal experience over divine revelation. This division between the orthodox and the progressives both unites religious traditions that had been at odds and divides religious traditions that had once been unified. Traditional Roman Catholics, Orthodox Jews, and conservative Protestants[85] will often make common cause. Meanwhile, progressive Catholics will find themselves in the same camp as progressive or secular Jews, many mainline Protestants, and thorough-going secularists. Whether one is more comfortable with secular views of life and the world or with religiously rooted, traditional views of life and the world is more important than one's religious tradition. The key point for our purposes here is that Hunter's orthodox and progressives are mutually exclusive worldviews that are engaged in active competition to shape individual lives and American culture generally. I will return to this observation shortly.

A third observation on religion in American society deals with the surprisingly recent secularization of governmental institutions and programs. Not that many years ago, government-established agencies and programs usually had a broadly religious coloration or nature. Marsden has noted: "In the 1890s, for instance, almost all state universities still held compulsory chapel services and some required Sunday church attendance as well. State-sponsored chapel services did not become rare until the World War II era."[86] When the public schools were established in the nineteenth century they were rooted in and reflected a broad, consensual Protestantism. In 1848 Horace Mann, generally recognized as the major force behind the development of the public school system, wrote approvingly that there is not "a member of the [Massachusetts] Board of Education who would not be disposed to recommend the daily reading of the Bible, devotional exercises, and the constant inculcation of the precepts of Christian morality in all the Public schools."[87] Until they were barred by the Supreme Court in the 1960s, public schools commonly had prayer, Bible reading, and observances of Christian holidays.

Religious neutrality is violated when broadly, but not universally, accepted religious elements are present in government sponsored programs, but one can argue with equal force that their removal from all governmental programs also violates religious neutrality. When all religious references, acknowledgments, ceremonies, and beliefs have been carefully removed from an activity or institution one does not end up with an activity or institution that occupies a neutral, middle ground between religion and secularism. One ends up with an activity or institution that, for most intents and purposes, is secular, not religious. Political scientist A. James Reichley has expressed it well: "[B]anishment of religion does not represent neutrality between religion and secularism; conduct of public institutions without any acknowledgment of religion *is* secularism."[88] What results when religion has been eliminated from the public realm is not a self-conscious, explicit promotion of an antireligious secularism—such would no doubt quickly be found unconstitutional by the courts—but what does result is what Hunter has termed a secular cultural ethos or a "latent moral ideology" that is supportive of a thoroughly secular view of life and the world.[89] The diffuse, latent nature of the secular outlook that is thereby promoted does not make it any less powerful a force in American society today. Its very diffuse, latent, and thereby subtle nature may make it a more effective force at shaping attitudes and expectations than would one that directly and explicitly attacked religion and religiously based views of life and the world.

The removal of all elements of religion from public programs thereby runs the risk of government taking sides in the religion-secular debate raging in American society today. As University of Chicago law professor Michael McConnell has framed the issue, "In the marketplace of ideas, secular viewpoints and ideologies are in competition with religious viewpoints and ideologies. It is no more neutral to favor the secular over the religious than it is to favor the religious over the secular."[90] The subtitle Marsden chose for his recent book—*The Soul of the American University: From Protestant Establishment to Established Nonbelief*—is striking. In today's struggle between religious and secular mindsets, many believe government agencies and programs have moved from supporting a generic, consensual Protestant establishment to supporting—implicitly, by default—the establishment of a generic secular cultural ethos. Neither one meets the norm of a genuine governmental religious neutrality.

The fourth observation on religion in American society today relates to the implications for religion of the emergence and growth of the comprehensive administrative state.[91] As the twentieth century draws to a close, government is involved in running programs, providing services, and enforcing regulations undreamed of at the start of the century. Government today reaches into education, health care, prevention of unwanted pregnancies, treatment for drug dependency, innumerable social welfare services, international aid and disaster relief, domestic disaster relief, civil rights protection, and protection of children from abusive parents, of spouses from abusive husbands or wives, and—most recently—of elderly parents from abusive adult children. In all these and many more areas, government now reaches out to assist, provide, and regulate. This growth in the scope and power of government continues to be a subject of sharp political debate, but even the conservative wing of the political mainstream—represented by public figures such as Bob Dole and Newt Gingrich—accept a level of government activity and involvement unknown a hundred years ago.

As government entered one area of activity after another, it was not entering virgin territory in which no organizations were already active.

Instead, the typical situation was that of a variety of nonprofit organizations—a majority of which were religiously based—being already present and actively working to provide certain services. Often these organizations were doing so very effectively and commendably; often they also were not fully adequate to meet the needs at hand. There was a hit-and-miss quality to their efforts at education, health care, and care for the homeless, orphaned, and abused.[92] In the latter half of the nineteenth century in the case of education and hospital care, and increasingly in other fields as the twentieth century has progressed, government has entered more and more fields of economic, social welfare, and health activity. As seen in Chapter 1, this has not meant the private, nonprofit, often religiously based organizations already active in these fields have faded away and disappeared. Government has time and again sought to achieve public policy goals through a government-nonprofit partnership.

The rise of the comprehensive administrative state means government and religion are now actively involved in similar or parallel activities: educating the youth, feeding the hungry, sheltering the homeless, counseling the drug dependent, and much more. Any conception of church-state relations must take into account the fact that government, secularly based organizations, and religiously based organizations—all three—now provide many of the same services. The rise of the comprehensive administrative state that regulates, licenses, and helps finance all sorts of private organizations also means it will normally regulate, license, and help finance many religiously based organizations.

As a result, issues concerning the nature and meaning of religious autonomy and the free exercise of religion are bound to arise in ways they did not in the past, especially when the existence of the comprehensive administrative state is combined with the secularization of government programs and the religious-secular struggle present in American society. McConnell has noted, "If all that the government touches must be secular, an increase in the scope of government activity inevitably reduces the sphere of religious choice."[93] If, as the comprehensive administrative state expands into new areas of endeavor, religious groups that had been active in those areas would have to retreat, then serious religious freedom issues would be raised.

These four observations on religion in American society today—the public, social aspects of religion; interreligious struggles being replaced by a religion-secular struggle; the secularization of government agencies and programs; and the intrusion of government into many areas in which religious organizations have traditionally been active—are highly relevant to any consideration of church-state relations generally and of the receipt of public money by religious nonprofit organizations specifically. Yet they are often ignored. The question in need of answering is whether or not either one of the Supreme Court's strains of First Amendment interpretation—as outlined earlier in this chapter—is adequate to safeguard the freedom and autonomy of religious nonprofit organizations. Are the distinctions and legal principles that are in place or are being developed adequate to assure that the American polity has not moved from the establishment of a generic Protestantism to an establishment of a secular cultural ethos? Part of the answer to this question lies in the terms and conditions under which in actual practice religious nonprofit organizations are receiving public funds. It is that topic to which the next chapter turns.

Notes

1. *Everson v. Board of Education*, 330 U.S. at 15 (1947). Emphasis added.
2. *Everson v. Board of Education*, at 16.
3. *Everson v. Board of Education*, at 17.
4. *Everson v. Board of Education*, at 18.
5. *Lemon v. Kurtzman*, 403 U.S. at 612–613 (1971).
6. *Lemon v. Kurtzman*, at 618.
7. *Lemon v. Kurtzman*, at 619.
8. See, for example, *Kiryas Joel Village v. Grumet*, 114 S.Ct. 2481 (1994), *Capitol Square Review Board v. Pinette*, 1995 WL 382063 (1995), and *Rosenberger v. Rector*, 1995 WL 382046 (1995).
9. *Meek v. Pittenger*, 421 U.S. at 365 (1975).
10. *Grand Rapids v. Ball*, 473 U.S. at 391 (1985).
11. *Grand Rapids v. Ball,*, at 392.
12. *Mueller v. Allen*, 463 U.S. at 399 (1983).
13. *Lemon v. Kurtzman*, at 665.
14. *Committee for Public Education v. Nyquist*, 413 U.S. at 820 (1973).
15. *Committee for Public Education v. Nyquist*, at 803.
16. *Tilton v. Richardson*, 403 U.S. at 679 (1971).
17. *Roemer v. Maryland Public Works Board*, 426 U.S. at 764 (1976).
18. *Roemer v. Maryland Public Works Board*, at 762.
19. *Tilton v. Richardson*, at 681.
20. *Hunt v. McNair*, 413 U.S. at 743 (1973).
21. *Roemer v. Maryland Public Works Board*, at 755.
22. *Roemer v. Maryland Public Works Board*, at 755.
23. *Roemer v. Maryland Public Works Board*, at 756.
24. *Roemer v. Maryland Public Works Board*, at 756. The quotation is from the district court decision.
25. *Roemer v. Maryland Public Works Board*, at 757, quoting from the district court opinion.

26. *Roemer v. Maryland Public Works Board,* at 758.

27. *Roemer v. Maryland Public Works Board,* at 758.

28. *Aguilar v. Felton,* 473 U.S. at 412 (1985).

29. *Aguilar v. Felton,* at 412.

30. *Grand Rapids v. Ball,* at 384, footnote 6.

31. *Roemer v. Maryland Public Works Board,* at 757.

32. See *Bowen v. Kendrick,* 487 U.S. at 631 (1988).

33. *Witters v. Washington Department of Services for the Blind,* 474 U.S. at 487 (1986).

34. *Tilton v. Richardson,* at 686.

35. *Roemer v. Maryland Public Works Board,* at 764.

36. See, for example, Blackmun's summary argument in *Roemer* where he refers to the "character-of-institution distinctions" as being "most impressive" and gives only passing reference to the differing ages of the students. *Roemer v. Maryland Public Works Board,* at 764–765.

37. *Bradfield v. Roberts,* 175 U.S. at 298–299 (1899).

38. *Bradfield v. Roberts,* at 299–300.

39. *Bowen v. Kendrick,* at 602.

40. *Bowen v. Kendrick,* at 599.

41. *Bowen v. Kendrick,* at 615.

42. *Bowen v. Kendrick,* at 610.

43. *Bowen v. Kendrick,* at 621.

44. *Widmar v. Vincent,* 454 U.S. at 271 (1981).

45. *Widmar v. Vincent,* at 275.

46. In addition to the cases discussed in this section, the equal-access strain also played a major role in *Westside Community Schools v. Mergens,* 58 LW 4720 (1990) and *Zobrest v. Catalina School District* (1993) 125 L Ed 2d 1.

47. *Lamb's Chapel v. Center Moriches School District,* 1993 LW 187864, at 5.

48. *Lamb's Chapel v. Center Moriches School District,* at 5–6.

49. The opinion at one point declared that "any benefit to religion or to the Church would have been no more than incidental." *Lamb's Chapel v. Center Moriches School District,* at 6.

50. *Capitol Square Review Board v. Pinette,* 1995 WL 38063, at 6.

51. *Rosenberger v. Rector,* at 10–11.

52. *Rosenberger v. Rector,* at 11.

53. *Rosenberger v. Rector,* at 24.

54. *Rosenberger v. Rector,* at 27.

55. *Grove City College v. Ball,* 465 U.S. at 569 (1984).

56. See "Grove City Bill Enacted Over Reagan's Veto," *Congressional Quarterly Almanac, 1988,* 44 (Washington, DC: Congressional Quarterly, 1989), 63–68.

57. The Williamsburg Charter Foundation, *The Williamsburg Charter Survey on Religion and Public Life* (Washington, DC: The Williamsburg Charter Foundation, 1988), Appendix, Table 37. Also see a study based in large part on this survey: Ted G. Gelen and Clyde Wilcox, *Public Attitudes Toward Church and State* (Armonk, NY: M. E. Sharpe, 1995).

58. *The Williamsburg Charter Survey.* More specifically the academics were a random sample of 155 university faculty members of Ph.D.-granting departments of political science, sociology, history, and English; the media leaders were a random sample of 100 radio and television news directors who were members of the Radio and Television News Directors Association and newspaper editors in cities of over 100,000 population; the government leaders were a random sample of 106 high-level federal executive branch political appointees; and the business leaders were a random sample of 202 executives listed in *Who's Who in Industry and Finance.*

59. On this proposal and the line up of persons and groups for and against it and the final vote see Laura A. Locke, "The Voucher Initiative: Breakthrough or Break-up for California Schools?" *The California Journal* 24 (October, 1993): 8–14; "Helping Schools—and Not Helping," *Los Angeles Times,* 30 October 1993, B7; and Laura A. Locke, "Proposition 174: Vouchers Lose Big," *The California Journal* 24 (December, 1993): 21–22.

60. *Journal of the House of Representatives, 1973 Regular Session,* vol. 4 (Lansing, MI: The State of Michigan, 1973), 2980, and *Journal of the Senate, 1974 Regular Session,* vol. 1 (Lansing, MI: The State of Michigan, 1974), 494–495.

61. Based on a content analysis done by the author. See *Church and State,* 42 (January, 1989) through 46 (December, 1993).

62. Telephone interview with Thomas Maier, April 7, 1994. See Thomas Maier, "Cardinal Rules," *Newsday* (May 16, 1993), 22–24, Thomas Maier and Tom Curran, "Church Services: Public Funds Help O'Connor to Help Others," *Newsday* (May 17, 1993), 6 and 26, and Thomas Maier, "Balancing Morality and Mortality," *Newsday* (May 17, 1993), 26–27.

63. Stephen V. Monsma, *Positive Neutrality: Letting Religious Freedom Ring* (Westport, CT: Greenwood, 1993), 242.

64. See Appendix A for copies of the three questionnaires and the exact wording of the questions on which I am reporting here.

65. Quoted in Nancy Traver, "Breakfast with the Speaker," *Time Bureau Chiefs' Report* (*Time* magazine company, 1991), 2.

66. Quoted in "Presbyterians Protest D.C. Zoning Regulations," *Church and State* 47 (1994): 51.

67. *Inner City Christian Federation 1993 Annual Report,* 3.

68. Quoted in Maier and Curran, "Church Services," 26.

69. Robert Bellah, Richard Madsen, William M. Sullivan, Ann Swindler, and Steven M. Tipton, *Habits of the Heart* (New York: Harper & Row, Perennial Library, 1986), 220.

70. National Conference of Catholic Bishops, "To Live in Christ Jesus, A Pastoral Reflection on the Moral Life," (November 11, 1976) in *Quest for Justice,* J. Brian Benestad and Francis J. Butler, eds. (Washington, DC: National Conference of Catholic Bishops, 1981), 36-37.

71. Such concepts can also, of course, be rooted in nonreligious, secular world-views, but that does not take away from the fact that many are religiously based.

72. Kenneth D. Wald, *Religion and Politics in the United States,* 2nd ed. (Washington, DC: Congressional Quarterly, 1992), 27.

73. It is not accurate, of course, to say secularism is without moral norms and standards or without any nonempirical beliefs. Most secularists hold to certain ethical and moral standards for whose validity there is no empirical proof, sometimes doing so explicitly and self-consciously, sometimes implicitly and unself-consciously.

74. See James Davison Hunter, *Culture Wars: The Struggle to Define America* (New York: Basic Books, 1991), 76.

75. See "The Rites of Americans," *Newsweek* (November 29, 1993): 80–82.

76. Linda S. Lichter, S. Robert Lichter, and Stanley Rothman, "Hollywood and America: The Odd Couple," *Public Opinion* 5 (December/January, 1983): 55.

77. See S. Robert Lichter, Stanley Rothman, and Linda S. Lichter, *The Media Elite* (Bethesda, MD: Adler and Adler, 1986), 22.

78. See George M. Marsden, *The Soul of the American University: From Protestant Establishment to Established Nonbelief* (New York: Oxford University Press, 1994), and George M. Marsden, "The Soul of the American University: An Historical Overview," in George M. Marsden and Bradley J. Longfield, eds., *The Secularization of the Academy* (New York: Oxford University Press, 1992), 9–45.

79. Stephen L. Carter, *The Culture of Disbelief* (New York: Basic Books, 1993), 6–7.

80. "Spiritual America," *U.S. News and World Report*, 116 (April 4, 1994), 50.

81. George Gallup Jr. and Jim Castelli, *The People's Religion* (New York: Macmillan, 1989), 20.

82. See Roger Finke and Rodney Stark, *The Churches of America: 1776–1990* (New Brunswick, NJ: Rutgers University Press, 1992), especially chap. 7.

83. See Hunter, *Culture Wars*, and James Davison Hunter, *Before the Shooting Begins: Searching for Democracy in America's Culture War* (New York: Free Press, 1994).

84. Hunter, *Culture Wars* , 118. Emphasis removed.

85. There is no consensus on the best terms with which to refer to the wing of Protestantism that accepts the traditional, historical teachings of Christianity and the Bible in a literal, orthodox manner. As I have done in some of my other writings, and have explained elsewhere, I have chosen the term *conservative Protestant* and will use it consistently in this book to refer to the *theologically* conservative wing of Protestantism, not prejudging whether this wing is also marked by political conservatism. Within this wing of Protestantism there are at least three distinct subgroupings or traditions. First, there are the fundamentalists, who take the Bible very literally, are suspicious of modern learning, and have a recent history of separation from the world. Their best-known leader is Jerry Falwell. Second, there are the charismatics, who are distinguished by an emphasis on the active work of the Holy Spirit in the world today, leading them to emphasize the reality of frequent miracles, speaking in tongues, and direct guidance by the Holy Spirit in the lives of individual believers. Their best known leaders are Pat Robertson and Oral Roberts. Third, there are the evangelicals, who emphasize a thought-out, rational approach to Christian truth and historically have sought to engage those outside of evangelicalism in discussion and debate. Their best-known leaders are evangelist Billy Graham and theologian Carl F.

H. Henry. For a helpful discussion of some of these distinctions, see George Marsden, *Evangelicalism and Modern America* (Grand Rapids, MI: Eerdmans, 1984), and Randall Balmer, *Mine Eyes Have Seen the Glory: A Journey into the Evangelical Subculture in America* (New York: Oxford University Press, 1989). This footnote is largely taken from Monsma, *Positive Neutrality*, 14–15, footnote 27.

86. Marsden, *The Soul of the American University*, 3.

87. Quoted in Charles Leslie Glenn Jr., *The Myth of the Common School* (Amherst, MA: University of Massachusetts Press, 1987), 166.

88. A. James Reichley, *Religion in American Public Life* (Washington, DC: Brookings Institution, 1985), 165. Emphasis present.

89. James Davison Hunter, "Religious Freedom and the Challenge of Modern Pluralism," in James Davison Hunter and Os Guinness, eds., *Articles of Faith, Articles of Peace* (Washington, DC: Brookings, 1990), 66–68.

90. Michael W. McConnell, from remarks prepared for delivery to the Subcommittee on the Constitution of the House Judiciary Committee (June 7, 1995), 3.

91. For a helpful discussion of the comprehensive administrative state and its implications for church-state relations, see Paul J. Weber, "Excessive Entanglement: A Wavering First Amendment Standard," *Review of Politics*, 46 (1984): 483–91.

92. Some have argued the nonprofits for the most part were doing a fully adequate job. See, for example, Marvin Olasky, *The Tragedy of American Compassion* (Washington, DC: Regnery Gateway, 1992).

93. Michael W. McConnell, "Political and Religious Disestablishment," *Brigham Young Law Review*, 1986 (1986): 462.

Chapter Three

Religious Nonprofit Organizations and Public Money: Patterns

In order to obtain a clearer picture of how the First Amendment interpretations and legal principles articulated by the Supreme Court are being carried out in actual practice and what impact they are having on the freedom of nonprofit organizations to carry out their religious missions, I developed and mailed out a questionnaire to the heads of three types of nonprofit organizations: agencies providing services to children and their families, international aid and relief agencies, and independent, degree-granting colleges and universities. I sent out 1,606 questionnaires and received a total of 766 completed questionnaires back, an overall return rate of 48 percent. The same basic questionnaire was used, although it was varied slightly in order to adapt it to the special circumstances of the three different types of organizations. (See Appendix A for copies of these three questionnaires.)

The questionnaires sought to elicit information concerning four distinguishable topics: (1) the general nature and programs of the organizations, (2) their religious or secular natures, including for the religiously based ones the nature of their religious affiliations and the practices motivated by them, (3) the extent and nature of the public money received by the organizations, and (4) the effects of receiving public money on the organizations, including the effects of receiving public funds on the freedom of the religiously based nonprofits to carry out their missions and practices.

The questionnaires were sent to the presidents of all of the 853 independent, degree-granting, nonprofit colleges and universities in the United States, and to the directors of 579 child service and 174 international aid agencies on nationwide lists of those types of agencies. The presidents of 390 independent colleges and universities completed their questionnaires (a return rate of 46 percent).[1] Directors of 286 child and family service

63

organizations completed the questionnaire (a return rate of 49 percent), and 90 international relief agency directors returned completed questionnaires (a return rate of 52 percent). By several measures the nonprofit organizations returning questionnaires appear not to differ significantly from those not doing so. Those completing the questionnaires represent a nationwide, diverse cross-section of nonprofit organizations of the three types surveyed. (See Appendix B for additional information on the survey, how it was conducted, and evidence indicating that the organizations whose heads completed the questionnaires did not differ greatly from those not doing so.) I supplemented the questionnaire results with numerous personal and telephone interviews with officials of the surveyed organizations, as well as with officials of umbrella associations composed of nonprofits of the three types.

This chapter reports on the results of this survey in four sections. First, it discusses the amount and type of public money the three types of nonprofit organizations reported receiving. Second, the chapter relates the religious nature of the nonprofit organizations reporting a religious orientation to their receipt of public funds, and third, it explores the effects the receipt of public funds has had on the religiously based nonprofit organizations and especially on their freedom to pursue their religiously motivated practices. The fourth section of the chapter summarizes and draws conclusions based on the previously presented information.

Nonprofit Organizations and Public Money

One basic, incontrovertible fact that emerged from the study is that most of the nonprofit organizations of all three types receive substantial amounts of public tax dollars. As Table 2 shows, strong majorities of all three reported receiving at least some public money, and many reported receiving substantial amounts of public money. Here and throughout the study I have defined "public money" very broadly to encompass a wide range of public funds, including indirect as well as direct funding programs, in-kind grants as well as cash grants, and loans, loan guarantees, and purchase of service contracts as well as grants. Tax exemptions or other tax benefits—often referred to as tax expenditures—were not included. A majority of the child service agencies indicated at least 60 percent of their funds came from the government. Colleges and universities reported receiving the least amount of public funds in terms of what they contribute to their overall budgets, but they were the highest among the three types of nonprofits in terms of receiving at least some public funds. A third of the international aid and

TABLE 2
Receipt of Public Money by Nonprofit Organizations

	Child Service Agencies	Colleges/ Universities	Internat'l Aid Agencies
Percentage receiving public money*	90%	98%	67%
Percent of total budget from public money:*			
None	10%	2%	33%
1% to 19%	13%	59%	23%
20% to 39%	8%	17%	11%
40% to 59%	9%	4%	9%
60% to 79%	17%	2%	13%
80% to 100%	37%	1%	8%
No response	5%	16%	2%
	99%	101%	99%
	(N=286)	(N=390)	(N=90)

*All forms of public money--direct and indirect, grants and loans, cash, and in-kind--are included. Thus among the included public funds are such items as purchase of services contracts, grants to individual users of a nonprofit's services, and in-kind materials. What are commonly referred to as tax expenditures are not included.

relief agencies reported receiving no public funds—the highest proportion of the three types of nonprofits included in this study. In terms of the proportion of their budgets received from government sources, the international aid agencies fall in between the colleges and universities and the child service agencies. They received a higher proportion than the former and a lower proportion than the latter. In short, the general pattern noted in Chapter 1 of a government-nonprofit partnership—in which nonprofits look to government for funding and government seeks to achieve certain public policy goals by way of funneling tax dollars to nonprofits—was abundantly documented by the results of the current study.

Among the child service agencies receiving public funds, the most frequent form of public money was purchase of service contracts, with 90 percent of them receiving some government funds of this type. Typically these agencies provide residential care and other services for children who are under state supervision or control due to their having been neglected or abused or being children and youths in the juvenile justice system. State or local governments then purchase residential care and other forms of education and counseling help for these children. As the head of one agency told me, "It's simply a business transaction. We provide a service for the state and they pay us for doing so."[2] The second most frequent form of government funds was grants of in-kind materials, with 41 percent reporting receipt of this type of assistance. Usually this consists of food or surplus government property.

Most of the colleges and universities that receive public funds do so indirectly by way of various student grant and loan programs, with 83 percent indicating they receive public funds by way of student scholarship grants, 93 percent by way of loans or government guaranteed loans to their students, and 96 percent by way of work-study funds for their students. Fifty-four percent also reported receiving low interest loans and 51 percent reported receiving direct grants. A majority (62 percent) receive government-financed faculty research grants. Clearly, independent colleges and universities receive a wide variety of public funds, but their other sources of funds—such as tuition payments, private contributions, and endowment funds—make the overall percentage of their budgets attributable to government funds less than that of the other nonprofits studied.

Among the sixty international aid and relief agencies that reported receiving public funds, by far the most common form was direct program grants, with 87 percent of those receiving public money reporting they receive this form of assistance. Next most common was transportation services, with 43 percent indicating they receive this form of aid (this usually consists of government assistance with the transportation of aid and relief materiel), while 35 percent receive institutional support grants (grants intended to improve the institutional strength of agencies involved in food relief programs), and another 35 percent receive grants of in-kind materials.[3]

In summary, a clear picture emerges that shows all three types of nonprofit organizations receiving substantial amounts of government funds, although the amounts and types of money received varies with the type of organization. Relative to their overall budgets, the child service agencies reported receiving the most and higher education the least. Child service agencies indicated they receive most of their government funds from purchase of service contracts, higher education indirectly from aid to students, and international aid agencies from direct grants.

I also analyzed whether or not the amount of government funds the nonprofit organizations reported receiving varied by the size, location, and age of the organizations. The most important conclusion to emerge from this analysis is that public funds are distributed very broadly. As a general rule, regardless of their size, location, and age, the nonprofit organizations studied reported receiving substantial amounts of public funds. It is not a matter of the government-nonprofit partnership encompassing only a narrow band of nonprofits. Large and small nonprofits, old, well-established and recently organized nonprofits, and nonprofits located throughout the United States—all are included in the partnership. The breadth and significance of the public tax dollars going to nonprofit organizations outweighed whatever variations in the public funding of nonprofits that emerged by their type, size, location, or age.

Two notable patterns, however, did emerge. First, the smaller organizations—and especially the very small ones—clearly reported receiving much smaller proportions of their budgets from public sources than did the medium-sized and large organizations. This is true of all three types of nonprofit organizations surveyed. Presumably the larger nonprofits, with their more professionalized nature and more internal resources, are better equipped to pursue and qualify for public funds. Or it may be a matter of the very small organizations having less need for public funds due to their lower budgets and, perhaps, stronger local support bases.

Second, in the case of the child service agencies and colleges and universities there was a tendency for the younger organizations to receive larger proportions of their budgets from government sources. Their founding and the defining of their missions may have taken into account the increase in public funds availability starting in the 1960s. Steven Smith and Michael Lipsky have argued that many nonprofit agencies came into existence starting in the 1960s specifically to take advantage of government funds that had become available.[4] A supplementary explanation could be that the younger nonprofits have not had the time that older organizations have had to develop strong alternative sources of funding, such as support networks in their communities and among alumni.

The study also explored the secular-religious nature of all three types of nonprofit organizations surveyed. At one point their heads were asked which of the following statements best describes their organizations:

- A private, secular agency with no religious base or history
- A private agency that at one time had a religious orientation, but today has evolved into an agency that is largely secularly based
- A private agency that continues to have a clear religious base and orientation[5]

Table 3 shows the responses to this question, both for all of the organizations of one type taken together and for the organizations broken down by their receipt of public funds. A bare majority of the child service agency directors and a strong majority of the college and university presidents chose the "continuing religious orientation" option. Only among the international

TABLE 3
Nonprofit Organizations' Secular-Religious Nature and Receipt of Public Funds

	Child Service Agencies			Internat'l Aid Agencies			Colleges/Universities		
	Secular	Religious in Past	Religious	Secular	Religious in Past	Religious	Secular	Religious in Past	Religious
All	33%	15%	51%	48%	15%	38%	13%	16%	70%
Percent budget from public funds:									
None	5%	0%	18%	29%	58%	30%	0%	2%	3%
1% to 19%	9%	7%	19%	10%	33%	39%	65%	75%	69%
20% to 39%	4%	7%	12%	17%	0%	6%	26%	20%	19%
40% to 59%	9%	10%	9%	15%	8%	3%	9%	2%	5%
60% to 79%	22%	15%	17%	17%	0%	15%	0%	0%	3%
80% to 100%	51%	61%	25%	12%	0%	6%	0%	2%	1%
Total	100% (N=92)	100% (N=41)	100% (N=137)	100% (N=41)	99% (N=12)	99% (N=33)	100% (N=43)	101% (N=60)	100% (N=226)

aid agency directors did a plurality choose the secular option. Further evidence was thereby given in support of the observation in Chapter 1 that many nonprofit agencies in the United States have a clear religious base or orientation. Only about 15 percent of the organization heads chose the option describing their organizations has having been religious in the past but now being "largely secularly based." Most nonprofits of the three types surveyed that started out being religious in nature still see themselves as maintaining a religious orientation. The assumption that most nonprofit organizations that started out religiously based have given up that orientation is not accurate—at least not in the eyes of their directors or presidents.

Table 3 also reveals the amount of government funds received by each of these three categories of nonprofit organizations. It clearly shows that the religiously based organizations of all three types reported receiving significant amounts of public funds. This is especially true of the child service agencies, a majority of whom reported receiving over 40 percent of their budgets from government sources. In the case of all three types of religiously based nonprofit organizations, strong majorities (from 70 to 97 percent) indicated they receive at least some public funds.

Table 3 also shows that among the child service and international aid agencies, the religiously oriented agencies receive less of their budgets from public funds than do the secular agencies, but among the colleges and universities the religiously based institutions, if anything, receive slightly more of their budgets from public funds than do the secular institutions. Among the child service agencies, more than twice as high a proportion of the secular agencies and those that once were religious reported receiving over 80 percent of their budgets from public money than did the religiously based agencies. Meanwhile, many more religious agencies get by without any government funds than is the case among their secular counterparts.

Among the international aid agencies, about 30 percent of both the secular and religious agencies get by without any government funds, but if one compares those receiving over 40 percent of their budgets from the government, one finds 44 percent of the secular agencies fall into this camp, but only 24 percent of the religious agencies do so. The religious agencies are notable for the large number that receive only small amounts of public funds (39 percent indicated they receive 1 to 19 percent of their budgets from the government, compared to 10 percent of the secular agencies that did so).

A surprising pattern emerged in regard to the receipt of public funds by the independent colleges and universities. The religiously based institutions tended to report receiving a slightly greater proportion of their funds from government sources than did the secularly based institutions. Table 3 gives some, but only limited support for this observation by showing more religiously oriented institutions in the higher categories of public funds received. It is more revealing, however, to divide the category of institutions receiving 1 to 19 percent of their budgets from government sources into two: those receiving 1 to 9 percent of their budgets and those receiving 10 to 19 percent. When this was done, 48 percent of the secular institutions were found to have reported receiving 1 to 9 percent of their budgets from government sources, while 33 percent of the religious institutions did so. Meanwhile, 18 percent of the secular institutions reported receiving 10 to 19 percent of their budgets from government sources, while 37 percent of the religious institutions did so. This means 65 percent of the religiously based institutions receive over 10 percent of their budgets from government sources, but a notably lower percent of the secularly based institutions (53 percent) do so. The institutions with a religious past fall inbetween these two figures, with 59 percent receiving over 10 percent of their budgets from public sources. There was a clear tendency for the secular colleges and universities to receive less money from the government than do the religious colleges and universities.

These findings confirm the observation in Chapter 1 that religiously based nonprofits fully share in the public-nonprofit partnership. Given the Supreme Court's finding of most forms of public funds for religiously based K–12 schools to be in violation of the First Amendment, and given the no-aid-to-religion position the Supreme Court has often taken, this finding—while not surprising to the knowledgeable observer—is nonetheless remarkable. In the case of one of the three types of nonprofits surveyed—independent colleges and universities—the religiously based ones actually tend to receive slightly larger proportions of their budgets from the government than do their secular counterparts.

Religious Nonprofit Organizations and Public Money

Looking more closely at the religious character of the nonprofit organizations receiving public funds sheds additional light on the nature of the public-religious nonprofit partnership. Given the Supreme Court's—and societal elites'—position that no public tax dollars may go in support of religion and given the Court's secular-sacred distinction and pervasively sectarian standard, one might suppose that those religious nonprofits that have managed to qualify for public funds without arousing public censure and legal findings of unconstitutionality would be the more nominally religious nonprofits and those associated with mainline Protestantism and Reform Judaism, both of which are culturally mainstream and high in status. And one might expect the nonprofit organizations that would not be sharing to the same degree in public funding programs would be from the Roman Catholic and the conservative Protestant traditions. Both of these traditions hold many beliefs that run counter to dominant trends among cultural elites, such as their belief in a literal supernatural realm that intervenes in human affairs and their positions on issues such as abortion, gay rights, and evolution. It is these two religious traditions that sponsor most of the K–12 schools that have largely been rejected for public funding by both Supreme Court First Amendment interpretations and elite and public attitudes. In addition, irregardless of the specific religious tradition, one might suppose that the nonprofits less thoroughly permeated with religiously based practices—those that are not "pervasively sectarian"—would be the ones receiving public funds. However, when one examines the religious traditions and religiously based practices of the nonprofits that receive public funds, none of these expectations are borne out.

Table 4 reveals the religious traditions of the 448 nonprofit organizations included in the study whose heads indicated they continue "to have a clear religious base and orientation," and Table 5 reveals what proportions of the budgets of the nonprofits of the various religious traditions can be traced to governmental sources. Table 4 shows that most of the nonprofit organizations surveyed fall into the Roman Catholic, conservative Protestant, or mainline Protestant camps. The Protestant organizations fell about equally into the mainline and conservative camps. There were roughly the same number of Catholic colleges and universities as there were mainline and conservative Protestant institutions, but in the case of the child service and international aid agencies the Catholic agencies included in the study were outnumbered by both the conservative and mainline Protestant agencies. There were a significant number of Jewish family service agencies, but no Jewish colleges or universities, and only two Jewish international aid agencies included in the survey. All of the Jewish agencies indicated they were in the Reform or conservative, rather than the orthodox, tradition or were rooted in all three traditions within Judaism.

Table 5 clearly demonstrates that the nonprofit organizations of all four religious traditions—Catholic, conservative Protestant, mainline Protestant, and Jewish—receive public funds. There are some variations among the four traditions in terms of the percentages of their budgets that they reported could be traced to government sources, but more striking than these differences is the widespread receipt of public funds across all religious traditions. In fact, the two traditions—Catholic and conservative Protestant—that one might expect to receive less public money actually tended to report larger proportions of their budgets coming from the government. Among the colleges and

TABLE 4

Religious Traditions of Religiously Based Nonprofit Organizations

Religious Tradition	Colleges & Universities	Child Service Agencies	Internat'l Aid Agencies
Jewish	0%	20%	6%
Catholic	35%	16%	12%
Conservative Prot.*	33%	31%	36%
Mainline Prot.*	30%	33%	36%
Other**	1%	0%	9%
Total	99% (N=271)	100% (N=144)	99% (N=33)

*An organization was considered mainline Protestant if it selected alternative 7 in Question 5 (see Appendix A) or if it chose alternative 5 and listed American Baptist, Disciples of Christ or Christian Church, Episcopal, Evangelical Lutheran Church in America, Presbyterian (USA), Unitarian, United Church of Christ or Congregational, or United Methodist. An organization was considered conservative Protestant if it chose alternative 6 or listed a denomination other than one of the eight listed above. If an organization gave a generic Protestant tradition corresponding to one of the eight mainline Protestant denominations, such as Presbyterian or Methodist, it was consider mainline, except if it simply gave "Baptist" it was considered conservative Protestant. I made the latter decision because the mainline American Baptist denomination is far overshadowed in the number of members by other, more conservative, Baptist denominations, such as the Southern Baptist denomination.

**"Other" organizations included Mormon, Orthodox, and organizations clearly cutting across Catholic, conservative Protestant, and mainline Protestant lines.

universities, 35 percent of the conservative Protestant institutions fall into the high category of receiving public funds and another 42 percent fall into the medium category, thereby outstripping the Catholic and mainline Protestant institutions in both of these categories. Among both the child service and the international aid agencies, it was the Catholic agencies that indicated they were receiving more public funds than were the other three traditions. Sixty-seven percent of the Catholic child service agencies and 75 percent of the Catholic international aid agencies fall into the high category in terms of receiving public funds. The surprising pattern is that the precise religious traditions one would expect to have the most difficulty qualifying for public

TABLE 5
Nonprofit Organizations' Religious Traditions and Receipt of Public Funds

| | Percentage of Annual Budgets from Public Funds* | | | | | |
	None	Low	Medium	High	Total	N
Colleges/universities						
Catholic	1%	43%	33%	23%	100%	82
Conservative Prot.	1%	22%	42%	35%	100%	74
Mainline Prot.	2%	37%	37%	25%	101%	63
Child service agencies						
Jewish	38%	46%	17%	0%	101%	24
Catholic	5%	5%	24%	67%	101%	21
Conservative Prot.	27%	16%	18%	39%	100%	44
Mainline Prot.	5%	14%	23%	59%	101%	44
Internat'l aid agencies						
Jewish	0%	100%	0%	0%	100%	2
Catholic	0%	25%	0%	75%	100%	4
Conservative Prot.	25%	58%	0%	17%	100%	12
Mainline Prot.	50%	25%	8%	17%	100%	12

*In the case of the colleges and universities low equals 1-9% of their budgets coming from public funds, medium equals 10-19% of their budgets coming from public funds, and high equals 20% or more coming from public funds. In the case of the child service agencies, low equals 1-19% of their budgets coming from public funds, medium equals 20-59% coming from public funds, and high equals 60% or more coming from public funds. In the case of the international aid agencies low equals 1-19% coming from public funds, medium equals 20-39% coming from public funds, and high equals 40% or more coming from public funds.

funds—and that have been turned down for public funds in the K–12 educational context—receive the highest proportions of their budgets from tax dollars in the areas of higher education, child and family services, and international aid and relief.

But perhaps the organizations that are receiving public funds—no matter what the religious tradition—have largely secularized, or at the least have significantly watered down their religious commitments and practices. As discussed in Chapter 2, this would not be surprising, given the Supreme Court's First Amendment interpretations under which religious nonprofits are allowed to receive public tax dollars. Thus it is important to raise the crucial question of the exact religious nature of those institutions that claim a continuing "religious base and orientation." This phrase could, of course, mean quite different things to different persons. Thus those heads of nonprofit organizations who indicated their organizations have a continuing religious orientation were asked whether or not their organizations engage in a number of practices with a religious motivation or aspect, such as having religious symbols or pictures in their facilities, having spoken prayers at meals, only hiring staff in keeping with their religious orientation, and encouraging their clients or students to make personal religious commitments. Fifteen such practices were listed in the higher education questionnaire, thirteen in the child services questionnaire, and nine in the international aid questionnaire, and the organization heads were asked to indicate in which ones their organizations engage.

Tables 6, 7, and 8 give for each of the three types of nonprofits studied the religious practices listed in the questionnaires and the percentage of organization heads that indicated their organizations engage in those practices, divided by religious tradition. The practices are listed not in the order

TABLE 6

Religious Practices of Religiously Based Colleges and Universities

Religious Practices	Catholic (N=95)	Conservative Protestant (N=89)	Mainline Protestant (N=82)	All* (N=269)
1) Spirit of service/love	99%	99%	89%	96%
2) A chapel on campus	99%	93%	90%	94%
3) Voluntary rel. exercises org. by the college or university	92%	96%	80%	89%
4) Taking rel. in account in student behavior policies	85%	96%	68%	84%
5) Mandatory rel./theology courses	82%	93%	65%	80%
6) Rel. symbols/pictures on campus	98%	74%	65%	80%
7) Voluntary chapel services	99%	40%	84%	74%
8) Encouraging student rel. commitments	62%	82%	35%	60%
9) Encourage faculty to integrate rel. concepts and ideas into courses	53%	88%	34%	59%
10) Compulsory chapel services	2%	72%	15%	29%
11) Only hire faculty in agreement with religious orientation	8%	67%	11%	29%
12) Give preference in hiring faculty to those in agree. with rel. orientation	26%	40%	13%	27%
13) Give preference in admitting students to those in agree. with rel. orientation	4%	34%	9%	15%
14) Compulsory rel. exercises org. by the college or university (in addition to compulsory chapel services)	3%	19%	2%	9%
15) Admitting only students in agreement with religious orientation	0%	10%	0%	3%

*Three institutions that fell in the "other" category in terms of religious tradition are included in the fourth "All" column.

TABLE 7
Religious Practices of Religiously Based Child Service Agencies

Religious Practices	Jewish (N=28)	Catholic (N=22)	Conservative Protestant (N=44)	Mainline Protestant (N=47)	All (N=141)
1) Spirit of service/love	68%	95%	100%	91%	90%
2) Voluntary religious activities	57%	68%	80%	87%	77%
3) Rel. symbols/pictures in facilities	85%	77%	64%	66%	71%
4) Informal references to religious ideas by staff with clients	61%	50%	82%	74%	70%
5) Spoken prayers at meals	7%	41%	87%	85%	64%
6) Required religious activities	0%	14%	57%	45%	35%
7) A paid chaplain on staff	4%	36%	39%	47%	34%
8) Encourage religious commitments by clients	4%	9%	73%	26%	33%
9) Taking rel. into account in making foster care or adoption placements	29%	32%	39%	21%	30%
10) Give preference in hiring staff to those in agree. with rel. orientation	43%	0%	45%	13%	27%
11) Only hire staff in agreement with religious orientation	14%	9%	32%	9%	17%
12) A volunteer chaplain on staff	7%	32%	16%	13%	16%
13) Giving preference in accepting clients to those in agree. with rel. orientation	36%	0%	2%	2%	9%

they were given in the three questionnaires, but from the most frequently mentioned to the least frequently mentioned. Two highly significant patterns stand out in these three tables. The first is that the respondents indicated that their organizations engage in many of these practices. One immediately receives the clear impression that the religious orientation these nonprofits claimed for themselves does indeed translate for most of them into distinctive practices. They are religious in more than name. This is especially true of the colleges and universities. A majority of the presidents indicated their institutions engage in nine out of the fifteen listed practices. (See the fourth, "all," column of Table 6.) Fewer practices were cited by the directors of the other two types of organizations, but among them significant numbers indicated that their agencies engage in many if not most of the practices listed. (See Tables 7 and 8.)

A second clear pattern is that in the case of all three types of organizations it was the conservative Protestant organizations that reported engaging in the most religious practices. If one compares the percentages of the conservative

TABLE 8
Religious Practices of Religiously Based International Aid Agencies

Religious Practices	Jewish (N=2)	Catholic (N=4)	Conservative Protestant (N=12)	Mainline Protestant (N=12)	All* (N=33)
1) Spirit of service/love	0%	75%	92%	100%	85%
2) Religious affiliation reflected in name or logo	100%	100%	83%	67%	79%
3) Informal references to religious ideas by staff with persons served	0%	0%	58%	67%	52%
4) Voluntary religious activities	0%	50%	58%	0%	30%
5) Give preference in hiring staff to those in agree. with rel. orientation	0%	0%	33%	17%	24%
6) Overt rel. activities by associated organization	50%	0%	33%	0%	21%
7) Only hire staff in agreement with religious orientation	0%	0%	50%	8%	21%
8) Encourage religious commitments by persons being served	0%	25%	33%	8%	21%
9) Helping construct religious centers	50%	0%	25%	8%	15%

*Three agencies that fell in the "other" category in terms of religious tradition are included in the fourth, "All" column.

Protestant organizations that indicated they engage in the various religious practices listed in Tables 6, 7, and 8 with the percentages of all the religiously based organizations taken together, higher percentages of the conservative Protestant organizations are found to be engaging in the listed practices than is the case for the religious organizations taken as a whole. This is true in the case of twelve out of the fifteen practices listed for the colleges and universities, ten out of the thirteen listed for the child service agencies, and all nine of the practices listed for the international aid agencies. (Compare the second column in Table 6 with the fourth column, and in Tables 7 and 8 the third column with the fifth one.) A higher percentage of the Catholic colleges and universities engaged in eight out of the fifteen listed practices than did all the religious colleges and universities taken together (compared to only one out of the fifteen for the mainline Protestant institutions), but among the child service and international aid agencies the Catholic agencies did not indicate a greater tendency to engage in the listed religious practices than did the Jewish or mainline Protestant agencies.

The conservative Protestant organizations, consistently, and the Catholic organizations of one of the three types of nonprofits were found to be engaging in more religiously based practices than were the mainline Protestant and Jewish organizations, thereby demonstrating that they apparently were not qualifying for public funds by making themselves more like the more culturally acceptable mainline Protestant and Reform Jewish organizations.

In order to study more directly the issue of the relationship between the receipt of public funds and the nature and extent of the religious practices pursued I developed the Religious Practices Scale (RPS), based on the organizations' responses to the listed religiously motivated practices. Depending on the degree to which a religious practice would tend to lead to religion permeating the entire organization and all its activities, points ranging from 1 to 5 were assigned for each practice listed in the questionnaire. Each organization was then assigned a total score, depending on how many and which practices its head indicated it engages in. The organizations were next grouped into three categories (two categories in the case of the international aid agencies), depending on their total number of points. (Appendix C describes in greater detail the construction and rationale of this scale.) Thus those organizations ranking high on the RPS are those that pursue many religious practices, and the ones they pursue are of a permeating nature that would tend to infuse the entire organization.

Table 9 reveals the amount of public funds received by the secular and religious organizations, with the religious organizations broken down by their position on the Religious Practices Scale. In the case of the colleges and universities it shows those ranking high or medium on the Religious Practices Scale reported receiving a greater percentage of their budgets from government sources than either the institutions ranking low on the RPS or the secular agencies. If one combines the institutions ranking medium and high in receipt of public funds (that is, all those institutions receiving over 10 percent of their budgets from public funds), one finds 56 percent of the secular and low RPS institutions, but 65 percent of the medium RPS institutions and 69 percent of the high RPS institutions. The previously noted, surprising pattern of the religiously based institutions receiving more public funds than do the secular institutions is a result, not of the less religious, but the *more* highly religious institutions receiving more public funds. This is the exact opposite pattern one would expect if one assumed that religious institutions were qualifying for public funds by reducing or playing down their religious nature.

In the case of both the child service agencies and the international aid agencies the opposite pattern held: the highly religious agencies reported receiving significantly lower proportions of their budgets from public sources than did the less religious agencies, and the secularly based agencies reported receiving more public funds than did the religious agencies, whether they

TABLE 9
The Religious Practices Scale and Receipt of Public Funds

| | Percentage of Annual Budgets from Public Funds* | | | | | |
	None	Low	Medium	High	Total	N
Colleges/Universities						
Presently secular**	2%	42%	29%	27%	100%	104
Low RPS	0%	44%	28%	28%	100%	36
Medium RPS	2%	34%	36%	29%	101%	103
High RPS	3%	28%	42%	27%	100%	86
Child Service Agencies						
Presently secular**	4%	8%	14%	74%	100%	133
Low RPS	9%	31%	15%	44%	99%	32
Medium RPS	12%	11%	28%	49%	100%	65
High RPS	33%	23%	18%	28%	102%	40
Internat'l Aid Agencies						
Presently secular**	36%	15%	13%	36%	100%	53
Low RPS	30%	40%	0%	30%	100%	20
High RPS	31%	39%	15%	15%	100%	13

*As is the case in Table 5, for the colleges and universities low equals 1-9% of their budgets coming from public funds, medium equals 10-19% of their budgets coming from public funds, and high equals 20% or more coming from public funds. For the child service agencies, low equals 1-19% of their budgets coming from public funds, medium equals 20-59% coming from public funds, and high equals 60% or more coming from public funds. For the international aid agencies low equals 1-19% coming from public funds, medium equals 20-39% coming from public funds, and high equals 40% or more coming from public funds.

**Includes organizations that indicated they always have been secular or once were religious but now are "largely secularly based."

ranked high, medium, or low on the RPS. Of the child service agencies ranking high on the RPS, only 28 percent receive over 60 percent of their budgets from public funds, while 74 percent of the secular agencies and slightly less than half of the low or medium RPS agencies do so. There is no clear pattern, however, between the agencies ranking low or medium on the RPS in terms of their receipt of public funds. That religion is indeed a factor in reducing the dependence of child service agencies on public funds is supported by the responses given to a question asked of all agencies that indicated they receive no public money. They were asked if their receiving no public money was due to a policy of not accepting government funds, or if it was just the way things had worked out. Of the thirteen agencies that receive no government funds and rank high on the RPS, eleven reported it was a policy not to accept government funds and only two said that was just the way things had worked out. But of the eleven agencies that score medium or low on the RPS and receive no public money, only four said not accepting public money was a policy and seven said it was the way things had happened to work out. The five secular agencies that receive no public money run counter to this pattern, however, in that three of the five said their not receiving public funds was due to a policy not to do so. (The numbers here are small, however, and thus caution must be exercised in interpreting their significance.) Whether due to fear of government control, other available sources of money, or other causes, it appears the religious nature of some child service agencies have led them to avoid public funds.

The international aid agencies showed a pattern similar to that of the child service agencies. Among the secular agencies, 36 percent reported receiving over 40 percent of their budgets from government sources, while only 15 percent of the highly religious agencies did so, with the agencies ranking low on the RPS falling inbetween these extremes. But this pattern is not fully consistent. More of the secular agencies get by with no public funds at all than do either of the rankings of religiously based agencies. As noted earlier, the religious agencies—whether low or high on the RPS—are distinguished by the large number of them that receive relatively small amounts of public funds. The international aid agencies are distinguishable from the child service agencies in that the secular ones seem, if anything, more leery of public funds than are the religious ones. Of the eighteen secularly based international aid agencies that receive no public funds, twelve, or 67 percent, indicated it is a policy of theirs not to accept public funds; among the ten religious agencies that receive no public funds only five identified their not doing so as the result of a policy they have adopted. This may be due to the fact that a continuing issue in the international aid community is the fear that accepting government grants may lead aid agencies to be come tools of American foreign policy. This fear was especially strong during certain periods of the Cold War era, when it was felt American aid—even when funneled through voluntary, nonprofit aid agencies—was being given in such a manner as to favor right-wing movements and to discourage left-wing or Marxist-tainted insurgency movements. It may be that the religious agencies—especially those with strong anti-Communist heritages—tended not to share the same hesitations as did many secular agencies to being identified with American government aid programs.[6]

In summary, religiously based nonprofit organizations of the three types studied are full partners in the public-nonprofit partnership. Nonprofits from all religious traditions and from all levels of religiosity, as measured by their religiously motivated practices, take part in this partnership. In fact, both conservative Protestant and Catholic organizations—for which there is some basis to expect they would be less involved in receiving public funds—in many instances reported receiving larger proportions of their budgets from government sources than did the more culturally mainstream, less distinctively religious mainline Protestant and Reform Jewish organizations. Especially among the colleges and universities it is the religious institutions, and, among them, the more religious institutions, that tended to report receiving larger proportions of their budgets from public sources. When it comes to public funds and religiously based nonprofit organizations, sacred and secular clearly mix.

The Impact of Public Money on Religious Organizations

This section explores whether or not the heads of the three types of religiously based nonprofit organizations studied perceive their organizations as losing some of their religious autonomy due to the receipt of public money. The importance of this question and the negative answers some researchers have given were first noted in Chapter 1. It is difficult to exaggerate the importance of the answer to this question. Given the pervasiveness of public funds going to religious nonprofits, given the crucial importance in many religious traditions of social and educational efforts as expressions of their faith, and given the existence of the comprehensive administrative state that has entered the same social and educational fields in which religious nonprofits are active, the United States is facing a freedom of religion problem of the first magnitude, if the receipt of public funds seriously compromises the religious autonomy of religiously based nonprofit organizations. This is an issue worth exploring carefully.

Theoretically, there are three possible sources of restrictions or limitations on the religiously inspired activities of nonprofit organizations that receive public money. One consists of government initiated and imposed restrictions and limitations. As a condition of receiving public money, government agencies could impose certain limitations on the "sectarian"—as it is often put—practices of the recipient nonprofits, or the receipt of public money could lead to court-imposed limitations based on First Amendment concerns. Such limitations would not be surprising, given the Supreme Court decisions holding that "pervasively sectarian" organizations are ineligible to receive public funds. Second, groups or persons outside of government itself—such as church-state separation advocacy groups, professional associations, and the news media—could pressure religiously based nonprofit organizations that receive public funds to refrain from certain religious practices. Third, the receipt of public money could trigger self-imposed restrictions or limitations on religiously motivated practices by leaders of nonprofit organizations, based on their beliefs that their receipt of public money means they ought not to or legally may not engage in certain religiously motivated practices, even in the absence of government-generated limitations.

It is not easy to determine whether these three potential sources of restraints on the three types of religiously based nonprofit organizations included in this study are in fact actual sources of restrictions on them. One is dealing with relationships and causes that may not be fully and self-consciously understood even by the nonprofit heads responding to the questionnaires. Subtle, hard-to-measure factors may be at play. Nevertheless, the information provided by the respondents gives some important insights into the question of the impact of public funds on their organizations' religious autonomy. This section explores the light shed by the questionnaire responses on each of the three potential sources of restrictions on the religious autonomy of nonprofits receiving public funds.

Government-Imposed Restrictions

The first potential source of limitations on the freedom of religious nonprofit organizations receiving public funds are those that originate with government itself. I explored three separate pieces of evidence from the questionnaire results that help indicate whether or not religiously based nonprofit organizations that receive public money have had to curtail religiously based practices due to governmental pressures and limitations: their responses to several open-ended questions asking directly about government pressures or limitations, whether they felt they could engage in their religiously motivated practices openly and directly or felt they had to do so subtly and indirectly, and their positive or negative assessments of the effects of their receiving public money.

Taking the colleges and universities first, three open-ended questions directly inquired whether or not the institutions have ever "had to curtail or eliminate any religiously based practices" due to their receipt of public funds, or have had any "disputes with government officials over what constitutes proper use of campus facilities constructed with government financial assistance," and whether or not they have had other disputes or have felt pressure from government officials on other matters related to their religiously-motivated practices. (See Questions 11, 12 and 14 in the questionnaire found in Appendix A.) Of the 267 colleges and universities with a continuing religious character that reported receiving public funds, nineteen, or 7 percent reported having to curtail or eliminate religious practices due to receiving public funds (Question 11), thirteen, or 5 percent, reported some sort of dispute over the use of buildings built with government assistance (Question 12), and the exact same number reported other pressures or disputes with government officials (Question 14). There was a total of forty-five mentions of some sort of a problem with government in response to the above three questions. Since some institutions responded positively to more than one of the open-ended questions, a total of 36 institutions (13 percent) cited one or more problems with government over their religious practices. (See Table 10.)

A careful survey of the instances of reported pressures and disputes with government officials reveals that they covered the whole range of possible issues or problems: hiring and promotion decisions based on religious considerations, compulsory chapel requirements, student behavior policies, and

TABLE 10

Government Pressures and Disputes by Religious Tradition and
Religious Practices Scale: Colleges and Universities

	Total Number*	Forced to Curtail Pract.**	Pressures on Building Use***	General Gov't Pressures****	Combined Problems*****
All religious institutions that receive public funds:	267	7%	5%	5%	13%
Religious tradition:					
Catholic	95	8%	3%	0%	11%
Conservative Prot.	88	9%	10%	11%	19%
Mainline Prot.	80	5%	3%	3%	8%
Religious Practices Scale:					
High	97	11%	10%	9%	22%
Medium	124	5%	1%	2%	8%
Low	46	4%	2%	2%	11%

*The total number consists of the number of religiously based institutions falling into that category that reported receiving public funds. Those institutions that did not respond to these open-ended questions were considered to have indicated they had not experienced pressures or problems, since I judged if they had had such experiences they would have reported them.

**The percentage of positive responses to Question 11 that asked concerning "any other religious practices you feel you have had to curtail or eliminate because you receive government funds?" Those who did not answer this question were counted as responding with a "No."

***The percentage of positive responses to Question 12 concerning "any disputes with government officials over what constitutes proper use of campus facilities constructed with government financial assistance." Those who did not answer this question were counted as responding with a "No."

****The percentage of positive responses to Question 14 concerning whether or not "any government officials [have] ever questioned any of your religiously based practices or brought pressure to bear on you to change any of them." Those who did not answer this question were counted as responding with a "No."

*****The percentage of institutions that gave a positive response to at least one of the three questions.

more. The one that came up most often concerned the use of buildings partially paid for by public funds (perhaps simply because one of the questions specifically concerned this). But even this problem was cited only thirteen times by the 267 religiously based colleges and universities that were receiving public funds. Six institutions mentioned that they had given up public funds that were otherwise available due to fears that accepting funds would interfere with their religious mission. As the president of a conservative Protestant college wrote, "We have forfeited government programs because of our religious nature—for instance state subsidies for child care for student mothers." The president of another conservative Protestant college wrote, "We did not pursue per capita assistance for each graduate provided by the State of _____ because it was clear we would have to modify our hiring practice of requiring a signed statement of Christian faith for all employees." Sometimes the problems indicated the authorities were more concerned with appearances than substance. The president of a Catholic university wrote that they "had to remove 'Catholic University' from our mission statement in order to receive _____ State money." A mainline Protestant institution reported it had been forced to stop the practice of prayer in classrooms. (In spite of a Supreme Court decision that specifically said prayer in classrooms did not necessarily mean a college was "pervasively sectarian" and thus ineligible for aid.[7]) The president of a conservative Protestant college stated, "We have felt inappropriate pressure from [the] state to compromise our rel. mission to obtain financial loans for building." As is the case in several of the above quotations, the reports of pressures and hassles more often seemed to come from state than from federal officials.

Reading through the thirty-six questionnaires that mentioned some sort of a problem with government officials one receives a picture of a greater potential for government pressures than has thus far materialized. Many practices over which some college presidents reported their institutions had received complaints or pressures are not practices unique to them, but are practices in which many other religiously based institutions also engage. The existence of challenges and pressures seem to have more to do with happenstance than the nature of the practices themselves. Thus there is a large potential for more pressures in the future. The president of one conservative Protestant college told me he feared this is exactly what the future holds: "Pressures are building to interfere with the religious mission of our college."

Additional insight into reported government pressures and restrictions is given in Table 10, which shows the percentages of the colleges and universities that reported government pressures on certain of their religiously based practices by religious tradition and the Religious Practices Scale. Clearly it is the conservative Protestant institutions that were feeling the most pressure. About one in ten reported some sort of problem or pressure in response to each of the questions, and a total of 19 percent of them—one in five—reported at least one problem with government in response to these three questions. Similarly, it is the institutions ranking high on the RPS that most frequently reported government pressures. (There is, of course, considerable overlap between the conservative Protestant institutions and those ranking high on the RPS.) It was the colleges and universities that are clearly and distinctively religious—whether Protestant or Catholic—that are feeling the pressures. Among those ranking high on the RPS 22 percent reported at least one problem with government officials in response to the three open-ended questions. But even among them it is important to bear in mind that 78 percent failed to report even one instance of pressures or problems over their religious practices from government.

A second measure throws some additional—if indirect—light on the question of government restrictions on the religious missions of religiously based colleges and universities that receive public funds. The presidents of religiously based institutions were asked, for each of the religiously motivated practices listed in the questionnaire that they reported their institutions do, whether they do them openly and directly or subtly and indirectly, and for the ones they reported their institutions do not do, whether they feel they ought not to do them, feel legally they cannot do them, or had no desire to do them. (See Question 10.) If the colleges and universities were feeling pressures or threats from government—and, possibly, from sources outside government—many presumably would indicate that of the religiously moti-vated practices in which they engage they do so indirectly and subtly rather than directly and openly. Table 11 shows that, on the average, 91 percent of the college and university presidents reported that for the religious practices in which they engage, they do so openly and directly, not subtly and indirectly. The only practices where even as many as 20 percent of the presidents said their institutions do them subtly and indirectly are those that encourage students to make personal religious commitments and that give preference in hiring faculty to those in agreement with their institutions' religious orientation. In the former of these, there are reasons other than fears of government pressures or restrictions to do them subtly or indirectly. Later we will also see that for those practices in which the presidents reported their institutions do not engage, an average of 88 percent reported they fail to do them, not out of feelings they should not or legally cannot do them, but because they have no desire to do them. (See Table 12.)

In short, the vast majority of the college and university presidents reported that their institutions either engage in the fifteen religiously based practices

TABLE 11
Manner of Doing Religious Practices*
(religiously based organizations receiving public funds only)

	Do openly	Do subtly	Total	N**
Colleges & universities	91%	10%	101%	152
Child service agencies	77%	24%	101%	60
International aid agencies	62%	38%	100%	11

*The percentages are the percentage of times, on the average, the organization heads indicated for the religious practices in which they engage whether their organizations engage in them openly and directly or subtly and indirectly. The percentages were found by taking each of the religiously based practices listed for each of the three types of organizations, determining the total number of responding organizations that indicated they did each of them and whether they indicated they did them openly and direct or subtly and indirectly, then for each practice the percentage of organizations giving each of these two responses was determined, and then the percentages for the listed practices were averaged. For the colleges and universities fifteen religiously based practices were listed in their questionnaire, for the child service agencies twelve were listed, and for the international aid agencies nine were listed. See Question 10 in the questionnaires in Appendix A.

**The Ns were found by taking the number of organizations indicating they did each of the religious practices listed in their questionnaire and averaging them.

listed in their questionnaire openly and directly or that they had no desire to engage in them. The pattern is not what one would expect to find if the presidents of the religiously based colleges and universities felt under strong governmental pressures to curtail or eliminate their institutions' religiously based practices.

A third measure that gives some insight into the issue of governmental pressures on religiously based colleges and universities that receive public funds is based on the more general perceived effects of public funds on the colleges and universities. The questionnaire at one point listed twelve possible effects that government funding could have had on the institutions. The presidents were then asked to indicate which of these effects had been

TABLE 12
Reasons for Not Doing Religious Practices*
(religiously based organizations receiving public funds only)

	Ought not do	Legally not do	No desire to do	Total	N**
College and universities	10%	1%	88%	99%	69
Child ·service agencies	17%	10%	73%	100%	40
International aid agencies	22%	14%	64%	100%	9

*The percentages are the percentage of times, on the average, the organization heads indicated for the religious practices in which they do not engage whether their organizations do not engage in them because the feel they ought not to do them, feel they legally cannot do them, or have no desire to do them. The percentages were found by taking each of the religiously based practices listed for each of the three types of organizations, determining the total number of responding organizations that indicated they did not do each of them and whether they indicated they did not do it because they felt they ought not to do so, felt they legally could not do it, or had no desire to do it, then for each practice the percentage of organizations giving each of these three responses was determined, and then the percentages for each of the three reasons were averaged. For the colleges and universities fifteen religiously based practices were listed in their questionnaire, but there was one that no college or university indicated it did not do and thus for them this table is based on fourteen practices, for the child service agencies twelve religiously based practices were listed, and for the international aid agencies nine were listed, but there was one that no international aid agency indicated it did not do and thus for them this table is based on eight practices. See Question 10 in the questionnaires in Appendix A.

**The Ns were found by taking the number of organizations indicating they did not engage in each of the religious practices listed in their questionnaire and averaging them.

experienced by their organizations. (See Question 9.) It is especially informative to observe the total number of effects that were selected and whether what could be considered positive effects or negative effects were the ones more frequently selected. If the religiously based institutions were suffering from serious constraints and limitations in their ability to carry out their religious missions, one would expect that their perception of the effects of government funds would be generally negative, and certainly more negative than their secular counterparts, who would not be suffering similar constraints and limitations.

The college and university presidents responding to this question reported a total of 1,483 effects, for an average of 4.1 effects per institution. The most frequently cited effect was the expansion of the student body and campus, cited by 70 percent of the presidents, followed by the expansion of services and programs, with 63 percent citing it, and then by more paperwork than should be necessary, cited by 61 percent of the presidents. The least frequently cited of the listed effects was the receipt of fewer private gifts, cited by only 1 percent of the presidents, while 3 percent cited changed research priorities as an effect and 6 percent cited changed building or development priorities. Two of the three most frequently cited effects were positive effects, and all three of the least frequently cited effects were negative effects. The college and university presidents perceived the effects of government funds in largely positive terms.

As noted earlier, one would suppose that if the presidents of the religiously based institutions are feeling pressures and tensions over their religious missions being stifled and limited, they would be reacting negatively, even in general terms, to the effects of government funds. When one looks at the extent to which the presidents of religiously based institutions cited either positive or negative effects of government funds on their institutions, there is, at the most, very slight support for the above supposition. (See Table 13.) The presidents of the 44 institutions ranking low on the Religious Practices Scale mentioned an average of 3.0 positive effects of government funds on their institutions, while the presidents of the institutions ranking high on the RPS mentioned an average of 2.4 positive effects; while the presidents of the colleges and universities ranking low on the RPS mentioned an average of 0.8 of a negative effect of government funds while the presidents of the institutions ranking high on the RPS mentioned an average of 1.0 negative effect. In other words, the more religious institutions named slightly fewer positive effects of government funds and slightly more negative effects. Making the interpretation of these figures more difficult, however, is the fact that the secular institutions (combining those that had always been secular and those that reported they once had a religious nature but are now largely secular in nature) cited slightly more negative effects than did the institutions ranking high in religious practices.

Table 13 also illustrates this pattern with several specific effects that were listed in the questionnaire. The positive effect of expanding one's "services and programs" decreased as one moves from institutions low to medium to high on the RPS. And the two specific negative effects included in Table 13 show the exact opposite pattern: the percentage of institutions citing them increases as one moves from those that are low on the RPS to those that are medium to those that are high. But again, complicating the interpretations of these figures is the fact that the secular institutions and the highly religious

TABLE 13

Effects of Public Funds, by Religious Nature: Colleges and Universities

| | | Religious Practices Scale | | |
	Secular*	Low	Medium	High
Average number of positive effects cited out of 6 listed	2.8	3.0	2.6	2.4
Average number of neutral effects cited out of 1 listed	.3	.5	.4	.4
Average number of negative effects cited out of 5 listed	1.1	.8	.9	1.0
Percentage of times specific effects were cited				
Expanded your services and programs	71%	73%	59%	56%
Put more time and effort into paper-work than should be necessary	67%	52%	53%	68%
Became more "bureaucratic" and less flexible and creative	26%	16%	18%	24%
N	110	44	120	90

*Included among secular institutions here are those that indicated they are secular in nature and those that indicated they once were religious but now are largely secular.

ones were about equally negative. Also, whether one takes the positive and negative effects grouped together or individual positive or negative effects, the differences among the secular, low-RPS, medium-RPS, and high-RPS institutions are not large. If the religiously based colleges and universities were suffering persistent and significant limitations due to their religious natures, one would expect a clearer pattern of dissatisfaction with the effects of government funds than is indicated by these figures.

Turning now to the child and family service agencies and evidence of governmental pressures and limitations on their religiously based practices, the three same measures used for the colleges and universities were employed. The directors of the child service agencies were asked, first, open-ended questions similar to the ones asked of the college and university presidents: one asked whether there were any religious practices other than those specifically listed in the questionnaire that they felt they "had to curtail or eliminate" due to their religious orientation and a second one asked if "any government officials [had] ever questioned any of your religiously based practices or brought pressure on you to change any of them." In response to either one or both of these questions, 30 percent of the heads of the 122 religious agencies receiving public funds reported government officials as having questioned or pressured them with regard to their religiously motivated practices. (See Table 14.)

A careful review of the sorts of issues or problems that have arisen reveal that most have to do with required religious activities, especially with required attendance at Sunday church services. Twenty-four agencies mentioned this as a point of contention with state officials. From many comments written on the returned questionnaires it is clear that different states and different agencies have worked out a variety of approaches to this issue. The head of one agency wrote, "In the past, religious services were mandatory, but we can no longer do that. However, we give incentives for attendance and encourage them to attend their own church." This approach has been explicitly rejected by the officials with whom another agency has had to deal: "We used to encourage church attendance by giving children extra free time if they went to church. We had to discontinue the practice. We may encourage church attendance but may not reward for church attendance." A third reported that required attendance at church services is being questioned but is still allowed: "[We experience] some informal leaning [on us] that youth should not be required to attend church—they say federal law mandates this, but no one has pushed us or other agencies yet." Other issues mentioned as sources of controversy or pressure run the gamut from religious symbols such as crosses and religious statues and a generalized suspiciousness or hostility from government officials toward religious practices.

TABLE 14

Government Pressures and Disputes by Religious Tradition and
Religious Practices Scale: Child Service Agencies

	Total Number*	Forced to Curtail Pract.**	General Pressures***	Combined Problems****
All religious agencies that receive public funds:	122	11%	25%	30%
Religious tradition:				
Jewish	20	10%	5%	15%
Catholic	21	10%	29%	33%
Conservative Prot.	32	22%	28%	34%
Mainline Prot.	45	4%	29%	31%
Religious Practices Scale:				
High	31	13%	26%	39%
Medium	59	12%	32%	32%
Low	32	9%	9%	19%

*The total number consists of the number of religiously based institutions falling into that category that reported receiving public funds. Those agencies that did not respond to these open-ended questions were considered to have indicated they had not experienced pressures or problems, since I judged if they had had such experiences they would have reported them.

**The percentage of positive responses to Question 11 that asked concerning "any other religious practices you feel you have had to curtail or eliminate because you receive government funds?" Those who did not answer this question were counted as responding with a "No."

***The percentage of positive responses to Question 13 concerning whether or not "any government officials [have] ever questioned any of your religiously-based practices or brought pressure to bear on you to change any of them." Those who did not answer this question were counted as responding with a "No."

****The percentage of positive response to either Question 11 or Question 13.

The picture that emerges is one of child service agencies facing more pressures from the government on their religious practices than are the colleges and universities. About 13 percent of the colleges and universities made reference to problems with the government in response to three open-ended questions probing this issue, while 30 percent of the child service agencies reported problems or issues in response to two open-ended questions. Seventy-eight (29 percent) of the religiously based colleges and universities have compulsory chapel services, for example, yet this hardly ever came up as an issue; forty-nine (39 percent) of the child service agencies have required religious activities and this came up repeatedly, especially as it relates to Sunday church services.

Table 14 also shows the positive responses to the two open-ended questions concerning government pressure to curtail or eliminate religiously inspired practices, broken down by religious tradition and the RPS. It is the conservative Protestant and Catholic agencies that tend to face the most pressure, although the mainline Protestant agencies did not lag far behind. It is also clearly the agencies ranking high or medium on the RPS that are experiencing pressures from government officials on their religious practices. This table also reveals the higher level of pressures child service agencies are facing as compared with colleges and universities. Among the latter the highest percentage of organizations reporting problems with government officials over their religious practices was 22 percent (the high RPS institutions), whereas among the child care agencies upwards of 35 percent were reporting problems with government officials (note the Catholic, conservative Protestant, and high and medium RPS agencies). The child service agencies ranking low on the Religious Practices Scale were experiencing about as many problems as were the colleges and universities ranking high on the same scale. In addition the Catholic and mainline Protestant agencies, as well as the conservative Protestant agencies, are feeling pressures, while among the colleges and universities it is only the conservative Protestant institutions that are experiencing heightened pressures. Nevertheless, a strong majority of the child service agencies were reporting no problems with government officials over their religiously based practices. This was true of all four religious traditions and for those ranking high as well as those ranking low on the Religious Practices Scale.

As was done with the colleges and universities, the child service agency directors were asked to indicate for each of the religiously based practices in which their agencies engage if they do so openly and directly or subtly and indirectly. Table 11 shows that, as with the college and university presidents, the strong majority of the child service agency directors (77 percent) reported that of the religiously based practices in which their agencies engage, they do so openly and directly, not subtly and indirectly. Similarly, 73 percent, on the average, of the child service agency directors reported that of the religious practices their agencies did not engage in, they refrained from engaging in them because they had no desire to do them, not because they felt they ought not to or could not do them. (See Table 12.)

As with the direct reports of governmental limitations or pressures, the evidence indicates the child service agencies felt more pressures than the colleges and universities to restrict their religiously based practices. An average of 24 percent of them—versus only 9 percent of the college and university presidents—reported that of the religious practices they do, they do them subtly and indirectly. And 27 percent—versus 12 percent of the colleges and universities—reported their agencies do not do the religious practices from which they refrain because they feel they ought not to or may not do them, not because they have no desire to do them. Compared with the colleges and universities, larger percentages of the child service agencies—although still minorities—were reporting that they engage in religious practices indirectly and subtly and that they refrain from certain religious practices because they believe they ought not to or may not do them. In short, a majority of the child service agencies, by this measure, were not experiencing governmental pressures to curtail or restrict the religiously based practices they wished to engage in, but a minority—and a much larger minority than among the colleges and universities—gave evidence of experiencing some pressures or constraints.

A third, indirect measure of the impact of receiving public funds on child service agencies' freedom to follow their religious missions is based on the reported effects of their receipt of public funds. The questionnaire listed ten possible effects the receipt of public funds could have and the agency directors were asked to indicate which ones in fact had been experienced by their agencies. The 243 agency heads responding to this question cited a total of 1,099 effects of government funding, for an average of 4.5 effects cited per agency director, a higher average number than the 4.1 cited by the college and university presidents. This is not surprising, since the child service agencies tend to receive a much higher proportion of their funds from government sources than do the colleges and universities.

The three most frequently cited effects were the expansion of services (cited by 71 percent of the agency heads), having to deal with clients with more severe emotional and behavioral problems (cited by 59 percent), and more paperwork than should be necessary (also cited by 59 percent). The least frequently cited effects were the receipt of fewer private gifts and volunteer hours (cited by only 7 percent of the agency heads), avoiding having to close down (cited by 24 percent), and becoming more bureaucratic and less flexible and creative (cited by 30 percent). As with the colleges and universities, the most frequently cited effects—except for the ubiquitous complaint about paperwork—were more likely to be favorable effects than were the least frequently cited effects. The agency directors cited an average of 2 positive effects (out of a possible 4); 1.5 neutral effects (out of a possible 3); and 1 negative effect (out of a possible 3). As just seen, the highly negative effect of becoming more bureaucratic and less flexible and creative was cited by 30 percent of the agency heads (the highest among the three types of nonprofit organizations). Nevertheless, the heads of the child service agencies basically perceive the effects of public money in a favorable light.

As with the college and university presidents, if the religiously based child service agencies were experiencing strong pressures on their religious practices, one would expect them to be evaluating the effects of their receipt of public funds in more negative terms than their secular counterparts, and the more religious agencies to be evaluating them more negatively than the less religious ones. But the pattern of responses indicates that the secular agencies actually cited somewhat fewer positive effects of government funds and more negative effects than did the religiously based agencies, and the highly religious agencies cited more positive effects and no more negative effects than did the less religious agencies. (See Table 15.) Each of the secularly based agencies named an average of 1.9 positive effects, while the religious agencies were naming an average of 2 positive effects. It is especially noteworthy that the religious agencies ranking the highest on the Religious Practices Scale cited the most positive effects. The secular agencies named an average of 1 negative effect, while the religious agencies named an average of slightly less than 1 negative effect. It is also noteworthy that more of the religious agencies were naming a positive effect such as "expanded your services and programs" than were the secular agencies (and the more religious agencies were naming this effect more frequently than were the less religious agencies). Meanwhile, the heavily negative effect of making the agencies less flexible and more "bureaucratic" was cited more often by the secular than the religious agencies, and more often by the agencies that were low rather than high on the RPS. One would expect the directors of religious agencies to be citing fewer positive effects and more negative effects of public funds if their agencies were experiencing widespread, serious limitations and restrictions on their religiously motivated practices, limitations and restrictions secularly based agencies by their very nature would not be experiencing. This was not the case.

In exploring the question of the impact of government funds on religiously based international aid agencies, I was somewhat handicapped by the fact that only thirty-three of the ninety agencies that responded to the questionnaire, indicated they had a continuing religious orientation. And of these thirty-three, ten reported they receive no public funds. Thus only twenty-three religiously based agencies that receive public funds are included in the study. Nevertheless, the responses of these twenty-three agencies reveal some interesting patterns.

The questionnaire asked the international aid agency directors the same two open-ended questions asked of the child service agency directors concern-

TABLE 15
Effects of Public Funds by Religious Nature: Child Services Agencies

	Secular*	Religious Practices Scale		
		Low	Medium	High
Average number of positive effects cited out of 4 listed	1.9	2.0	1.9	2.2
Average number of neutral effects cited out of 3 listed	1.7	1.1	.5	1.4
Average number of negative effects cited out of 3 listed	1.0	.8	.9	.8
Percentage of times specific effects were cited:				
Expanded your services and programs	66%	84%	71%	89%
Put more time and effort into paper-work than should be necessary	59%	58%	64%	48%
Became more "bureaucratic" and less flexible and creative	34%	26%	27%	22%
N	128	31	55	27

*Included among secular institutions here are those that indicated they are secular in nature and those that indicated they once were religious but now are largely secular.

ing any government pressures on their religious practices. Five of the twenty-three religiously based agencies that receive public money (22 percent) mentioned some sort of pressure or problem in response to the two open-ended questions. None of the Jewish agencies, one Catholic agency, one mainline Protestant agency, and three out of the nine conservative Protestant agencies did so. Even with the small numbers, a pattern observed with the other types of nonprofits held true. The conservative Protestant organizations more often reported running into problems carrying out their religious practices than did the organizations of other religious traditions. Also, the percentage of agencies reporting problems with government officials is at about the same level as it is for the child service agencies. The previously observed pattern of nonprofits that rank high on the RPS experiencing more problems with government officials did not hold true with international aid agencies, however. Two of the nine high RPS agencies reported experiencing a problem, and three of the fourteen low RPS agencies did so.

Of the five issues or problems mentioned by the agency directors, one dealt with the use of a building constructed in part with government funds that was being used for "voluntary services on Sunday" (the issue was worked out so that the building could continue to be used for worship services), one dealt with some questions raised about a fundraising letter, one concerned some questions about the use of overtly religious language in some technical publications, one dealt with questions about alleged proselytizing efforts, and one concerned sexual behavior standards in an overseas foster care program. There was no pattern or consistency with the five issues. One comes away from a series of interviews with international aid officials and a careful review of the written questionnaires with the impression that as long as the religiously based aid agencies are not too overt or up-front with their religious practices, they can get by with a significant amount of mixing religious elements into publicly funded activities and programs. A high-level official with a conservative Protestant international aid agency indicated that the only problems his agency has had with government officials over the religiously motivated practices have been very minor. He reported that often he has been assured by the Agency for International Development (AID) officials that they enjoy working with his and other religiously based nonprofit aid agencies because they appreciate their moral framework, feel they can trust them, and know they deliver. He pointed out that when faced with an overseas crisis or disaster of one type or another AID officials will often come to them and ask for advice and help in dealing with it. "It's a cooperative relationship," is how he summed it up. One does not get the picture of agency heads struggling and squirming to live up to their religious missions in the face of strong government opposition.

As Table 11 shows, when the directors of the international aid agencies were asked whether their agencies engage in the religiously motivated practices that they do directly and openly or indirectly and subtly, an average of 38 percent—the highest for the three types of organizations studied—reported they do them subtly and indirectly. The international aid agencies were also the highest in reporting for the religious practices in which they do not engage that they refrain from them because they feel they ought not to do them or legally cannot do them, rather than having no desire to them. For the nine listed practices, an average of 64 percent of the agencies that do not do them said that is the case because they have no desire to do them; over a third reported they were not doing them because they felt they ought not to or legally could not do them. (See Table 12.) By this measure one would conclude the international aid agencies were feeling under more scrutiny or under more governmental restrictions than were the other two types of nonprofit organizations studied here. But it must be noted that a strong majority of even the international aid agencies were indicating that they were either doing the listed religiously based practices openly and directly or had no desire to do them.

A third means of throwing light on the question of government interference with the religiously based international aid agencies—as was done with the other two types of nonprofits—is to look at their assessment of the effects of government funds. The international aid questionnaire listed ten possible effects of receiving public funds and asked the directors of the agencies to indicate which ones are effects their agencies had experienced. Dividing those ten potential effects into four that are positive, two that are neutral, and four that are negative in nature, Table 16 shows there are few differences between the religiously based and secularly based aid agencies in terms of their perceiving positive versus negative effects of public money. If anything, the secular agencies were slightly more likely to cite negative effects of receiving public funds (although they also cited slightly more positive effects). In addition, there are no real differences between the religious agencies ranking high on the RPS and those ranking low on it. When the same three specific effects that were considered for the other two types of nonprofits are examined, one finds the religiously based agencies being equally positive and somewhat less negative. It is especially interesting to note that the agencies ranking high on the RPS were significantly less likely than the other agencies to cite the highly negative effect of becoming "more bureaucratic and less flexible and creative." One of the other effects posed by the questionnaire was whether or not government funds had caused the agencies to change "your relief or development priorities to meet government desires or priorities." Only two of the twenty-one religious agencies responding to this

TABLE 16
Effects of Public Funds by Religious Nature: International Aid Agencies

		Religious Practices Scale	
	Secular*	Low	High
Average number of positive effects cited out of 4 listed:	1.9	1.9	1.7
Average number of neutral effects cited out of 2 listed:	.1	.6	.6
Average number of negative effects cited out of 4 listed:	1.2	1.0	.9
Percentage of times specific effects were cited:			
Expanded your services and programs	91%	100%	89%
Put more times and effort into paper-work than should be necessary	65%	67%	56%
Became more "bureaucratic" and less flexible and creative	26%	25%	11%
N	34	12	9

*Included among secular institutions here are those that indicated they are secular in nature and those that indicated they once were religious but now are largely secular.

question—less that 10 percent—selected this as an effect, while eight of the thirty-four secular agencies—24 percent—did so. If the religious agencies were in fact feeling squeezed and pressured by the government due to their religious practices, it seems they would surely have been selecting this effect in higher numbers than they were. At the very least, the responses to the question asking concerning the effects of government funds reveals no firestorm of dissatisfaction.

What can one conclude from this lengthy exploration of possible governmental pressures and restrictions on the ability of religiously based nonprofit organizations to freely pursue religiously based practices important to them? The old adage about whether a glass of water is half full or half empty applies here. The child service agencies, the conservative Protestant organizations, and organizations ranking high on the Religious Practices Scale reported the most problems, but even among them 70 percent or more reported no problems. Nonprofits from the other religious traditions and those lower on the RPS tended to report even fewer problems. And the nonprofit organizations' assessments of the effects of receiving public money and their strong tendencies either to engage in religious practices openly and directly or to fail to engage in them simply because they had no desire to do so adds to the picture of religious nonprofits receiving public funds being relatively free to pursue religiously based practices without governmental interference.

This picture leads to two important observations. One is the surprising nature of this situation from the point of view of church-state jurisprudence and societal elites' attitudes. Not only are religiously based nonprofit organizations able to participate in the public-nonprofit partnership as full members, not only are Catholic and conservative Protestant organizations and the deeply religious organizations able to participate fully in this partnership, but they are also apparently able to do so without having to compromise—for the most part—their religious missions as they see them. The anomaly between the Supreme Court's sometimes ringing declarations of no public funds for religion and religious institutions and actual, real-world practice grows deeper. This anomaly is explored in much greater depth in the next two chapters.

The second observation based on the evidence cited in this section of the chapter is that all is not necessarily well in terms of the religious autonomy of religious nonprofit organizations receiving public money. The glass is half full; it is also half empty. The lack of uniform standards and the sort of restrictions sometimes applied suggest the partially empty glass is a danger signal indicating the religious autonomy of the religious nonprofit organizations receiving public funds may be in a precarious position. Restrictions that have been applied to some religiously based nonprofits by government officials—restrictions on hiring practices, religious exercises, required behavior standards, and more—are ones that would result in the serious compromise of their religious autonomy, if suddenly they were uniformly applied to all religious nonprofits receiving public funds. Even today, the hit and miss quality of the restrictions that have been imposed poses a threat to their religious autonomy. Running into problems is something like getting hit by lightning. The odds of it happening to any particular person are not very high, but when it happens the results are highly negative.

Pressures and Threats from Outside Government

A second potential source of limitations on the pursuit of religiously motivated practices by religious nonprofit organizations—in addition to government-imposed limitations—consists of pressures and threats of pressures from private individuals and groups. The president of one conservative Protestant college, for example, recounted the following incident in a letter to me:

> This past April I wrote a generic letter to adjunct faculty in a business program related to _____ College simply informing them we intended to continue to use religious criteria in the hiring of faculty in an effort to ensure that we did not compromise the religious mission of the school. What we anticipated would be understood to be simply a reassertion of who we are, was interpreted by some members of the local community as an action which was discriminatory and bigoted.

Local newspapers pilloried the college for a "bigoted" hiring policy and a religious "cleansing" of the faculty.

In addition to public and media criticism such as this, pressures or threats from outside sources can take such forms as criticisms from supporters, employees, or clients, pressures from licensing or accrediting agencies, and lawsuits or threats of lawsuits from individuals or church-state watchdog groups, such as the American Civil Liberties Union, People for the American Way, and Americans United for the Separation of Church and State.

The questionnaires therefore asked the heads of all three types of organizations in an open-ended question whether their organizations had been subjected to "any other [that is, other than from government officials] criticism or pressure, or law suits or threats of law suits due to any of your religiously-based practices." (See Question 15 on the college and university questionnaire and question 14 on the other two.) As Table 17 shows, of the 267 religiously based colleges and universities receiving public funds thirty-

TABLE 17
Nongovernmental Pressures, by Religious Nature*

	Colleges/ Universities	Child Services	Internat'l Aid
All religious non-profits receiving public funds	13% (N=267)	15% (N=122)	4% (N=23)
Religious tradition			
Jewish	—	18% (N=17)	0% (N=2)
Catholic	9% (N=86)	5% (N=18)	0% (N=4)
Conservative Prot.	25% (N=81)	17% (N=30)	13% (N=8)
Mainline Prot.	9% (N=75)	17% (N=42)	0% (N=6)
Religious Practices Scale			
High	26% (N=88)	31% (N=26)	11% (N=9)
Medium	4% (N=115)	13% (N=55)	—
Low	16% (N=43)	10% (N=30)	0% (N=13)

*The percentage of religiously based organizations that received public funds and reported they have "received any other [i.e., other than from government officials] criticism or pressure, or law suits or threats of law suits due to any of your religiously based practices."

five, or 13 percent, reported experiencing some sort of a problem from persons and groups outside government; eighteen, or 15 percent, of the 122 religious child care agencies did so, and one, or 4 percent, of the twenty-three religious international aid agencies did so. Table 17 also shows the percentages of positive responses to this question, broken down by religious tradition and the RPS.

Three patterns stand out in Table 17's figures. One is similar to the pattern found in the case of governmental pressures or problems: the small proportion of nonprofit organizations reporting having experienced problems. Eighty-five to ninety-six percent of the organizations reported having experienced no problems from nongovernmental sources.

A second pattern observable in Table 17 is the relatively large number of problems or pressures the college and university presidents reported having experienced. They had reported the lowest level of governmental pressures among the three types of nonprofits, but were very close to the child service agencies and ahead of the international aid agencies in experiencing problems or challenges from sources outside of government. They reported about the same number of problems or pressures from nongovernmental sources in response to one open-ended question as they did in response to three open-ended questions asking about governmental pressures. In contrast, the child service agencies reported twice the level of problems from governmental sources as from nongovernmental sources, and the international aid agencies reported over five times the level of governmental problems as of nongovernmental problems.

The lower visibility and the less mainstream clientele of most child service and international aid agencies may work to lessen the public's concerns and pressures below what would otherwise be expected. Child service agencies tend to work with lower status children and families who are often far removed from the purview of community leadership groups, the public, and the media; and international relief and aid agencies operate largely outside the United States and usually with the "poorest of the poor." Meanwhile, the higher visibility of colleges and universities in their communities and the higher status, more mainstream nature of their students and faculty may work to heighten the public's knowledge of and concern over their religiously based practices. Most persons and groups who tend to be concerned with the religiously based practices of nonprofits seem to turn their attentions to nonprofits whose actions have a more visible, direct impact on them and their communities.

The third pattern seen in Table 17 is the now familiar tendency for the conservative Protestant organizations and those ranking high on the RPS to report more problems than did the other organizations. This pattern parallels those found with regard to governmental pressures. This general pattern, however, did not hold up in the case of the child service agencies, where the Jewish and mainline Protestant agencies reported as many problems as did the conservative Protestant agencies.

In the case of the colleges and universities the issue over which nongovernmental pressures and criticisms most frequently arose was that of hiring, firing, and promoting faculty or staff. Seventeen institutions mentioned pressures or lawsuits challenging policies to hire only or to give preference in hiring persons in agreement with the religious orientation of their institutions. The concept of a hiring policy that discriminates in favor of one's co-religionists apparently is a concept many find difficult to understand and accept, thereby spawning a significant number of lawsuits or threats or pressures of one type or another.

Several presidents also mentioned the pressures they have felt from some elements in their own religious constituencies to be more thoroughly religious or to push certain pet religious perspectives. One president of a Catholic institution revealed a level of frustration with which I suspect more presidents could identify when he or she wrote, "Extremists left and right threaten law suits or withholding contributions. 'The truth lies somewhere in the middle,' as Thomas Aquinas said. Beware the zealots and wackos! God bless the moderates with open hearts and minds."

Among the child service agency directors there was no clear pattern of nongovernmental pressures centering on the hiring issue. The complaints they reported cover a wide range of issues with no real pattern. The hiring issue came up once or twice but the complaints ranged widely, from being closed on religious holidays (a Jewish agency), to the United Way questioning a lack of religious diversity on a governing board, to parents of children questioning certain religious activities, or pressures in regard to the religious atmosphere more generally. The one religiously based international aid agency reporting a nongovernmental pressure or threat involved a threatened lawsuit by an employee who had been let go and claimed religious discrimination.

After all is said and done, however, the key fact that emerges from the open-ended question asking about nongovernmental pressures and problems is that the vast majority of religious nonprofits reported not having experienced them. Even within the categories of religious nonprofits experiencing the most problems—the high RPS child service agencies and conservative Protestant colleges and universities—70 to 75 percent had not experienced problems or pressures. Nevertheless, for the highly religious organizations, and especially for conservative Protestant colleges and universities with policies of hiring only persons in agreement with their religious tradition, it remains a potential source of trouble. When added to the previously discussed level of governmental pressures or threats these same nonprofits have experienced, the nongovernmental pressures and threats on their religious autonomy becomes a factor to be reckoned with.

Self-Imposed Restrictions

A third possible source of limitations on the religious missions of religiously based nonprofit organizations that receive public funds consists of certain limitations that the organizations have imposed on themselves. The next chapter explores more fully the existence and nature of indirect, subtle forces that may be encouraging nonprofits to restrict or limit their religious facets and the role the receipt of public funds may play in such tendencies. The very indirect, subtle nature of forces such as these—if in fact they exist—makes it difficult to inquire about them in a written questionnaire. The responses to one of the questions, however, may throw some light on the existence of self-imposed restrictions.

As noted earlier the heads of religiously based nonprofit organizations that receive public money were asked for each of the religiously motivated practices listed in the questionnaires in which they reported their organizations do not engage, whether their organizations do not do them because they feel they ought not to do them, legally cannot do them, or have no desire to do them. (See Question 10.) If self-imposed restrictions are playing a significant role in limiting religiously motivated practices, one would expect many organization heads to indicate they do not engage in certain practices due to their belief they either ought not to do them or legally cannot do them.

Table 12 shows the results of this question. For all three types of nonprofit organizations strong majorities indicated the reason for their not doing the listed practices from which they refrain is that they have no desire to do them. Few indicated they do not do them because they felt they ought not to or legally cannot do them. The college and university presidents were especially strong in insisting that when they refrain from certain religiously based practices, they do so because the have no desire to do them. An average of 88 percent gave this as the reason for not doing those religiously based practices they reported they do not do, compared to 73 percent for the child service agencies, and 64 percent for the international aid agencies. In other words, an average of over one-third of the international aid agencies and one-fourth of the child services agencies implied that the religious practices from which they refrain they would like to do, if it were not for their belief they either ought not to do them or legally cannot do them. For example, 37 percent of the fifty-nine child service agency directors whose agencies do not require religious exercises reported they refrain from them because they feel they either ought not to or legally cannot do them, not because they have no desire to do them. The evidence is far from conclusive, but it seems to indicate that a significant minority of the religiously based child service and international aid agencies are cutting back on their religiously based practices due to their understanding of what they legally or morally can do. For them, self-imposed concepts of what is and is not proper seems to be limiting their religiously based activities.

Adding to the self-imposed nature of this factor is the fact that for all three types of nonprofit organizations the percentage of organization heads reporting they do not engage in certain religiously motivated practices because they "ought not to do" them tends to be larger than the percentage reporting they "legally cannot do" them. From 10 to 22 percent of the organization heads whose organizations had decided not to engage in certain religiously based practices, seem to have decided not to do so due to certain internalized, self-imposed concepts of what would or would not be proper, a figure that—with only a few exceptions—is significantly higher than the percentage of organization heads who said their organizations did not do certain religious practices because they felt they legally could not do them.[8]

In brief, self-imposed restrictions on religious practices seem to be a very minor factor for colleges and universities receiving public funds, but play a more significant role for child service agencies and even more so for international aid agencies. The responses to this question are, however, far from definitive when it comes to the existence of subtle, indirect pressures on the religious practices of nonprofits receiving public funds. Certain cultural, professional, or legal norms may—perhaps even unself-consciously—be leading the heads of religious nonprofits to conclude they do not want to engage in certain religious practices, even practices normally associated with the religious traditions of which their nonprofits are a part. This difficult-to-research question is explored more fully in the next chapter.

Conclusions

What conclusions can one reach from the mass of information garnered from the 766 completed questionnaires on which in this chapter reports? Several stand out. One is the basic fact that all three types of nonprofit organizations included in this study receive substantial amounts of public money and that this is true of the religiously based and secularly based nonprofit organizations alike. This is hardly surprising, but it is added evidence that the pattern noted by some researchers, yet often ignored by others, continues to hold true for these three types of nonprofits today.

A second basic conclusion is that most of the religiously based nonprofits that receive public funds are religious in more than a nominal sense. Included among them are many Roman Catholic and conservative Protestant agencies and institutions, the two largest religious traditions in the United States, whose belief in a literal supernatural realm that has a continuing relevance to human affairs and whose stands on public policy issues such as abortion and gay rights often put them out of step with the cultural and public policy elites in the United States. Whether Catholic, conservative Protestant, or of some other religious tradition, most religiously based nonprofits receiving public funds take their religious commitments seriously and live out those commitments in many identifiable practices and activities. In fact, as will be developed more fully in the following chapter, an observer could conclude that many appear to be "pervasively sectarian," as that term has been defined by the Supreme Court.

A third basic conclusion is that most of the nonprofits studied here appear to experience a surprisingly low level of problems or pressures due to the religious practices in which they engage. They seem for the most part to be able to operate free from severe limitations on their freedom to live out their religious commitments and beliefs—whether from the government itself, limitations arising from private individuals and groups, or self-imposed limitations. There are exceptions to this general rule. Serious problems have been experienced by some individual organizations and by significant minorities among those nonprofits whose religious practices tend to color or permeate many of their activities. Often the conservative Protestant agencies and institutions were found in the latter group. But even among those categories of nonprofits that have experienced the most problems and restrictions, a majority of organizations have not experienced them.

A fourth basic conclusion is that in spite of the religious autonomy currently enjoyed by most of the religious nonprofit organizations receiving public funds studied here, there are warning signs on the horizon indicating their religious autonomy is in an unsafe, precarious position. Three aspects of the findings presented in this chapter point in the direction of this precariousness. The first is that a minority—and for the more highly religious nonprofit organizations and those in some religious traditions, a sizable minority—are already experiencing limitations on their religious autonomy. They are not as free to pursue the religiously based practices that inhere in their religious traditions as what they would be if they did not receive public funds. Especially among the religious child service agencies, many have given up public funds that similar or parallel agencies receive, thereby putting themselves at a comparative disadvantage.

Second, some of this study's findings indicate much more serious restrictions could be imposed in the future on religious nonprofits receiving public funds. Especially telling are the inconsistencies and uncertainties facing any nonprofit organization receiving public funds. As documented at several points in this chapter, what one nonprofit is allowed to do another is not allowed to do; what leads one nonprofit to endure public censure or law suits, another does as a matter of course with no controversy; what some nonprofit officials are concerned they should not or legally cannot do, others do openly and have done so for years. As I noted earlier in the chapter, finding one's self being condemned or in trouble for engaging in a certain religiously based practice is like being struck by lightning. It is seemingly arbitrary, capricious, and—thus far—rare. Yet the very uncertainty thereby created can have an inhibiting effect on religious freedom. Serving as a top official in a nonprofit organization—many of which employ hundreds of persons, serve thousands of clients, and have budgets running into the millions of dollars—is at best a difficult job. In such a situation the natural tendency is to avoid conflict and problems whenever possible. Thus hearing about a nonprofit of the same type as one heads that has run afoul a government official, or been challenged in the courts or by the news media on some of its religious practices, the natural tendency is to seek to avoid a similar situation arising for one's own organization.

A third aspect of the findings presented in this chapter suggesting the vulnerable position of nonprofits receiving public funds is the crucial nature of some of the religious practices that have been challenged. The very reason many religious traditions have founded colleges and universities, agencies designed to serve troubled children and their families, and agencies engaged in international aid and relief in the face of natural and human-made disasters, is to live out their faith in the world. Just as deeply religious parents attempt to raise their own children within the beliefs, values, and traditions of their faith, so they have helped establish, for example, homes for troubled youth so that what they perceive as the blessings and healing properties of their faith can be extended to others whose lives are in turmoil. But this chapter has shown that practices as simple as offering a prayer before meals, requiring children to attend worship services, or having religious symbols on campus have at times been drawn into question. And all three types of nonprofit organizations studied here have at times had the practices of hiring only persons in agreement with their religious tradition challenged. If a religious nonprofit organization should ever find that it must strip its facility of identifying religious pictures and symbols, desist from requiring minor children to participate in religious practices crucial to its tradition, or must hire persons in open disagreement with the religious background and mission of the nonprofit, its religious autonomy would have been effectively destroyed. It would virtually cease to exist as a religious organization. No one should minimize the stakes at issue here. The findings presented in this chapter indicate that religious nonprofits receiving public funds have, as a rule, not been subjected to restraints such as these, but they have also indicated that all of these restrictions have been experienced by some nonprofits at some times.

The minority of religiously based nonprofit organizations that have experienced problems or pressures in regard to their religious practices, the confused, uncertain situation concerning what religious practices nonprofit organizations receiving public funds may and may not engage in, and the significance of the practices that have sometimes been at issue, all point to the vulnerable position their religious autonomy and freedoms are in. When more theoretical, legal, and constitutional issues and popular and elite attitudes are added to the mix even more serious problems are evident. I turn to them in the next two chapters.

Notes

1. Although the questionnaire was sent to the presidents of the colleges and universities, it is evident that sometimes they passed the questionnaires along to a subordinate official to fill out. Presumably in such cases the person to whom the president delegated the task of filling out the questionnaire was someone able to speak for him or her. Thus in this study I will refer to the "presidents" who responded to the questionnaire even though in some cases the task was delegated to another official of the college or university.

2. Here and elsewhere throughout the book I do not identify the nonprofit institutions and agencies that I use for illustrative purposes. Given the sensitive nature of the subject matter, the continuing threat of lawsuits or public controversy, and the absence of a need to do so I have decided this is the appropriate path to take.

3. For the various government support programs for private, voluntary aid and relief agencies, see United States Agency for International Development, *Voluntary Foreign Aid Programs, 1993* (Washington, DC: Agency for International Development, Office of Private and Voluntary Cooperation, 1993), 8–10.

4. See Steven Rathgeb Smith and Michael Lipsky, *Nonprofits for Hire* (Cambridge, MA: Harvard University Press, 1993), 76.

5. In the questionnaire used for the colleges and universities the term *institution* was used instead of *agency* in this question.

6. See J. Bruce Nichols, *An Uneasy Alliance* (New York: Oxford University Press, 1988), 100–31.

7. *Roemer v. Maryland Public Works Board*, 426 U.S. at 756–757 (1976).

8. This does not mean, of course, that 10 to 22 percent of all the organization heads said that they were not engaging in certain practices due to self-imposed concepts of what is or is not appropriate. These percentages are based only on those organization heads who first reported they did not pursue a certain religiously based activity. For example, of the child service agency directors that reported they do not

have spoken prayers at meals, 26 percent reported their agencies do not have them because they felt it would be inappropriate for them to do so. But only nineteen of ninety-nine religious agencies receiving public funds reported not having spoken prayers. Thus of all religious agencies receiving public funds only 5 percent reported they do not have spoken prayers due to their believing they ought to do so.

Chapter 4

Mixing Sacred and Secular: Tensions and Problems

The public-nonprofit partnership is not only surviving, but prospering, and religiously based nonprofit organizations are taking part in this partnership as full members without, for the most part, having to give up their religious autonomy. The prior chapter documented this conclusion from many angles and in many ways. All appears to be well with the public-religious nonprofit partnership. Nevertheless I argue in this chapter and the next that all is not well. The general public, public policy elites, and the nonprofit sector all desire a certain outcome, so things have been arranged to achieve it; but the legal, theoretical foundation for doing so is askew. As a result some religious nonprofit organizations have been left out of the public-nonprofit partnership altogether, and those taking part in it have had their religious autonomy put in a vulnerable position.

The basic problem is that the legal doctrines the Supreme Court has used to interpret the First Amendment as it applies to public funds for religious nonprofit organizations are—in light of the actual practices being followed—seriously flawed. If they would ever be strictly followed, religious freedom—as it relates to religiously based public service and educational organizations—would be severely compromised. But practice is better than theory. Religious nonprofit organizations still possess the freedom to pursue their religious commitments because the legal doctrines set down by the Supreme Court are simply ignored when policy elites and nonprofits find it convenient to do so.

These conclusions are controversial and rooted in a jumble of legal precedents, definitions, distinctions, and widely varying practices. Thus I will proceed carefully in developing the bases on which I have reached them. In the first three sections of this chapter I revisit the three legal principles, described in Chapter 2, on which the Supreme Court has thus far found public money for most types of religious nonprofits to be in keeping with the establishment and free exercise clauses of the First Amendment: no-aid-to-religion, the sacred-secular distinction, and the pervasively sectarian standard. In doing so I seek to show that all three of these legal principles have theoretical problems that pose threats to the religious freedom of nonprofits receiving public funds, but that in practice, they are not being followed, or, at the most, are being followed in a hit and miss fashion. The last section of the chapter hazards a historical explanation for many of the tensions and confusions considered here. Then the following chapter considers some of the negative consequences of this situation for the government-religious nonprofit partnership, and for the religious autonomy of religious nonprofit organizations receiving public money in particular.

It would be as easy as it is tempting to ignore the tensions and problems to be explored in this chapter and the next . After all, outside of elementary and secondary schools, enormous amounts of public money flow to nonprofits, religiously and secularly based alike. As the previous chapter's survey results made clear, many religiously based organizations from almost all religious traditions receive substantial portions of their budgets from government sources. And they do so with few perceived problems and limitations. The system—jerry-built and haphazard though it may be—works. Why then rock the boat and risk capsizing a *modus operandi* the American Civil Liberties Union and Americans United for the Separation of Church and State, on the one hand, and the United States Catholic Conference and the National Association of Evangelicals, on the other, find satisfactory? The religious among us are pleased with the public dollars conservative Protestant colleges, Catholic child service agencies, and Jewish refugee resettlement agencies all receive; the ACLU and Americans United—who sound the alarm at the slightest amount of aid in the case of K–12 schools—seem to have made their peace with other types of religious nonprofits receiving large amounts of public money. If everyone is happy, why worry about a few untidy definitions or an occasional problem? After all, is not the real world of law and public policies often like this? Not-fully-worked-out concepts and occasional missteps are to be expected.

This chapter argues, however, that this is not merely a matter of a few untidy loose ends in a still-evolving area of public policy. Instead, I believe there are fundamental contradictions and unresolved issues running all through this policy area. American society's basic concepts with which it seeks to view, comprehend, and shape this area of public policy and law are fundamentally flawed. Until these flaws are addressed, we cannot help but end up with contradictions and uncertainties. Until they are replaced with more adequate ones, the religious nonprofit organizations that receive public funds and American society that depends on them for many of its educational and social programs are both in peril—and the religious freedom we all cherish with our words is in danger from our practices. Thus it is important that what to some may appear to be the sleeping dog of an acceptable *modus operandi* be awakened and challenged.

No Aid to Religion as a Means to Neutrality

The Supreme Court has held that under the First Amendment government may not aid religion, even religion generally or all religions equally. Although it has recently been challenged by the developing equal-treatment strain in the Supreme court's reasoning, it remains the official position of the Court in regard to nonprofit organizations and public funds. This principle at first glance appears to be fair and proper. It seems to be self-evident that government ought not to be giving money to churches, synagogues, or other religiously based nonprofit organizations. In a passage Supreme Court Justices have quoted more than once, James Madison, in his famous "Memorial and Remonstrance," wrote against any law that compels a person "to contribute three pence only of his property for the support of any one [religious] establishment."[1] To compel persons of the Jewish faith to support Christian organizations with their taxes, or persons committed to a thoroughly secular view of life to support deeply religious organizations would seem to be clear violations of such persons' basic freedom. Fairness would seem to demand a strict separation of church and state that bars public funds going to support any particular religion or all religions equally.

The reason this approach to church-state relations has so much inherent appeal is the value of governmental neutrality, or evenhandedness, on matters of religion that implicitly underlies it. Compelling persons to support with their taxes religious organizations at variance with their beliefs appears both to violate individual conscience and to result in government favoring or endorsing some religious beliefs over others. The state would no longer be neutral among persons of all faiths and of none, but would be weighing in on one side or the other.[2] Neutrality demands, in the eloquent words of Justice Potter Stewart, the freedom for "each of us, be he Jew or Agnostic, Christian or Atheist, Buddhist or Freethinker, to believe or disbelieve, to worship or not worship, to pray or keep silent, according to his own conscience, uncoerced and unrestrained by government."[3]

Supreme Court justices have often made clear that they see a strict church-state separation that allows no money to flow from government in support of religion as being essential to maintaining government neutrality in matters of religion. Justice Hugo Black made this point in his majority opinion in the early landmark *Everson* case. In it he articulated his and the Court's commitment to strict church-state separation:

> No tax in any amount, large or small, can be levied to support any religious activities or institutions, whatever they may be called, or whatever form they may adopt to teach or practice religion. Neither a state nor the Federal Government can, openly or secretly, participate in the affairs of any religious organization and vice versa. In the words of Jefferson, the clause against establishment of religion by law was intended to erect "a wall of separation between church and State."[4]

In Justice Black's thinking, this "wall of separation" doctrine was part and parcel of governmental neutrality in matters of religion. He made this clear when he wrote two pages later that the First Amendment "requires the state to be a neutral in its relations with groups of religious believers and non-believers; it does not require the state to be their adversary. State power is no more to be used so as to handicap religions than it is to favor them."[5]

Church-state separation and neutrality were explicitly linked by Justice Tom Clark in his majority opinion in *Abington v. Schempp:* "We have come to recognize through bitter experience that it is not within the power of government to invade that citadel [of religion], whether its purpose or effect be to aid or oppose, to advance or retard. In the relationship between man and religion, the State is firmly committed to a position of neutrality."[6]

There is scattered evidence that societal elites think in similar terms. A 1993 editorial in the *New York Times*, for example, referred to "the 'wall of separation' that is a foundation of American religious liberty" and concluded: "The Supreme Court's constant vigilance has preserved the religious liberty of all Americans by keeping churches and governments from meddling in each other's business. . . . Surely this is no time to pull down a wall that has served the nation well."[7] Such statements and those quoted from the Supreme Court resonate well with the American people. Common sense supports this position. After all, if religion and government are kept separate, government will not be able to aid or hinder religion generally nor any particular religious belief or organization. Religion will be left free to act as it sees fit and to prosper as it is able. No person will be forced to support or oppose religion against his or her will.

All this makes good sense if one is thinking in terms of government tax dollars going to fund the development, celebration, or propagation of a group's core religious beliefs. If one thinks in terms of centers of worship, religious rituals, and attempts to convince others to accept and take part in certain core religious beliefs and rituals, Madison's "three pence" surely ought not to go to their support. If tax dollars ever would go to support such activities, the ideal of governmental neutrality towards persons and communities of all faiths and of none would be broken.

When one turns, however, from institutions and programs directly involved in a religious community's core religious beliefs to the more public facets of religion—to a religious community's institutions and programs involved in practicing and living out the social, public implications of its core religious beliefs—one encounters a radically different situation. If the strict no-aid doctrine would ever be consistently followed in the context of religiously based, nonprofit organizations actively seeking to live out the public, social dimensions of the faith of the religious communities in which they are rooted, a trap would be sprung that would severely disadvantage religion. The free exercise of religion and governmental religious neutrality would be violated.

To understand why this is the case it is important to recall that in present-day American society—as seen earlier in Chapter 2—the major religious division is between religious believers and nonbelieving secularists, the government has largely secularized its own programs and agencies, and government is itself playing an active role in almost all areas of American life. Under these conditions, if government—seeking to strictly follow the no-aid-to-religion doctrine—would run public service programs in a secular manner or if it would fund public service programs of secular nonprofit organizations, but would not fund the public service programs of the same or parallel nature of religious nonprofit organizations, religion would be put at a government-created disadvantage. Both the government-run secular programs and the government-funded secular programs would be in competition with the religiously based programs. Thereby the thumb of government would clearly be on the secular side of the scales in the religionist-secularist struggle. It would not be neutral.

Government would collect taxes from all citizens—the religious and the nonreligious alike—and then dispense it only to the educational and social service programs in keeping with the values and beliefs of the nonreligious. Those desiring drug treatment for themselves, hospice care for a dying relative, or counseling for a troubled teenager—and who are themselves secularists and have no desire for such services within a religious context—could go to a government agency or a government-supported secular agency and receive such services in keeping with their beliefs. Those desiring such services within a context supportive of their deeply held religious views would, first, have to pay taxes to fund the government or the government-supported agencies providing such services within a secular context, and then would have to pay to fund religious agencies to provide such services within the context of their religious views. Religiously based organizations would have to struggle to survive in a field dominated by secular government and government-supported agencies with vastly superior financial and legal resources. Under such conditions, religious nonprofit, public service agencies and institutions would clearly be disadvantaged by public policy.

Government's advantaging of the secular over the religious could be avoided if government would simply stay out of a given policy area. For example, the government itself might not offer college education, nor grant any funds to either secular or religious private colleges. Under such circumstances a no-aid-to-religion approach would not violate religious neutrality. No religious institution would be favored over any other, nor would either religious or secular institutions as a whole be favored over the other. Since the government itself would be sponsoring no colleges, there would be no secular public institutions with a competitive advantage over private colleges, religious or secular. All would be fair. There would be a level playing field. But the day when government abandonment of higher education—or a host of other educational, social, and economic programs— would be a viable public policy is long since past. That day is not going to return. This option is religiously neutral, but practically impossible.

This leads to the possibility of the government funding religiously and secularly based nonprofits alike. Under the Supreme Court's no-aid-to-religion doctrine the money could only go the secular activities of the religiously based nonprofit organizations. This, as we have seen, is the solution the United States government and society have largely adopted in regard to religious nonprofit, service organizations, except in the case of K–12 education. In theory there is much to commend it. Its workability and actual religious neutrality, however, rests upon it being possible to make a clear-cut secular-sacred division among the activities of religiously based nonprofits and to fund only the secular without either harming or aiding the sacred. The next section examines more closely the sacred-secular distinction.

The Secular-Sacred Distinction

The sacred-secular distinction lies at the heart of the Supreme Court's— and, implicitly, American society's—approach to public funds for religious nonprofit organizations. In spite of the no-aid-to-religion doctrine, public funds may go to religious nonprofits without assisting religion, since such funds are only going to support their secular activities that have been carefully split off from their religious activities. That is the theory.

The results of the survey reported in the prior chapter, however, raise a host of troubling questions in regard to this sacred-secular distinction. They show that the secular and sacred activities of many of the religious nonprofit organizations are not in neatly separated boxes. Tables 6, 7, and 8 of Chapter 3—which reveal the religiously motivated practices in which the three types religious nonprofits surveyed engage—clearly show that for many religiously based nonprofits the Supreme Court's sacred-secular distinction is more myth than reality. Fifty-nine percent of the religiously based colleges and universities (and 88 percent of the conservative Protestant ones) indicated their faculty members are encouraged to integrate religious concepts and ideas into their courses. Among the religiously based child service agencies, 70 percent reported that staff members make informal references to religious ideas when working with their clients. And fifty-two percent of the religiously based international aid agencies reported their staff members do the same.

Sometimes this integration of the secular and sacred was made explicit by the nonprofit heads who responded to the questionnaire, as when the director of a child service agency wrote, "Religious life goals [are] built right into individual service plans which are agreed to by client, state and agency staff." Another agency director told me that since most of their clients come from some sort of a religious background, to develop treatment plans with no reference to religion would not be good therapy: "If what we do here has no reference to religion, we would not be properly preparing our boys to cope with the worlds to which they will be returning."

Take, for example, a home that provides education, living quarters, recreation opportunities, and counseling for troubled youth, most of whom have been placed there by the juvenile justice system. The home has roots deep in conservative Protestantism. Table 7 reveals that typically such a home has prayers before meals, its staff makes informal references to religious ideas as it councils the youth in its care, and it has certain religious activities in which its youths are required to take part. In such a situation how does one begin to sort out the sacred and the secular? If they are not actually intertwined, they are so closely juxtaposed that in real life they are not distinct, separable aspects of the agency's program. The youths being served have spiritual as well as physical, emotional, and mental dimensions to their persons. Thus the agency tries to meet their spiritual needs and to integrate a spiritual dimension into its overall efforts to help the youths to overcome problems in their lives and become balanced, contributing members of society. If counselors provide both religious and secular counseling, often intermixed or in the same counseling session, does one pro-rate their salaries based on an estimate of how much time is spent in one and the other? Does a spoken prayer before meals make them a sacred, non-fundable activity?

Similarly, an advertisement recently placed in a periodical by a Catholic university reads in part: "In the tradition of Catholic Education, the University seeks to educate its students so they may achieve excellence of mind and heart, develop a mature understanding of their faith and become leaders able to act responsibly for the good of their community." In a separate boxed statement the advertisement reads: "The Curriculum at _____ is based on the supposition that truth and virtue exist and are the proper objects of search in an education." I personally find this to be a well-written description of what I would expect to be offered in a college or university rooted in the Catholic tradition (and, for that matter, in other religious traditions). Yet one immediately senses that at this particular university—if what its advertisement claims is accurate—separating the secular from the sacred would be an impossible task. Education, the ad says, is aimed at achieving "excellence of heart *and* mind" and that "truth *and* virtue" are the objects of education. Clearly the advertisement is not saying in such and such classes we will conduct a secular search for truth or will develop a secular mind, and in other classes or in devotional services we will conduct a sacred search for virtue or develop excellence of heart. The intent is that mind and heart, truth and virtue be pursued and developed together.

The point here is that as an agency's staff member or a college's faculty member switches back and forth—at one time wearing a "secular" hat and another time a "sacred" hat, perhaps even several times during the course of a one-hour counseling session or a fifty-minute class period—the sacred-secular distinction, on which public money to religiously based nonprofit organizations hinges, is very quickly lost. It becomes impossible to say what is sacred and what is secular.

If public money may only support what is secular in an organization's activities, yet in actual practice many of its activities have religious aspects integrated into them, the organization is likely to face overt or subtle pressures to play down its religious orientation, to pretend it affects only certain limited aspects of its programming, or to jettison aspects of it altogether. When this occurs it is relinquishing some of its religious autonomy as the price for receiving public money. More on this in the following chapter.

A second problem with the sacred-secular distinction is that even if it were possible to neatly segregate the secular and sacred aspects of a single organization, giving public funds in support of the secular is as much help to the sacred as giving money directly to the sacred. It is really a bookkeeping operation. An example may illustrate what I am contending here. Take a homeless shelter sponsored by a group of deeply committed religious believers. It provides safe sleeping quarters and a warm breakfast for those out on the streets. It also offers counseling aimed at helping the homeless to understand and overcome whatever problems lie at the heart of their homelessness. All these activities are presumably "secular" in nature and eligible for public funding. But it also has a chaplain on staff who runs a voluntary bible study and prayer session each evening and conducts a public prayer prior to breakfast each morning. His or her activities would be "sacred" and not eligible for public funding. The shelter originally had no government funding and struggled to meet its annual $200,000 budget (of which the chaplain's salary and a supply of bibles and other devotional literature was about one-fifth or $40,000). The city government, fearing the shelter would close and compound the homeless problem in the city, appropriated an annual grant of $100,000, funding that it made clear was to go only toward meeting the $160,000 "secular" portion of the shelter's budget. Thus the shelter now only has to raise $100,000 a year, 40 percent of which covers the sacred portion of its expenses and 60 percent of which covers the portion of its secular activities not covered by the city's grant. Has the city government aided religion? Technically the answer is no, but realistically, in terms of the shelter's financial condition, it makes no difference had the $100,000 gone to fund the programs of the shelter as a whole, sacred and secular alike.

At times the Supreme Court has been willing to recognize this fact, but has dismissed it as inconsequential. In a case dealing with aid to religiously based colleges, for example, Justice Blackmun stated in his plurality opinion: "The Court has not been blind to the fact that in aiding a religious institution to perform a secular task, the State frees the institution's resources to be put to sectarian ends."[8] How did he justify this in light of the Court's no-aid standard he professed to uphold? He did so on the basis that the state grants at issue in this case had only an "incidental effect on facilitating religious activity" and were equivalent to police and fire protection afforded churches.[9] But this does not seem to square with the Supreme Court's ringing reiteration the year before of its strict no-aid-to-religion doctrine, especially its insistence that no tax money at all may go to support any religious institution: "The Court has broadly stated that '[n]o tax in any amount, large or small, can be levied to support *any religious* activities or *institutions*, whatever they may be called, or whatever form they may adopt to teach or practice religion.' "[10] It is especially interesting to note the Supreme Court boldly proclaims no tax money may go to support any religious "institutions, whatever they may be called."

There is a third, more theoretical problem in the Court's sacred-secular distinction. The activities and programs of both religious and secular organizations are rooted in certain presuppositions, values, and perspectives that are ultimately based on faith, not empirical proof. It is increasingly recognized and accepted by scholars that the traditional fact-value bifurcation is less certain and clear-cut than was previously thought. All learning and all knowledge (and thereby all service philosophies, therapies, and motivational techniques) are increasingly seen as being rooted in particular perspectives, presuppositions, and values.

In her classic work on human cultures, Ruth Benedict noted that all persons see the world through culturally conditioned perspectives:

> No man ever looks at the world with pristine eyes. He sees it edited by a definite set of customs and institutions and ways of thinking. Even in his philosophical probings he cannot go behind these stereotypes; his very concepts of the true and the false will still have reference to his particular traditional customs.[11]

And ever since the work of Thomas Kuhn, Michael Polanyi, Fritjof Capra, and others, few scholars argue for a clear cut fact-value distinction and for the existence of value-free, objective human knowledge.[12] Most recognize that what theories are accepted or rejected, what facts are considered relevant or irrelevant, or what studies are deemed important or ignored are dependent on one's presuppositions, perspectives, and values—on one's worldview or mindset. Capra has expressed it well: "The patterns scientists observe in nature are intimately connected with the patterns of their minds; with their concepts, thoughts and values. Thus the scientific results they obtain and the technological applications they investigate will be conditioned by their frame of mind."[13] Harold Brown has summarized succinctly where this leaves science:

> Science consists of a sequence of research projects structured by accepted presuppositions which determine what observations are to be made, how they are to be interpreted, what phenomena are problematic, and how these problems are to be dealt with. When the presuppositions of a scientific discipline change, both the structure of that discipline and the scientist's picture of reality are changed.[14]

Roy Clouser has made the needed additional point that one's worldview or mindset is religiously based:

> [O]ne religious belief or another controls theory making in such a way that *the contents of the theories differ depending on the contents of the religious belief they presuppose.* In fact, so extensive is this religious influence that virtually all the major disagreements between competing theories in the sciences and in philoso-

phy can ultimately be traced back to differences in their religious presuppositions.[15]

In short, basic values, perspectives, and presuppositions underlie *all* knowledge and *all* social theories and programs. These worldviews or mindsets may be clearly religious in a traditional sense or they may be nontheistic or secular in nature, but in either case they are "religious" in the sense of being nonempirical givens that condition or structure one's intellectual explorations, counseling theories and practices, approaches to complex social welfare needs, and other such activities. Whether knowledge and theories are, in a formal sense, religiously rooted or secularly rooted, they are rooted in perspectives and presuppositions that have strong subjective elements. All are rooted in certain commitments that are given, not empirically or rationally proven. They are rooted ultimately in faith.

If this is so one can still make a sacred-secular distinction in the sense that the sacred is rooted in the belief in a supernatural realm and the secular is not, but it is a distinction without a difference. Both are rooted in a faith commitment. Attempts to segregate out the sacred and the secular in nonprofit organizations in any meaningful sense is suddenly seen as being impossible. A Catholic therapist working in a Catholic drug rehabilitation agency, an Orthodox Jewish counselor working in a Jewish family services agency, a conservative Protestant professor teaching in an evangelical liberal arts college, and a nonbeliever working as a counselor in a secularly based spouse abuse shelter all bring certain presuppositions, perspectives, and underlying beliefs of a "religious" nature—a faith commitment—even to their "secular" activities and duties. In a theoretical sense, the logical, substantive basis for the Supreme Court's sacred-secular distinction is hard to justify. For the Court to interpret the First Amendment so as to favor programs rooted in a secularly based faith commitment over ones rooted in a religiously based faith commitment is to disadvantage religion.

In summary, the Supreme Court's sacred-secular distinction fails as a workable guide to funding religiously based nonprofit organizations without funding religion. Out in the real world of religious agencies and educational institutions, the sacred and the secular cannot be neatly separated out due to their intertwined nature. And even if this were not the case, funding secular aspects of a religious organization's activities also supports its religious aspects, and both sacred and secular aspects of nonprofits' activities are rooted in certain mindsets or worldviews that are ultimately faith based.

The only way in which the secular-sacred distinction makes any real sense as a guide to funding religious nonprofits without supporting religion is if a nonprofit is religious only in a nominal sense. Such an agency or institution might have a religious reference in its name or its logo and might have as part of its program or activities a religious or devotional service once a week, but otherwise it does not differ from its secular counterparts. In its hiring policies, services provided, standards of behavior encouraged, assumptions underlying its therapies, and other aspects of fulfilling its mission, it would be indistinguishable from similar or parallel agencies and institutions that are secularly based. In the case of this sort of religious nonprofit, the secular-sacred distinction makes some sense. Its religious aspects are few and almost totally segregated from its other, secularized activities. Thus sending public money to the organization means aiding religion only in a most limited, inconsequential sense: the few, largely formal religious aspects are in practice clearly separable from its overwhelmingly secular programs and activities. But Chapter 3 demonstrated that a majority of the nonprofit agencies and institutions receiving public funds are religious in more than a nominal sense. The tension remains.

The Pervasively Sectarian Standard

Public funds going to religiously based K–12 schools have generally been held to be in violation of the First Amendment by the Supreme Court, but public funds going to other types of religious nonprofit, service organizations have been held to be fully constitutional. As seen in Chapter 2 the Court has done so on the basis that the secular and religious functions of nonprofits other than K–12 schools can be separated, and thus government funds are able to support secular functions without supporting religious ones. This is possible because religious nonprofits other than K–12 schools are not pervasively sectarian, while religiously based K–12 schools are pervasively sectarian and thus their sacred and secular facets cannot be separated out and only the secular funded. Public funds going to the latter, therefore, would advance religion in violation of the First Amendment establishment clause, while public funds going to the former do not.

Given the crucial nature of the concept of pervasively sectarian organizations it is surprising that the Supreme Court has never clearly defined it. It has sometimes listed characteristics of pervasively sectarian organizations, but one is still left wondering what of the various characteristics of a pervasively sectarian organization could be present and that organization still not be so pervasively sectarian that it becomes ineligible for public funds. As seen in Chapter 2, Justice Blackmun, who in *Roemer* was the justice that made the most thorough attempt at defining "pervasively sectarian," twelve years later admitted it was "a vaguely defined work of art."[16] The Supreme Court seems to have taken a similar position to that once taken by Justice Potter Stewart when he wrote concerning obscenity: "I may not be able to define it, but I know it when I see it."[17] The puzzle deepens when one recalls that K–12 schools generally have been judged to be pervasively sectarian, but a Catholic agency providing counseling in an area as closely associated with religiously rooted beliefs and values as teen-age sexuality and pregnancies is not pervasively sectarian. Also escaping the pervasively sectarian label are religiously based colleges, which presumably would include a conservative Protestant college whose catalog states its mission in these terms: "_____ is a Christian liberal arts college. Its mission is to provide Biblically informed liberal arts education. . . . Its heritage is in the historic Christian faith . . . and its fundamental basis of governance and instruction is the infallible Word of God." One is tempted to conclude that, in the Supreme Court's view, a pervasively sectarian institution is a religiously based K–12 school, and that a nonpervasively sectarian institution is any other kind of religiously based nonprofit association.

The picture of religious nonprofits that emerges from the information uncovered by the survey reported in the previous chapter reveals even more problems with the pervasively sectarian concept. The Religious Practices Scale (RPS) is relevant here. As Appendix C, which describes the construction of the RPS, makes clear, this scale seeks to reflect the number of religiously motivated practices the organizations surveyed practice and the extent to which the religious practices they pursue tend to permeate entire organizations and all their activities. Thus those organizations ranking high on the RPS would seem to be "pervasively sectarian," although whether or not the Supreme Court would ever hold them to be such is unknown. I am only saying that to the extent one can apply "a vaguely defined work of art," those organizations ranking high on the RPS would seem to be something like what the Supreme Court has in mind in referring to "pervasively sectarian" organizations.

Table 9 of Chapter 3 clearly reveals that the large majority of religiously based nonprofits ranking high on the RPS—that is, the nonprofits possessing characteristics that would appear to place them in the "pervasively sectarian" camp—receive public funds, often substantial amounts of public funds. This is true of all three types of nonprofit organizations studied. Among the colleges and universities 26 percent rank high on the RPS, and all but 3 percent of them reported receiving public money. Sixty-nine percent of the high-RPS institutions indicated they receive over 10 percent of their budgets from public money, and 27 percent that they receive over 20 percent from public sources. In fact, as pointed out in Chapter 3, the colleges and universities ranking high in religious practices tend to receive a larger proportion of their budgets from government sources than do the secular institutions and those ranking lower in religious practices. Among the child service agencies, 15 percent ranked high on the RPS, and of them 67 percent reported receiving public funds, with 28 percent receiving over 60 percent and 46 percent receiving over 20 percent of their funding from public sources. Fifteen percent of the international aid agencies rank high on the RPS. Of them, 69 percent receive public funds, with 15 percent receiving over 40 percent of their budgets from government sources.

Table 18 gives additional insight into the "pervasively sectarian" nature of the nonprofits surveyed in this study. The table lists the six marks of a "pervasively sectarian" college Justice Blackmun gave in the *Roemer* decision, plus the more summary concept of "pervasively sectarian" Justice Powell articulated in *Hunt v. McNair*. Then it indicates what percentage of each of the three types of religiously based nonprofits included in my survey that reported receiving public funds appears to be marked by each of the seven. The first one—formally autonomous from control by a church—is unknown for the three types of nonprofits surveyed since I did not ask concerning this in the questionnaire. There is no indication that the third and fourth characteristics—a lack of academic freedom and of normal academic standards—characterize any of the colleges and universities receiving government funds. Any college or university lacking basic academic qualities such as these would not even be accredited by their regional accrediting bodies. Similarly, any child service agency that did not maintain basic professional standards in such areas as financial records, health and sanitation, and treatment plans would clearly not be allowed to operate by various licensing authorities. Any international aid agency would not be eligible to receive public funds if it would not maintain comparable professional standards. Thus I conclude none of the religious agencies or institutions receiving public funds lacked academic freedom or normal academic standards or, in the case of child service and international aid agencies, their professional equivalents.

Justice Blackmun also suggested the existence of "religious indoctrination" would in part be signaled by the presence of required religious exercises. Table 18 reveals that significant minorities of the religious nonprofits receiving public funds practice "religious indoctrination" as thus conceived by Blackmun. From 15 to 25 percent of the religious nonprofits that receive public funds indicated they seek to affect the religious views of those receiving their services *and* have certain required religious exercises (or voluntary religious exercises in the case of international aid agencies).

Significant minorities of the religious institutions and agencies that receive

TABLE 18
Religious Organizations Receiving Public Funds Marked by "Pervasively Sectarian" Characteristics*

	Child Service Agencies (N=122)	Colleges & Universities (N=267)	Internat'l Aid Agencies (N=23)
1) Formal ties with a church	unknown	unknown	unknown
2) Religious indoctrination common**	16%	25%	13%
3) A lack of academic freedom	none	none	none
4) A lack of normal academic standards	none	none	none
5) Religion a factor in hiring***	38%	49%	36%
6) Religion a factor in student/client admission****	8%	18%	unknown
7) If a substantial portion of their functions are subsumed in its religious mission*****	23%	36%	39%

*The first six characterizations are taken from Justice Blackmun's opinion in *Roemer v. Maryland Public Works Board*, 426 U.S. at 755-759 (1976), and the seventh is taken from Justice Powell's summary description of a "pervasively sectarian" organization in *Hunt v. McNair*, 413 U.S. at 743 (1972).

**The percentage of the religious organizations receiving public funds that, in the case of the child service agencies and the colleges and universities, reported they encourage religious commitments by their clients or students and have some required religious exercises; and, in the case of the international aid agencies, reported they encourage religious commitments by their clients and have some voluntary religious exercises.

***The percentage of the religious organizations receiving public funds that reported they either only hire staff in agreement with their religious orientation or give preference in hiring to those in agreement with their religious orientation.

****In the case of child service agencies the percentage of agencies receiving public funds that reported they give preference in accepting clients to those in agreement with their religious orientation, and in the case of colleges and universities the percentage of institutions receiving public funds that reported they only accept students in agreement with their religious orientation or give preference in accepting students to those in agreement with their religious orientation.

*****The percentages of the religious organizations receiving public funds that rank high on the Religious Practices Scale, as described in Appendix C.

public funds—and almost a majority of the colleges and universities—take religion into account in hiring their professional staff members, or, to put it into the lower court's pejorative terms quoted by Blackmun, "stack" their staffs "with members of a particular religious group."[18] Religion is a factor in admitting students in only a small percentage of the religious colleges and universities and in religious child service agencies accepting clients, although even here almost one in five of the religiously based colleges and universities that receive government funds give preference in admitting students to persons from their own religious tradition.

Finally, if the Religious Practices Scale is accepted as a measure of whether or not "a substantial portion of [an organization's] functions are subsumed in [its] religious mission,"[19] roughly one-third to one-fourth of all religious nonprofits surveyed that receive public funds fall into this category.

The composite picture that emerges is one of a majority of the religious nonprofits surveyed receiving public money probably not being pervasively sectarian, as this term seems to be conceived by the Supreme Court, but of a significant minority—roughly 30 to 40 percent—probably being so. The pervasively sectarian standard is seemingly not being followed in the case of a host of religiously based nonprofit organizations throughout the nation.

Problems in the pervasively sectarian standard are also shown by the fact that not only are many nonprofits receiving public funds that under its terms presumably ought not to be receiving them, but there are also many nonprofits denied public funds that do not materially differ from those receiving them. This standard was developed to distinguish elementary and secondary schools from colleges and universities and to defend denying public funds to the former and allowing them for the latter. But just as there are many colleges and universities, child service agencies, and international aid agencies that appear to be "pervasively sectarian," there also appear to be many K–12 schools that are not "pervasively sectarian," or—at the very least—are no more sectarian than are many other religious nonprofit organizations that receive public funds. This was the precise conclusion, for example, reached by the Ninth Circuit Court of Appeals in *EEOC v. Kamehameha* (1993).[20] This case concerned a private, nonprofit, Protestant school in Hawaii that had a policy of hiring only Protestant teachers. A non-Protestant denied employment brought her case to the EEOC. The school claimed exemption from religious anti-discrimination laws under exemptions the civil rights law provides religious educational institutions. But the Circuit Court ruled against the school, holding that it was not religious enough—was not, in effect, pervasively sectarian—and thus the exemption Congress had granted religious educational institutions did not apply: "We conclude the general picture of the Schools reflects a primarily secular rather than a primarily religious orientation."[21] Presumably the Kamehameha Schools would not be able to receive state funds—even if Hawaii should decide to establish a program of state grants to private, nonprofit schools—because it is pervasively sectarian, and it cannot discriminate on the basis of religion in its hiring policies because it is not pervasively sectarian!

I interviewed several key nonpublic school officials in both the conservative

Protestant and Catholic traditions. The picture of the "pervasively sectarian" nature of these schools that emerged from these interviews is very similar to those of colleges and universities and other of the nonprofits surveyed that rank high on the Religious Practices Scale.[22] They are religious in a significant sense, but neither are they indoctrination factories where children are forced into some rigid religious mold. An official of a national association of conservative Protestant schools made the explicit point that almost all of their member schools have no formal church ties. Instead, they all are independently established as nonprofit bodies. The person interviewed reported that students from the sponsoring groups' own religious traditions are normally given preference in admission, but other students are also accepted. This is confirmed by news reports that show roughly 14 percent of the children in the New York City Catholic schools and 13 percent in the Brooklyn Catholic schools are non-Catholics. Some Catholic schools in the New York area—largely in low-income, inner-city areas—have a non-Catholic enrollment as high as 80 percent.[23] All the persons I interviewed reported that in their schools there is no requirement that teachers be members of a particular denomination or church, although all take the religious beliefs and memberships of prospective teachers into consideration in making hiring decisions. All maintain normal educational standards and give their teachers normal freedom to run their classes and the flexibility to meet their individual classes' and students' needs. Almost all of their teachers are certified under their states' certification requirements. In other words, these conservative Protestant and Catholic K–12 schools look very much like the conservative Protestant and Catholic nonprofit agencies and institutions included in my study. The pervasively sectarian standard simply does not distinguish between religious secondary and elementary schools and other religious nonprofit organizations.

An additional problem with the pervasively sectarian standard is that at least one of its presumed characteristics, were it ever strictly followed, would virtually destroy the religious autonomy of nonprofit organizations receiving public funds. This is the characteristic both Blackmun in the *Roemer* opinion and Brennan in his *Grand Rapids* opinion mentioned: both insisted that one mark of pervasively sectarian organizations is that they take religion into account in hiring decisions. If this would ever be taken seriously as a criterion it would destroy not just the "pervasively sectarian" character, but any religious character of nonprofit organizations receiving public funds. Their religious autonomy would be destroyed for they no longer could define their own boundaries. It would mean an orthodox Jewish school would improve its chances of being found not pervasively sectarian and thus eligible for public funds if it hires Christian teachers, a Nation of Islam drug treatment center if it hires Jewish counselors, a Catholic family services agency if it hires mainline Protestants as family planning councilors, and a conservative Protestant college if it hires secularists as faculty members. On the surface such a standard says the religious orientation of a school, drug rehabilitation center, family services agency, or a college is to be jettisoned. If the teachers or other staff of a nonprofit agency cannot be hired on the basis of their faith commitments, the religious character of that nonprofit would be destroyed. Religion would be at most a nominal characteristic of the organization, a quaint, historical tradition long buried in the past that no one takes seriously any longer.

This is where the myth of a sacred-secular distinction leads. If at least some professors in a religious college or some counselors at a home for troubled youth are engaged in purely secular activities—ones the government can fund—there are few bases upon which to argue their religious beliefs and memberships are a relevant job qualification. But if they are engaged in activities with sacred as well as secular aspects—as I have claimed is often the case—then their personal religious beliefs and commitments become highly relevant to the continued character and integrity of the organization. But then their organization is presumably pervasively sectarian and not eligible for public funding. If consistently followed and applied, the pervasively sectarian standard would mean religious nonprofits would have to choose between giving up their religious autonomy or giving up public funds.

There is a free exercise issue here. If, to receive the normal benefits of public policies that similar, secularly-based organizations are receiving, a religious nonprofit organization must downplay or give up certain of its religious practices, public policy is interfering with its free exercise of religion. A parallel can be drawn between a nonprofit organization having to choose between giving up public funds or qualifying for such funds by giving up some of its religiously based practices so as not to be "pervasively sectarian," and individuals having to choose between certain public benefits and certain of their religiously based practices. The Supreme Court has been able to recognize the free exercise problem present in the latter situation. In 1962, for example, it overturned a lower court decision denying unemployment compensation to a person refusing to work on her Sabbath since, the Court said, that decision would force her

to choose between following the precepts of her religion and forfeiting benefits, on the one hand, and abandoning one of the precepts of her religion in order to accept work, on the other hand. Governmental imposition of such a choice puts the same kind of burden upon the free exercise of religion as would a fine imposed against appellant for her Saturday worship.[24]

Similarly, a religious nonprofit that would forfeit public funds available to its secular counterparts because it is unwilling to give up practices that make it too religious—that make it "pervasively sectarian"—would be put in as much a government-created disadvantage as would a government-levied fine on it for engaging in those practices. The free exercise problem is clear.

What saves most religious nonprofit organizations is that out in the real world the pervasively sectarian standard is not being consistently followed, and thus many possibly "pervasively sectarian" organizations are receiving public funds without having to abort their religious practices. While this has an advantage for religious nonprofits receiving public funds, it does not alter the fact that the pervasively sectarian standard is failing as a principled basis by which to determine what religious nonprofit organizations may constitutionally receive public funds and those that may not. Nor does it offer a principled basis on which to determine what religiously based practices nonprofits receiving public funds may engage in and what ones they may not. The standard is not doing the job it was put forward to do. Later in the chapter I suggest the pervasively sectarian standard may have more to do with a prejudicial view of Catholic K–12 schools prevalent a generation ago than any present-day, real-world assessment of the nature of religiously based K–12 schools and other types of religious nonprofit organizations.

If the courts and government agencies administrating public funds going to religious nonprofit organizations would ever insist that public tax dollars could never end up supporting programs or institutions permeated with religious ideals and practices, could only support activities of religious nonprofit organizations from which all religious elements have been purged, and could not go to religious nonprofits that seek to hire persons in keeping with their own religious beliefs or in other ways exhibit characteristics of "pervasively sectarian" institutions, then most current funding programs for religious nonprofits would have to be ended. But no one wants this result, and thus the no-aid-to-religion, secular-sacred distinction and the pervasively sectarian standard are not strictly followed. The end result is a confusion of practices.

A Confusion of Practices

Confusion results from legal standards out of synch with actual practice. This can be seen in the extent to which certain specific practices are routinely followed by many religiously based nonprofits receiving substantial public money that in other contexts—and especially in K–12 education—have been the source of great controversy. Two examples stand out. One is the matter of prayer. When it comes to prayer or other religious exercises in the public schools the Supreme Court has drawn a clear line in the sand. No prayer in the public schools. Why? One reason, as Justice Douglas proclaimed in a concurring opinion holding prayer and bible reading in the public schools unconstitutional, is that ". . . public funds, though small in amount, are being used to promote a religious exercise. Through the mechanism of the State, all of the people are being required to finance a religious exercise that only some of the people want and violates the sensibilities of others."[25] The majority opinion in the same case, written by Justice Clark, insisted that the voluntary nature of student attendance at the Bible reading exercises made no constitutional difference since the voluntary nature "furnishes no defense to a claim of unconstitutionality under the Establishment Clause."[26] Yet in my survey, 65 percent of the religiously based child service agencies receiving public funds have spoken prayers at meals, 31 percent have required religious activities, and 81 percent have voluntary religious exercises (participation is usually encouraged by agency staff). Meanwhile, 29 percent of the religiously based colleges and universities receiving public funds require their students to attend chapel services, 74 percent have voluntary chapel services, and 88 percent have voluntary religious activities organized by the college or university.[27] The confusion is compounded by the fact that in Blackmun's *Roemer* opinion he specifically ruled the fact that many classes were opened with prayer at some of the colleges receiving public funds under the challenged program was "peripheral to the subject of religious permeation."[28] What the Supreme Court has reacted against with indignation in one setting it ignores or counts as inconsequential in another.

Policy elites fit this same pattern. Editorial writers, watchdog groups like the American Civil Liberties Union and Americans United for the Separation of Church and State, and academic writers alike often express deep concern over prayers or other religious exercises supported by public funds in the public schools, but simply ignore the prayers and other religious exercises supported in part by public funds in nonprofit organizations receiving public funds.

Similarly, the issue of religious pictures or symbols periodically emerges as an issue when public funds are involved. In the late 1980s Congress debated and finally passed legislation to create a program for the subsidization of child care. Prominent in the debates over this legislation were church-state concerns, since many of the child care centers that would potentially be eligible for subsidization were located in churches.[29] Legislation as originally introduced included a provision—among others seeking to keep church and state separate—that if funds would flow to a church-based child care center any religious pictures or symbols would have to be removed or covered up.

There were protests over this and certain other church-state provisions by religiously based associations and their allies in Congress. As a result this provision was removed from the bill, only to stimulate protests from legislators and groups favoring a strict church-state separation. The strict separationist association, Americans United for the Separation of Church and State, became deeply involved in this legislation and actively worked against it because it feared public funds going to church-based child care centers. Several times it called attention to the fact that religious symbols and pictures could be permitted in government-subsidized child care centers, and its director declared, "The ABC bill remains a nightmare of church-state entanglement. It still poses a grave threat to the separation of church and state."[30]

The issue of religious pictures in the facilities of nonprofits receiving public funds has come up more often. In 1989 a Salvation Army homeless shelter in New Britain, Connecticut, was refused a $7,000 government grant by the Department of Housing and Urban Development because it had a picture of Jesus in its facility.[31]

While some agencies are denied funds due to religious symbols or pictures and while Congress and church-state watchdog groups struggle mightily over whether or not to fund child care centers with religious pictures and symbols in them, 72 percent of the child service agencies receiving public funds in my survey reported having religious pictures or symbols in their facilities, 81 percent of the religiously based colleges and universities receiving public funds reported the same, and 83 percent of the religious international aid agencies receiving public funds reported having a religious identification or symbol in their name or logo.

Countless other examples of seemingly arbitrary distinctions could be cited. Although 65 percent of the religiously based child service agencies receiving public dollars reported they have spoken prayers at meals, another agency head reported that a "county worker removed foster children because foster parents had them saying prayers at meal-time." Sometimes a slight subterfuge will gain a bureaucrat the figleaf needed to back off. The director of a Catholic child service agency reported: "Our campus ministry activities were originally disallowed by our Department of Social Services but are now allowed because we include them under the auspices of 'Values education.' "

A conservative Protestant college president reported that his state's "Post Secondary Educational Options Act permits students to attend college in lieu of [their] last year of high school—with modest direct subsidy from the state. These students may not take required religion classes while receiving that one year state subsidy. State Agency reviews course enrollments of each PSEO student to insure compliance." The problem here is that if these are really secondary school courses, the Supreme Court has ruled no government funds may be used to support even "secular" courses; if they are college courses, the Supreme Court has ruled even academic courses in religion may be covered by government funds. Confusion rules.

An example of the bizarre results of this situation was related by the head of a child service agency when asked in the questionnaire about having to curtail any of his or her agency's religious practices. He or she wrote, "Our only curtailment involves our operation of a school. We do not have religious symbols displayed in our school and do not mention religious activities there. However we are not restricted at our residential facility." (The same children, of course, that use the school use the residential facility and tax dollars help fund both.) This is a pragmatic response to a mixed-up system that says religion must be kept out of publicly funded schools, but does not have to be kept out of publicly funded homes for children. It makes no sense from the point of view of a consistent, principled church-state policy.

The Supreme Court on occasion has cited the younger, more impression-able age of K–12 students as compared to college students as a basis for denying public funds to religiously based K–12 schools and for allowing them to go to religiously based colleges and universities. Policy elites, if anything, place even greater weight on this factor and sometimes add the more episodic, less continuous, and less intensive contact it is claimed nonprofit agencies have with their clients. But this factor does no better than the pervasively sectarian standard and the secular-sacred distinction in sorting out the patterns found in Chapter 3 into a rational, principled order. The child service agencies included in my study, many of which run residential and foster care programs for youths, obviously are dealing with the same age children as are K–12 schools, and even do so in a more intensive, continuous manner than do K–12 schools. The potential for "indoctrination" is even greater with them than it is in the case of K–12 schools. Much the same point can be made with regard to some of the programs of international aid and relief agencies, such as the orphanages many run for the overseas victims of famine, disease, or war. A similar point can be made for a host of other religiously based nonprofit organizations that receive public funds: drug treatment programs, teenage runaway shelters, spouse abuse shelters, child care centers, and more.

In summary, when one looks at various specific practices engaged in by religiously based nonprofit organizations that receive public money, one finds a host of practices that in other contexts have been rejected by the Supreme Court as violations of First Amendment religious freedom provi-sions or, at the least, are subjects of intense controversy among policy elites. The results of the survey demonstrate that the policies being followed in regard to what types of religious nonprofits may receive public money and what religious practices nonprofits receiving public money may follow make little sense on the basis of the objective nature of the nonprofits and the practices they are following. Nor are the legal standards put forward by the Supreme Court being followed in a consistent manner. It is this confusion of standards that has led to the vulnerability of nonprofits' religious autonomy. This is considered in the next chapter.

Before moving on, however, it is important to note that all three of the legal principles considered in this chapter and found lacking—no-aid-to-religion, the sacred-secular distinction, and the pervasively sectarian standard—are aspects of the Supreme Court's no-aid-to-religion strain or line of reasoning. This leaves the recent, developing equal treatment strain identified earlier in Chapter 2. Two points are important to keep in mind concerning it. One is that the equal-treatment line of reasoning has never been used by the Supreme Court in the context of public funds for K–12 schools, colleges and universities, or other nonprofit, public service organizations of the type that are the subject of this study. Thus this study can only deal with projections and possibilities, not actual cases. Second, having acknowledged this, the equal treatment strain clearly offers a refreshing, promising basis for weighing the constitutional validity of public funding for nonprofit organizations, one that is respectful of both the religious autonomy of nonprofit organizations and the need for governmental neutrality towards organizations of all faiths and of none. Under the equal-treatment line of reasoning, religion is singled out for neither special limitations nor special favors. The final chapter considers how the equal-treatment line of reasoning, if more firmly grounded and more fully developed, could form the basis for a new, more principled standard for dealing with public funds and religiously based nonprofit organizations.

The Unconstitutionality of Public Funds for Religious K–12 Schools

The previous sections of this chapter, the results of the survey reported in Chapter 3, and material presented in Chapter 2 all note that American society, its leaders, and the courts largely agree in approving public money for most religious nonprofit organizations while rejecting it for religious K–12 schools. Why is this? The answer to this question can tell us much about how the American polity views church and state as they relate to religious nonprofits of all types, and may give insight into a way out of today's tensions and problems. I am convinced that much of the confusion existing in regard to government funds and religious nonprofits can be traced back to the felt need and inadequate attempts to distinguish between K–12 schools and their programs and other nonprofits and their programs.

I suggest in this section that the basic explanation for the anomaly of differing responses the American polity has given to the question of public money and religious K–12 schools, on the one hand, and the question of public money and other religious nonprofits, on the other, is to be found primarily in the conjunction of nineteenth-century attitudes towards the emerging common schools as the preeminent tool for social leveling and integration and a strong strain of anti-Catholic prejudice. Together these two factors do much to explain the anomaly mentioned above. I will take these two factors in turn.

The Common School Ideal

Robert Bellah tells the story of how in the early 1920s Henry Ford sponsored a festival: "A giant pot was built outside the gates of his factory into which danced groups of gaily dressed immigrants singing their native songs. From the other side of the pot emerged a single stream of Americans dressed alike in the contemporary standard dress and singing the national anthem."[32] This pageant represents the myth of the great American melting pot: persons coming from all the countries of the world, bringing their different customs, languages, and identifications, have been molded into one people, with one language and one American national identity: "*E Pluribus Unum.*" Ever since the early 1800s it was free, universal public schooling—the common school—that has been seen as the key element in this "melting-pot," Americanization process.

The common school ideal had its roots in the French Enlightenment, with its vision of national unity and loyalty to Enlightenment ideals.[33] This vision took hold in the early nineteenth century in several European countries. In France, for example, Francois Guizot (1787–1874) served as the minister for public instruction in the 1830s. At one point he sent a letter to all the teachers in France and required them to respond in writing with their thoughts and reactions to it. The letter, in part, said:

[L]iberty can neither be assured nor regular, except with a people sufficiently enlightened to listen, under all circumstances, to the voice of reason. Universal elementary education will become henceforward a guarantee for order and social stability. . . . Faith in Providence, the sanctity of duty, submission to parental authority, respect to the laws, to the sovereign, and to the common rights of all;—such are the sentiments which the teacher must labour to develop.[34]

Similar attempts at creating an enlightened national citizenry by way of universal elementary schools were also attempted in the nineteenth century in other European nations, especially in the Netherlands and Prussia.

In the early nineteenth century these European efforts caught the attention of Horace Mann and others of the New England elite, who worried about how to maintain—or create—national unity and to develop the virtues needed in a free, democratic nation, especially in light of an early-nine-teenth-century urbanization trend that was bringing large numbers of poor, provincial, and often uneducated farmers to the cities. The common school was seen by these reformers as the basic means by which the children of all classes—but especially the children of the lower, uneducated classes—would be taught social and political virtues. The common school advocates consis-tently saw the common school primarily in terms not of teaching skills in areas such as reading and mathematics, but in teaching the virtues thought necessary for national unity and free, democratic society. As Os Guinness has observed, "It [the public school] was to move beyond instruction in mere skills to education in character, ideals, and loyalties; and thus to be a moral force for character-forming and nation-building."[35]

David Tyack and Elisabeth Hansot have noted this commitment to education as the path to inculcating essential virtues already existed right after the War for Independence: "After the Revolution the majority of the early state constitutions expressed a common conviction, that education was essential to civil peace and prosperity as well as to individual morality. Hence education was in the public interest, and many forms of schooling deserved the favor of government."[36] In 1819 the famous Noah Webster wrote to the Massachusetts governor the following words:

> To form plans for diffusing literacy and moral improvement among the poorer classes of citizens, in connection with religious instruction, will be no less our pleasure than it is our duty. To draw from the obscure retreats of poverty the miserable victims of ignorance and vice, to enlighten their minds and correct their evil habits, to raise them to the rank of intelligent, industrious, and useful members of society will never cease to be the object of deep solicitude with a wise legislature.[37]

The concept of the common school as a molder of character and inculcator of virtue predated the big surge of immigration of the middle decades of the nineteenth century. When, however, immigration surged in the 1840s and especially when immigration from Ireland increased, bringing in immigrants more desperately poor and certainly more Catholic than seen before, the concept of the common school was already well launched among the elites of the young American nation and readily available for application to the new and, to many, frightening turn of events. It was the fear of American society being overwhelmed and undermined by the unwashed millions streaming into the United States in the middle decades of the nineteenth century that turned the common school ideal from an elite theory into a popular ideal broadly held in American society. Charles Glenn reports, "What in the 1830s was a cause appealing to a relatively limited elite, concerned to shape the American people in their own image, came in the next two decades to be perceived as an urgent necessity by virtually all Americans of social and political influence."[38]

As the nineteenth century progressed, each shift in the nations from which successive waves of immigrants originated seemed to bring in persons more difficult to assimilate and more lacking in the virtues thought necessary for democratic governance than the one before. First there were the Irish, then the Poles, then the Russian Jews, then the Italians, and so forth. Emma Lazarus's words, carved in the base of the Statue of Liberty ("Give me your tired, your poor,/Your huddled masses . . . /The wretched refuse of your teeming shores . . ."), were seen as an accurate description of the people reaching America, not as an exercise in hyperbole or poetic license. As each new wave of difficult-to-assimilate, "wretched refuse" washed ashore, the common school came to be seen as an increasingly crucial means for achieving national unity, assimilation, and the inculcation of habits of good citizenship.

William Issel has clearly documented the role assigned the common schools in late-nineteenth-century Pennsylvania in assimilating new immigrant groups. At one point he reports:

> By the mid 1890's Pennsylvania's state superintendent of schools had taken up the call for Americanization. Superintendent Schaeffer urged the readers of his annual report for 1896 to give their attention to the social consequences of "foreign immigration and to the employment of cheap labor in our mines and elsewhere." He specifically recommended to the state's school superintendents that they create public support in their communities for "the necessity of assimilating the foreign element by a system of public instruction."[39]

Later, Issel goes on to state, "As the numbers of southern and eastern European immigrants and their children increased after 1896, the consensus of the desirability of Americanization broadened, and the conviction about its necessity hardened."[40] Education historian Edward Cubberley, in 1909, described the problem as seen by his generation:

> These southern and eastern Europeans are of a very different type from the north Europeans who preceded them. Illiterate, docile, lacking in self-reliance

and initiative, and not possessing the Anglo-Teutonic conceptions of law, order, and government, their coming has served to dilute tremendously our national stock, and to corrupt our civic life. . . . Everywhere these people tend to settle in groups or settlements, and to set up here their national manners, customs, and observances. Our task is to break up these groups or settlements, to assimilate and amalgamate these people as a part of our American race, and to implant in their children, so far as can be done, the Anglo-Saxon conception of righteousness, law and order, and popular government. . . .[41]

To meet the above problem, Cubberley saw the common school as being "called upon anew to help assimilate the increasing number and the changing type of aliens coming to our shores."[42]

In the vision of the common school as the crucial inculcator of civic virtue and as the crucial instrument of cultural and national assimilation, religion was to play an important role, but it was religion of a particular type. Horace Mann was a Unitarian—as were many of his fellow New England education reformers—and as such rejected both particularistic religion and a nonreligious secularism. The schools were to be rational, Christian, and consensual. Calvin Stowe wrote in the 1830s a highly popular, influential book that described in positive terms the Prussian school system. Concerning religion he wrote,

> The *religious* spirit which pervades the whole of the Prussian system is greatly needed among ourselves.—Without religion—and, indeed, without the religion of the bible—there can be no efficient school discipline. . . . Religion is an essential element of human nature; and it must be cultivated, or there will be distortion of the intellect and affections. . . . [T]here is enough of common ground here to unite all the different sects in this great object. . . . If our republic is to be prosperous and happy, all our children must be instructed in the elements of science and religion.[43]

David Tyack has noted, "Religious and clerical influence turned up everywhere in the common school movement in an interlocking directorate of reform."[44]

But the religion of the common school was more reflective of Unitarianism than any other tradition within Christianity. Glenn writes,

> Unitarians believed that they were preserving the essence of Christianity, purged of "sectarian" and divisive doctrines which—they argued—were no part of the message of Jesus. This essential Christianity could and should be taught in the common schools, since it represented a "religion of heaven" to which no right-minded parent could object, whatever additional doctrines he might hold privately and teach to his children at home.[45]

Thus the Christianity to be taught in the common schools was—in the eyes of the Unitarian backers of the common school—rational and consensual. One ended up with a nonsectarian, generalized Protestantism. Horace Mann once wrote:

> Although it may not be easy theoretically, to draw the line between those views of religious truth and of christian faith which are common to all, and may, therefore, with propriety be inculcated in school, and those which, being peculiar to individual sects, are therefore by law excluded; still it is believed that no practical difficulty occurs in the conduct of our schools in this respect.[46]

Carl Kaestle has described the resulting common school ideology as being "centered on republicanism, Protestantism, and capitalism, three sources of social belief that were intertwined and mutually supporting."[47]

There were some protests to this form of religion both from the more evangelical, conservative Protestants and from Roman Catholics, but Catholics in the nineteenth century were largely marginalized politically and socially, and conservative Protestants surprisingly came largely to accept the vision of the common school religion Mann and others were espousing. Especially in light of the perceived threat arising from large numbers of Catholic immigrants flooding into the United States, many conservative Protestants—by far the numerically dominant group within nineteenth-century Protestantism—felt common schools that included bible readings and moral lessons represented a bulwark against the Catholic threat, even if it was not exactly biblical, orthodox Christianity that was being taught. Guinness has expressed it well, "In the nineteenth century, therefore, Protestant evangelicals were public-spirited in supporting state-run public schools. But it was also their way of 'establishing' a vague, nonsectarian, and moralistic Protestantism as the de facto civil religion."[48] There was virtual unanimity among the culturally dominant Protestant elites that in the common school the ideals of democracy, America, and Christianity were joined together in a powerful device for uniting the nation. The elements of Christianity in the common schools meant the then dominant conservative, evangelical Protestants saw no need for their own separate schools, and enabled them to join fully in the common school enterprise.

Anti-Catholic Prejudice

Running alongside and helping to stimulate the development of the common school was a deep-seated prejudice against the Roman Catholics, who—to many in the nineteenth century—seemed to represent a foreign element that was in tension with, if not in outright opposition to, the developing democratic American heritage. Anti-Catholic feelings were not limited to Protestant extremists, but marked both the mainstream and the very liberal, Unitarian wing of Protestantism. Glenn reports, "The General Association of the Congregational Churches of Massachusetts adopted, in 1844, a *Report on Popery* which stated that the Catholic church was in fact more idolatrous and abominable than the pagans themselves."[49] In 1849, on the founding of the College of the Holy Cross, the Unitarian *Christian Examiner*, referred to the "debasing and corrupting influence of the Roman Catholic religion" and declared:

> We should grieve for our beloved Commonwealth if we saw any reason to apprehend that the gross perversion of the Christian faith and life which Romanism involves would ever renew its blighting influences here. . . . [O]ur fathers sought this wild, dreary region, hard and inhospitable as it was, for the sake of an everlasting riddance of Popery, with all its forms and substance. . . . It is almost too much . . . [to bear that out] from the heart of our beloved Commonwealth are now to graduate, from year to year, Jesuit priests,—O'Briens, the O'Flahertys, and the McNamaras. Ireland and Rome together make a combination of a not very attractive character to the sons of New England sires.[50]

Historian John Higham has identified three distinguishable currents within American nativism: anti-Catholicism, anti-foreign radicalism, and a belief in Anglo-Saxon racial superiority.[51] "By far the oldest and—in early America— the most powerful of the anti-foreign traditions" Higham identifies as being "Protestant hatred of Rome."[52] Throughout his book he identifies periodic waves of anti-Catholic prejudice. Two aspects of recurrent anti-Catholic feelings that Higham points out are especially noteworthy. One is that the hatred of Roman Catholicism tended to focus not so much on the simple Catholic believers as on the pope and the church hierarchy. Concerning the 1870s, which experienced one of the recurrent waves of anti-Catholicism, Higham writes:

> Above all, anti-Catholics dealt gently with the immigrants. Blame fell instead on the clergy. One foe of Rome contended that the Irish would assimilate if the priests did not keep them separate. Another thought that the priesthood drove the Irish into reluctant hostility to public education. Another acknowledged the innocence of Catholic laymen and held the hierarchy alone disloyal.[53]

Similarly, he reports concerning the 1890s, which witnessed another surge in anti-Catholic feeling:

Since religious nativists had always regarded Catholics as disloyal adherents of a foreign potentate, the anti-Catholic tradition was easily susceptible to jingoist influence. Eyeing their Catholic neighbors, Protestant nationalists could enjoy a tingling sense of confronting the waiting soldiery of an enemy state. In the mid-nineties, without the provocation of actual international friction, the papacy took on place alongside Chile, Italy, and Great Britain as one of the powers against which an inflamed populace prepared to do battle.[54]

A second aspect of anti-Catholic feelings identified by Higham is the frequency with which it concerned the common school and the Catholic proclivity to create separate Catholic schools. Higham writes of the 1880s:

[E]ach parish strove to build a school, and Catholic parents felt increased pressure to send their children there. At the same time non-Catholics were becoming increasingly insistent on a standard, compulsory system of education dominated by the secular state. . . . To great numbers of Americans the common school was becoming a potent patriotic symbol.[55]

Any attempt to gain public funds for Catholic schools was met with strident anti-Catholic rhetoric. The common school espoused a morality based on a generalized religion that came suspiciously close to the Unitarian view of the virtues of a nonsectarian religion, consisting of broad moral ideas without particularistic religious beliefs.

This, of course, Catholics who took the particularities of their faith seriously could never accept. In addition, they rightly saw the common school as largely reflecting a generalized Protestantism. After all, when the Bible was read without comment it was the Protestant King James Version of the Bible that was read, and the very act of reading the Bible without comment implied the endorsement of the Protestant concept of the individual believer being able to interpret and appropriate biblical truth for him or herself without the need for church authority. Thus Catholics saw the common school as a potential force for undermining the faith of their children.

Meanwhile, the political elites of American society and much of the Protestant populace saw the waves of Catholic immigrants posing a major problem of assimilation and education. The common school was *the* institution for educating, training, and assimilating the foreign-born immigrants, and especially their children. Catholics' loyalty was already suspect due to their loyalty to the pope and what was seen as a foreign church hierarchy. Thus their rejection of the common schools was seen as a clear indication they were still committed to a foreign potentate and were determined that neither they nor their children were going to Americanize. Cubberley revealed a mindset typical of the day when in 1909 he made reference to the difficulties in getting the children of German immigrants "into our American public schools instead of their alien parochial schools."[56] Robert Handy has observed that "to many Protestants and some others the concern that every Catholic child have an opportunity for parochial school education appeared as an attack on the common schools."[57] Catholics were seen as posing a major threat to national unity and the creation of a common political culture.

In short, anti-Catholicism and the common school ideal worked to reinforce each other. Catholics, to the extent they rejected the common schools, proved the worst suspicions of nativist Americans. They, it was held, were determined to hold unto their allegiance to a foreign potentate and to resist the democratizing, character-building, Americanizing efforts of the common schools of their adopted land.

This mindset that developed in the nineteenth century did not simply die out in the twentieth century. Paul Blanshard is a revealing figure. In 1949 he published a book entitled, *American Freedom and Catholic Power*. In it he made two basic charges that directly echo the nineteenth century's anti-Catholic prejudices: first, the power of the church hierarchy, culminating in a foreign Pope, was absolute, and, second, the system of separate, parochial schools was subversive of American national unity.[58] Historian Barbara Welter has written that Blanshard's book "verges on absurdity."[59] Its prejudicial nature can be seen in its title, which juxtaposes American freedom and Catholic power as though they are mutually exclusive, and on almost every page, as when he refers more than once to the dangers posed by "American Catholics outbreeding the non-Catholic elements in our population."[60] At one point Blanshard clearly brought together fears over the power of the church hierarchy and over the distinctive Catholic schools:

> My own conviction is that the outcome of the struggle between American democracy and the Catholic hierarchy depends upon the survival and expansion of the public school. Even if the differential Catholic birth rate should soar in the United States, as it has soared in Quebec under the goading of the priests, the Catholic hierarchy could never make the United States into a clerical state unless it captured the public-school system or regimented a majority of American children into its own parochial-school system. There is no doubt that the hierarchy . . . would like to fragmentize our "godless" culture, under the guise of "Christianizing" it, by establishing strong competing schools of its own in every American community.[61]

Blanshard could be dismissed as having no significance for our present concerns if he were a fringe player with no following. This was not the case. It would be more accurate to say he was an establishment figure, respected and taken seriously by elite figures and institutions in the mid-twentieth century. He was a Congregational clergyman, and his book was published by Beacon Press (with its ties to the Unitarian Church). The first edition of the book sold a quarter of a million copies and went through twenty-six printings.[62] It was favorably reviewed in *The New Yorker* and the mainline Protestant journal, *The Christian Century*.[63] Blanshard was a leading figure in the well-known, respected church-state separationist organization, Americans United for Separation of Church and State (then revealingly called, Protestants and Others United for the Separation of Church and State). Blanshard and his popularity and acceptance in elite circles demonstrate that nineteenth-century anti-Catholic prejudices were alive and well in the mid-twentieth-century United States.

Conclusions

There is strong evidence that both the common school ideal and the suspicion of Catholic private education rooted in an anti-Catholic prejudice are continuing factors shaping the mindset with which Supreme Court justices and other policy elites approach the issue of public funds and K–12 schools. They certainly were present in the 1960s and 1970s, when the Supreme Court's basic precedents governing aid to K–12 schools were established.

One does not have to look long to find Supreme Court opinions that reveal a mindset that embraces the common school ideal and a prejudicial view of Catholic schools. One can imagine the ghost of Horace Mann hovering over the Supreme Court building when Justice Brennan, for example, wrote in a concurring opinion in *Abbington v. Schempp*:

> It is implicit in the history and character of American public education that the public schools serve a uniquely *public* function: the training of American citizens in an atmosphere free of parochial, divisive, or separatists influences of any sort—an atmosphere in which children may assimilate a heritage common to all American groups and religions. This is a heritage neither theistic nor atheistic, but simply civic and patriotic.[64]

Justice Frankfurter wrote in another concurring opinion, in which Justices Jackson, Rutledge, and Burton joined: "Designed to serve as perhaps the most powerful agency for promoting cohesion among a heterogeneous democratic people, the public school must keep scrupulously free from the entanglement of the strife of sects."[65] It is significant that among the justices clearly reflecting the common school ideal as it has been seen and described since the days of Horace Mann in the 1830s were justices such as Jackson, Frankfurter, and Brennan, some of the most respected and influential justices on the Supreme Court in the twentieth century.

In contrast to this highly positive, unifying view of the common school is the caricature of Catholic schools presented by Justices William Douglas and Hugo Black in a 1971 concurring opinion. In it they quote favorably from a 1961 anti-Catholic diatribe by Loraine Boettner, who begins his book by declaring: "Our American freedoms are being threatened today by two totalitarian systems, Communism and Roman Catholicism."[66] It is this book that Justices Douglas and Black turned to for this description of Catholic schools that they put forward as factually accurate:

> The whole education of the child is filled with propaganda. That, of course, is the very purpose of such schools, the very reason for going to all of the work and expense of maintaining a dual school system. Their purpose is not so much to educate, but to indoctrinate and train, *not to teach* Scripture truths and *Americanism, but to make loyal Roman Catholics.* The children are regimented, and are told what to wear, what to do, and what to think.[67]

It is significant to note that Boettner, and Justices Douglas and Black by quoting him favorably, not only revealed a highly negative view of Catholic schools, but also contrasted teaching Americanism and making loyal Catholics. The assumption is that one cannot be both a loyal American and a loyal Catholic. As seen earlier, that was the basic assumption on which much of nineteenth-century anti-Catholic prejudice was based—and was a key part of Blanshard's case against the Catholic Church. This quotation is the "smoking gun" of anti-Catholic prejudice on the Supreme Court, but other Justices have echoed similar views of Catholicism. The highly respected Justice Robert Jackson, for example, wrote in a dissenting opinion in which Justice Frankfurter joined: "Our public school, if not a product of Protestantism, at least is more consistent with it than with the Catholic culture and scheme of values."[68] Similarly, in another, dissenting opinion, Justice Black noted that the law under challenge in that case did "not as yet formally adopt or establish a state religion," but warned that the Catholic Church was "looking toward complete domination and supremacy of their particular brand of religion."[69] In short, when the Supreme Court was establishing its basic precedents concerning public funds and religiously based K–12 schools in the 1960s and 1970s, anti-Catholic prejudices were still alive and well among some Supreme Court justices.

After reading the caricature of Catholic schools quoted by Justices Douglas and Black, at least some of the marks of a "pervasively sectarian" institution put forward by Justice Blackmun in *Roemer* suddenly make more sense. Three of the six marks he cited were religious indoctrination of students, a lack of academic freedom, and a lack of normal academic standards. Blackmun, writing for a plurality of three justices, was saying that aid to colleges and universities could be approved because they were not marked by characteristics such as these, as he apparently supposed was the case with Catholic K–12 schools.

The picture that emerges is one of a Supreme Court that, when determining the basic precedents governing aid to religiously based schools, was still deeply affected by a belief in the present-day public schools as an embodiment of the common school ideal, and by a suspicion of Catholic K–12 schools as subversive of that ideal and thereby not in the American mainstream. One can debate the extent to which and whether such a mindset ever had a basis in reality, but it surely is based on a blatantly false view of the world as it is today. James Coleman and his associates have demonstrated that the Catholic schools "come closer to the American ideal of the 'common school,' educating all alike than do the public schools."[70] In any case, Catholic schools today account for only 55 percent of the students in private schools, with 31 percent in schools of other religious traditions, and 14 percent in secularly based private schools.[71] To equate "nonpublic school" with "Catholic school," as the Supreme Court consistently did in the 1960s and 1970s, is today clearly inaccurate.

It is hard to get away from the impression that in the 1960s and 1970s the general public, the policy elites, and the Supreme Court justices did not want tax money to go to support the Catholic hierarchy in its attempts to maintain a separate school system they saw as clearly inferior to the public schools and less supportive of consensual American values. Thus they found the constitutional principles on which to reach such a result. The problem was that the same elites wanted public money to flow to—from their point of view—the nonthreatening, less Catholic, and more mainstream colleges and universities, hospitals, disaster relief agencies, child service agencies, homeless shelters, and a host of other such educational and social service nonprofit organizations. The result was a series of legal principles of dubious constitutional merit out of touch with the real world. The resulting vulnerability of religious nonprofit organizations receiving public funds is considered in the next chapter.

Notes

1. James Madison, "Memorial and Remonstrance Against Religious Assessments," in *The Supreme Court on Church and State*, Robert S. Alley, ed. (New York: Oxford University Press, 1988), 20.

2. On religious neutrality, see Douglas Laycock, "Formal, Substantive, and Disaggregated Neutrality Toward Religion," *DePaul Law Review*, 39 (1990), 993–1018. The concept of neutrality I am presenting here is what Laycock termed substantive neutrality.

3. From Stewart's dissenting opinion in *Abington v. Schempp*, 372 U.S. at 319–20 (1963).

4. *Everson v. Board of Education*, 330 U.S. at 16 (1947).

5. *Everson v. Board of Education*, at 18.

6. *Abington School District v. Schempp*, at 226. Other especially clear linkings of strict church-state separation with governmental neutrality were made by Justice Abe Fortas in *Epperson v. Arkansas*, 393 U.S. at 103–104 (1968) and Justice Thurgood Marshall in his dissenting opinion in *Mueller v. Allen*, 463 U.S. at 404 (1983).

7. "Keeping the Church-State Wall," *The New York Times* (December 1, 1993), A16.

8. *Roemer v. Maryland Public Works Board*, 426 U.S. at 747 (1976).

9. *Roemer v. Maryland Public Works Board*, at 747.

10. *Meek v. Pittenger*, 421 U.S. at 359 (1975). Emphasis added. The quotation is one I have cited earlier from *Everson v. Board of Education*.

11. Ruth Benedict, *Patterns of Culture*, 2nd ed. (New York: Houghton Mifflin, 1959), 2.

12. See Thomas S. Kuhn, *The Structure of Scientific Revolutions* (Chicago: University of Chicago Press, 1962); Michael Polanyi, *Personal Knowledge: Towards a Post-Critical Philosophy* (Chicago: University of Chicago Press, 1962); and Fritjof Capra, *The Turning Point* (New York: Simon and Schuster, 1982).

13. Capra, *The Turning Point*, 87.

14. Harold I. Brown, *Perception, Theory and Commitment: The New Philosophy of Science* (Chicago: Precedent, 1977), 166.

15. Roy A. Clouser, *The Myth of Religious Neutrality* (Notre Dame, IN: University of Notre Dame Press, 1991), 3. Emphasis present.

16. *Bowen v. Kendrick*, 487 U.S. at 631 (1988).

17. *Jacobellis v. Ohio*, 378 U.S. at 197 (1964).

18. *Roemer v. Board of Public Works*, at 757.

19. *Hunt v. McNair*, 413 U.S. at 743 (1973).

20. *Equal Employment Opportunity Commission v. Kamehameha Schools*, 990 F.2nd 458 (1993).

21. *EEOC v. Kamehameha Schools*, at 461.

22. This is the same picture as the one presented in *Religious Schools in America*, James C. Carper and Thomas C. Hunt, eds., (Birmingham, AL: Religious Education Press, 1984).

23. For the figures on non-Catholic enrollments in Catholic schools, see Dennis Hevesi, "Brooklyn's Bishop Outlines Policies for Parish Schools, *New York Times* (December 1, 1993), A18. I also interviewed a high-ranking official in the New York Archdiocese and he confirmed these figures.

24. *Sherbert v. Verner*, 374 U.S. at 404 (1963).

25. *Abington School District v. Schempp*, at 229.

26. *Abington School District v. Schempp*, at 225.

27. Admittedly the sponsorship of religious exercises in public schools and in tax-supported nonprofit agencies can be distinguished in that the state's authority or imprimatur is not being placed behind religion in the case of the nonprofit agency in the same way as in the case of the public schools. Justice Brennan, in a concurring opinion, especially emphasized the importance of implicit government endorsement of prayers and bible reading led by public schools officials. Nevertheless, the importance of the financial facet and the non-importance of the voluntary nature of the religious exercises that were found unconstitutional in the *Schempp* case run throughout the opinions of the majority justices.

28. *Roemer v. Board of Public Works*, at 756.

29. On this whole issue, see *Congressional Quarterly Almanac*, 46 (Washington, DC: Congressional Quarterly Service, 1990), 547–51; "Church-Based Centers: A Funding Dilemma," *Congressional Quarterly Weekly Report*, (February 27, 1988): 515; "ABC Bill Sets Off New Church-State Debate," *Congressional Quarterly Weekly Report*, (August 6, 1988): 2201; Rob Boston, "To Raise Up a Child," *Church and State*, 41 (March, 1988): 52–54; and Joseph L. Conn, "Churches and Child Care," *Church and State*, 41 (July/August, 1988): 148-49.

30. Quoted in "ABC Bill Advances to Senate Floor, Despite Church-State Conflicts," *Church and State*, 42 (April, 1989): 85.

31. See "Picture of Jesus Blocks Public Funds for Salvation Army," *Church and State*, 42 (October, 1989): 207.

32. Robert N. Bellah, *The Broken Covenant: American Civil Religion in Time of Trial* (New York: Seabury Press, 1975), 94.

33. On the Enlightenment and its views on the importance of universal education as a means of socialization, see Charles Leslie Glenn Jr., *The Myth of the Common School* (Amherst, MA: University of Massachusetts Press, 1987), 15–37.

34. Quoted in Glenn, *The Myth of the Common School*, 37.

35. Os Guinness, *The American Hour* (New York: The Free Press, 1993), 228. Also very helpful on this point is Carl F. Kaestle, *Pillars of the Republic: Common Schools and American Society, 1780–1860* (New York: Hill and Wang, 1983), especially Chapter 5.

36. David Tyack and Elisabeth Hansot, *Managers of Virtue: Public School Leadership in America, 1820–1980* (New York: Basic Books, 1982), 28.

37. Quoted by Glenn, *The Myth of the Common School*, 77.

38. Glenn, *The Myth of the Common School*, 84.

39. William Issel, "Americanization, Acculturation and Social Control: School Reform Ideology in Industrial Pennsylvania, 1880–1910," *Journal of Social History*, 12 (1979): 575.

40. Issel, "Americanization, Acculturation and Social Control," 576.

41. Ellwood P. Cubberley, *Changing Conceptions of Education* (Boston: Houghton Mifflin, 1909), 15.

42. Cubberley, *Changing Conceptions of Education*, 41.

43. Quoted by Glenn, *The Myth of the Common School*, 149. Emphasis present in the original. The original book is Calvin E. Stowe, *The Prussian System of Public Instruction and Its Applicability to the United States* (Cincinnati, OH: Truman & Smith, 1836), 73–75.

44. David Tyack "The Kingdom of God and the Common School," *Harvard Educational Review*, 36 (1966): 454.

45. Glenn, *The Myth of the Common School*, 154. Also noting the Unitarian nature of the Christianity of the common schools is George M. Marsden, *The Soul of the American University* (New York: Oxford University Press, 1994), 89.

46. Quoted in Glenn, *The Myth of the Common School*, 164.

47. Kaestle, *Pillars of the Republic*, 76.

48. Guinness, *The American Hour*, 229.

49. Glenn, *The Myth of the Common School*, 70.

50. Quoted in Glenn, *The Myth of the Common School*, 70–71.

51. See John Higham, *Strangers in the Land: Patterns of American Nativism, 1860–1925* (New Brunswick, NJ: Rutgers University Press, 1955), 5–11.

52. Higham, *Strangers in the Land*, 5.

53. Higham, *Strangers in the Land*, 29.

54. Higham, *Strangers in the Land*, 84.

55. Higham, *Strangers in the Land*, 59–60.

56. Cubberley, *Changing Conceptions of Education*, 42.

57. Robert T. Handy, "Why It Took 150 Years for Supreme Court Church-State Cases to Escalate," in *An Unsettled Arena: Religion and the Bill of Rights*, Ronald C. White and Albright G. Zimmerman, eds. (Grand Rapids, MI: Eerdmans, 1990), 60–61.

58. See Paul Blanshard, *American Freedom and Catholic Power* (Boston: Beacon, 1949). After large sales the book was reissued in an expanded second edition in 1958.

59. Barbara Welter, "From Maria Monk to Paul Blanshard: A Century of Protestant Anti-Catholicism," in *Uncivil Religion: Interreligious Hostility in America*, Robert N. Bellah and Frederick E. Greenspahn, eds. (New York: Crossroad, 1987), 54.

60. Paul Blanshard, *American Freedom and Catholic Power*, 2nd ed., 322. Also see 313. My key point here, of course, is that Blanshard uses the term, "breeding," to refer to procreation, a term normally used to refer to procreation among animals.

61. Blanshard, *American Freedom and Catholic Power*, 2nd ed., 323.

62. Blanshard, *American Freedom and Catholic Power*, 2nd ed. Jacket cover.

63. See *The New Yorker* (August 27, 1949): 25, and *The Christian Century*, 66 (June 8, 1949): 709–10. Excerpts from the book were also printed in *The Nation* and *The Christian Century*. It did, however, receive an unfavorable review in the *New York Times*, 15 May 1949, 15.

64. *Abington School District v. Schempp*, at 241–42. Emphasis present in the original.

65. *McCollum v. Board of Education* 333 U.S. at 216–17 (1948).

66. Loraine Boettner, *Roman Catholicism* (Philadelphia: Presbyterian and Re-

formed Publishing, 1962), 3. At another point Boettner makes the absurd claim that if priests were offered ten thousand dollars "there would not be enough priests left to man the churches." Boettner, *Roman Catholicism*, 72. Almost every page of this book offers examples of patently false, prejudicial attacks on Roman Catholicism.

67. *Lemon v. Kurtzman*, 403 U.S. at 635 (1971). Emphasis added.

68. *Board of Education v. Everson*, 330 U.S. at 23 (1947).

69. *Board of Education v. Allen*, 235 U.S. at 250 (1968).

70. James S. Coleman, Thomas Hoffer, and Sally Kilgore, *High School Achievement: Public, Catholic, and Private Schools Compared* (New York: Basic Books, 1982), 144. Chapter 5 of this book cites additional studies that have concluded Catholic schools are today doing a better job of educating minority and low-income students than are public schools.

71. U. S. Bureau of the Census, *Statistical Abstract of the United States: 1994*, 114th ed. (Washington, DC: GPO, 1994), 172.

Chapter Five

When Legal Principles Confuse

The previous chapter noted tensions and problems in the Supreme Court's legal principles and distinctions as they apply to religious nonprofit organizations receiving public funds. This leaves the question, however, of the actual impact these tensions and problems have on nonprofit organizations, and especially on their religious autonomy. The questionnaire results presented in Chapter 3 reveal that in practice nonprofit organizations receiving public funds have greater religious autonomy than one would expect, given the tensions and problems in the legal principles under which they receive those funds.

This chapter argues that there are three identifiable consequences for religious nonprofit organizations resulting from the current legal principles and, implicitly, the public and elite attitudes under which they receive public funds. First, religious nonprofit organizations receiving public funds are left vulnerable to attempts to limit or restrict the expression of their religious beliefs, since their religious autonomy is largely undefined and unprotected by legal-constitutional guarantees. Second, the legal doctrines and public and elite attitudes under which religious nonprofits receive public funds may be exerting subtle, indirect pressures on them slowly to give up crucial aspects of their religious beliefs and practices. Third, one of the most vital types of religiously based nonprofit organizations with much to offer in meeting persistent societal problems—K–12 schools—has been left out of the public-nonprofit partnership. This chapter considers each of these three consequences in turn.

Religious Nonprofit Organizations' Vulnerability

The questionnaire results reported in Chapter 3 indicate that in actual practice the religious autonomy of most nonprofit organizations receiving public funds has not been violated, at least not in a direct, large-scale fashion. The responses indicate that only a minority—and usually a small minority—of even the most highly religious nonprofit organizations receiving public money are experiencing invasions of their freedom to live out their religious beliefs and practices as their consciences dictate. Various measures consistently support this conclusion.

This situation in many ways is fair and equitable to religiously based nonprofits. They are not being forced to choose between losing their religious autonomy and their freedom to pursue the practices their religious consciences demand, on the one hand, or, on the other hand, losing public funds all other similarly situated organizations, public and private alike, are receiving. Most religious nonprofits have managed to avoid this dilemma. In a glorious application of the "muddling through" dynamic, a confusion of legal standards is used to block almost all public funds from going to religiously based elementary and secondary schools, but allows them to flow to all other religiously based educational and social service nonprofits, and to do so largely without violating their religious autonomy.

However, the religious autonomy of religiously based nonprofits receiving public funds is—legally, constitutionally—largely unprotected. The possibility of being impaled on either the no-public-funds horn of the above dilemma or the no-more-religious-autonomy horn is real. The extent to which religious nonprofits have been able thus far largely to escape this dilemma appears to be a result of a usually sympathetic public, supportive policy elites, the nonprofits' provision of services others have no desire to provide, the savings they often achieve for public programs, and the perceived effectiveness of the services they provide. They are not being protected—but in fact are being made more vulnerable—by the courts and their interpretations of the First Amendment religious freedom guarantees. There is an irony here. The First Amendment was designed to protect unpopular religious minorities from public and legislative majorities; today it is public and legislative majorities that are protecting religious nonprofits from current interpretations of the First Amendment.

Thus whenever state or federal bureaucratic agencies, lower courts, church-state separation groups, disgruntled individuals, or the news media question or seek to block certain of the religiously based practices of religious nonprofits receiving public funds, those nonprofit organizations have few legal protections. The confusion of legal standards means that legally they are likely to find themselves standing not on firm ground, but quicksand. Amy Sherman of the Ethics and Public Policy Center has described the situation in these words:

Many religious nonprofits that choose to accept state funding have a relationship of convenience with government. Government provides funds and the ministry provides effective services among clientele the government has not been able to reach. Some of these nonprofits report that government officials will "look the other way" when the ministries undertake activities that, technically, may be in violation of church-state separation regulations. This has allowed the ministries to maintain the distinctives of their outreach (namely, Biblical teaching and moral challenge) which make them effective. It is, however, a precarious situation: at some point, a more zealous social worker or government bureaucrat could enforce more rigorously regulations that can squelch the religious expression of the ministry.[1]

Two Key Areas of Concern

The difficult situation in which religious nonprofits receiving public funds have been placed due to the absence of constitutional protections for their religious autonomy can be most clearly seen in two crucial areas. One relates to hiring policies and whether or not religiously based organizations that receive public funds may favor persons of their own faith in hiring staff, and the other relates to the freedom to integrate religiously based practices and beliefs into their organizations' activities. Time and again in the returned questionnaires, in my discussions with organization officials, and in the literature these two issues arise.

First, it is important to note that these two issues are vital in terms of the religious autonomy of an organization. As seen earlier, if an organization cannot insist its staff members be in agreement with its religious beliefs, but must hire persons of other religious traditions and nonbelievers, that organization effectively ceases to exist as a religious organization. It will have lost its ability to define itself. It may be able to carry on for a while by hiring only a token number of staff members in disagreement with its religious nature or by keeping them in lower level, less sensitive positions, but if the principle of making hiring decisions without reference to the religious beliefs of the applicants were ever to be followed fully and consistently, that organization would cease to exist as an organization with a particular religious orientation. It no longer would be a Muslim, Jewish, Catholic, or Baptist organization.

Similarly—even if not quite as clearly—an organization needs to be free to integrate religiously based practices and beliefs into its activities if its religious autonomy is to be preserved. If a religious organization is told it cannot engage in prayer and other religious exercises, or cannot have pictures or symbols in its facilities honoring its religious tradition, or cannot establish behavior norms based on its religious beliefs, its autonomy will be seriously eroded. As with hiring decisions, it is a matter of self-definition, of being free to be what its religiously-shaped collective conscience says it should be. If an orthodox Jewish nursing home would be pressured not to keep Kosher, if a Catholic child service agency would be pressured to give abortion referral information to its teenage clients, or if a conservative Protestant college would be pressured to recognize and financially support a gay-lesbian student organization, those religiously based organizations would be forced to engage in actions their consciences tell them is wrong. The long hand of the administrative state would be reaching into their internal affairs, forcing them to do what their religious traditions tell them they have no choice but not to do.

Sometimes the Supreme Court has been willing to recognize the importance to a religious nonprofit organization of making hiring decisions on the basis of religion. Its 1987 decision in *Corporation of Presiding Bishop v. Amos* is particularly instructive. A unanimous Court upheld a federal civil rights law that specifically allows religious organizations to discriminate in their hiring policies on the basis of religion as constitutional, even in the instance of a church-sponsored Mormon recreation center and its hiring of a maintenance worker. Writing for the Court, Justice Byron White stated that "as applied to the nonprofit activities of religious employers" the federal law that allows religious discrimination in hiring "is rationally related to the legitimate purpose of alleviating significant governmental interference with the ability of religious organizations to define and carry out their religious missions."[2] Thus the law allowing religious nonprofit organizations to make hiring decisions based on religion was held not to be a violation of the establishment clause. In a concurring opinion, Justice Brennan clearly made a free exercise argument when he noted that for government to allow religious discrimination in hiring only for religious positions and not secular positions, such as was at issue here, would give rise to a "prospect of government intrusion [that] raises concern that a religious organization may be chilled in its free exercise activity."[3] No public funds were involved in this case, and the Supreme Court could clearly see the religious autonomy implications if religious nonprofit organizations could not hire on the basis of religious beliefs and membership, even for as nonsensitive a position as that of a maintenance worker.

When public money is involved, however, the situation is radically different. Earlier it was seen that one of the marks of a "pervasively sectarian" institution that would help make it ineligible for public money is its use of religious criteria in its hiring decisions. In addition, the same Justice Brennan who clearly saw in *Amos* the negative effects for a religious organization of its not being able to hire staff in keeping with its religious beliefs, once flatly stated in a concurring opinion from the K–12 education level that "when a sectarian institution accepts state financial aid it becomes obligated under the Equal Protection Clause of the Fourteenth Amendment not to discriminate in admissions policies and faculty selection."[4] In other words, a religious organization that receives public funds does not have the same religious autonomy as one that does not receive such funds. If a church-sponsored recreation center would have its free exercise rights undermined by not being able to insist on hiring a fellow believer as a maintenance worker, surely a religious college that could not insist on hiring a fellow believer as a professor would have its free exercise rights undermined. Yet if a religious agency or institution that has received public funds should have its right to insist on hiring fellow believers questioned, it would have few protections under current Supreme Court legal doctrines.

The Supreme Court's decision in *Bowen v. Kendrick* also helps illustrate the jeopardy in which a religious organization's religiously based practices are put under Supreme Court doctrines when they receive public dollars. As noted earlier in Chapter 2, this case dealt with the issue of whether or not Congress could constitutionally grant funds to religiously based agencies under the Adolescent Family Life Act (AFLA), which sought to prevent teenage pregnancies and encourage teenage sexual responsibility. By a close 5–4 vote, the Supreme Court held that on its face AFLA was constitutional and remanded the case to the lower courts to determine whether or not as actually carried out it met constitutional standards.

The decision was rooted firmly in the sacred-secular distinction and the pervasively sectarian standard. A bare majority of the Supreme Court upheld AFLA as it was written because it was fulfilling a primarily secular, not religious purpose, and the agencies receiving public funds were not pervasively sectarian (thereby enabling them to separate the religious from the secular). At one point Chief Justice Rehnquist, writing for the Court majority, said that "nothing in our prior cases warrants the presumption adopted by the District Court that religiously affiliated AFLA grantees are not capable of carrying out their functions under the AFLA in a lawful, *secular manner.*"[5] In other words, the counseling the religious agencies was to provide had to be done in a secular manner. Later he went on to write:

> The facially neutral projects authorized by the AFLA—including pregnancy testing, adoption counseling and referral services, prenatal and postnatal care, educational services, residential care, child care, consumer education, etc.—are not themselves 'specifically religious activities,' and they are not converted into such activities by the fact that they are carried out by organizations with religious affiliations.[6]

There is a critical ambiguity here. True, the activities cited in this quotation are not religious activities in the same way as explicitly religious worship services or other religious rituals are, but they touch so close to the nature and meaning of personhood and other deeply moral, ethical issues that it is hard to contemplate their being devoid of religious content.

The dissenting justices quoted these words of Dr. Paul Simmons, a Baptist clergyman and professor of Christian Ethics:

> The very purpose of religion is to transmit certain values, and those values associated with sex, marriage, chastity and abortion involve religious values and theological or doctrinal issues. In encouraging premarital chastity, it would be extremely difficult for a religiously affiliated group not to impart its own religious values and doctrinal perspectives when teaching a subject that has always been central to its religious teachings.[7]

It is hard to deny the accuracy of Simmons' words. But does the majority opinion mean that any religious agency receiving funds under AFLA must teach about "sex, marriage, chastity, and abortion" without any reference to the religious traditions and beliefs of that agency? If the answer is yes, the religious autonomy of that agency has been invaded. The dissenting justices also declared, "It should be undeniable by now that religious dogma may not be employed by government even to accomplish laudable secular purposes."[8] If taken literally, it is hard to argue against this statement, but if "government" is extended to include private, nonprofit organizations that receive public funds, then those organizations' freedom to integrate religious values and perspectives in their programs is left unprotected.

The basic problem lies in the basis on which religious nonprofits' participation in public funding programs has been justified. The Supreme Court has stated, in ruling against aid to religious K–12 schools, that no aid may go to religion. Thus the only way in which one can justify public money flowing to religiously based nonprofits has been to make a sacred-secular distinction, and then insist public funds are only funding the secular programs and activities. Once this justification for government funding of nonprofits' activities is accepted, a trap snaps shut, a trap that legally puts their religious autonomy in a vulnerable position. If a religious nonprofit agency or institution is performing certain secular functions that are clearly and cleanly separable from its religious functions, what rationale does it have to defend its practice of hiring only fellow religious believers to perform those supposedly secular functions? Or on what basis can one justify introducing any religious values or practices at all into supposedly purely secular programs or activities? If a certain program or activity of a religious nonprofit is purely secular in nature, there is no rationale left to defend insisting on a fellow believer running it, or requiring—or encouraging—participants to engage in certain religious practices, or even to have certain religious symbols or pictures in the facility where it is being held. Seeking to bring religion into a purely secular activity in ways such as these is, at the worst, to act on the basis of prejudice, or, at best, to indulge one's sentimental traditions. To do so would bring religion into a secular program where religion has no rational, defensible role to play.

Thus when public funds flow, for example, to a conservative Protestant or Catholic college on the basis that it performs "essentially secular education functions . . . that are distinct and separable from religious activity" and the public money only supports the "secular educational functions,"[9] what basis is left for that college to insist only a conservative Protestant or only a Catholic should teach such courses? There is none. After all, if religiously rooted worldviews or values are irrelevant to the subject matter of a course, a conservative Protestant, Catholic, Jew, Muslim, Marxist, or totally nonreligious humanist would teach the course in the exact same way.

This is why the artifices and subterfuges under which the Supreme Court has approved funding programs for religious nonprofits other than K–12 schools have left the religious autonomy of nonprofits receiving public funds in a legally precarious position. The basic fact is that at least for many religious traditions—including both the Catholic and conservative Protestant traditions used in the preceding example—it makes a great deal of difference if a course in literature, sociology, history, psychology, and a host of other subjects is taught by a Catholic, Jew, conservative Protestant, Muslim, Marxist, or nonreligious humanist. The exact same point is true of a therapist in a drug abuse center, a counselor in a child service agency, or a rural development worker in an international aid agency. To pretend otherwise may enable programs of nonprofit-public partnership and cooperation to slip by the Supreme Court, but the end result is that the religious autonomy of the nonprofits taking part in such programs is left unprotected by the First Amendment.

One is back to the previously noted dilemma. If religious nonprofit organizations accept public dollars, their religious autonomy is put in an uncertain, vulnerable position. If they do not accept public dollars in the context of the comprehensive administrative state that is funding all sorts of competing secular programs run by the government itself or by secular nonprofit organizations, they are severely disadvantaged. The pressures to accept public funds, even at the cost of giving up some of their religious freedoms, is evident. Especially when one recalls the "culture war," as discussed in Chapter 2, between secularly grounded and religiously grounded mindsets, government's funding of secular nonprofits and running of its own secular programs, but funding of religious nonprofits only on the condition of their giving up some of their religious freedom is anything but neutral.

When the First Amendment Does Not Protect

Most of the time the lack of clear First Amendment protections for religious nonprofits receiving public money does not create major problems for them. As long as they are able to maintain the good will of the public, policy leaders, and overseeing officials, and as long as they provide effective services that few care to provide anyway, they are likely to be able to integrate religious practices and values into their programs and to make hiring decisions in part on the basis of the religious beliefs and memberships of the applicants. But when a terminated employee, or an applicant for a position who was not hired, or a church-state separation watchdog group brings legal action against a religious nonprofit, or when even a low level bureaucrat in an overseeing government office informs a religious nonprofit it can no longer engage in a certain religiously based practice, that nonprofit has few legal protections.

As Chapter 3 demonstrated, most , but not all, religiously based nonprofits receiving public funds have escaped such problems. As noted there, 30 percent of the religious child service agencies receiving public funds reported having received some sort of government pressures or questions in response to their religious practices, as did 13 percent of the religious colleges and universities, and 22 percent of the religious international aid agencies. Among those ranking high on the Religious Practices Scale, the percentages, while still below 50 percent, were higher, approaching 40 percent in the case of child service agencies. In addition to governmental pressures and problems were those arising from individuals and the news media, with over one-fourth of the highly religious colleges and universities and child service agencies experiencing problems of this nature. The minority of religious nonprofits receiving public funds experiencing difficulties over their religious practices from the governmental or private sources truly is a minority, but for the more thoroughly religious nonprofits it is a sizable minority.

As noted in Chapter 3, having a problem of one type or another suddenly arise is like being hit by lightning. It is unpredictable, rare—and also often disastrous. When it does occur the head of the nonprofit agency or institution can rally whatever political resources he or she may have in the community and among public office holders. A friendly newspaper editor, a powerful board member, a helpful legislator: these are the resources she or he may be able to call upon. Legally, constitutionally, however, she or he is likely to face an uphill struggle.

Periodic reports that surface of problems encountered by religious non-profits receiving public funds are revealing of the difficulties nonprofits can experience due to the lack of clear First Amendment protections. Three are considered here as examples of the difficulties religious nonprofits receiving public funds can experience and of their vulnerability due to existing legal principles governing such funds.

One such case is *Dodge v. Salvation Army*. The Salvation Army in Pascagoula, Mississippi, had received public funding for a domestic violence shelter, and had hired Jamie Dodge as a "Victim's Assistance Coordinator."[10] Her duties included interviewing victims of domestic violence, helping clients in case planning, assisting with community education, and providing for any special needs of shelter residents. Thus the job involved many contacts with the victims of abuse and violence to whom the Salvation Army—in its tradition of Christian compassion for the hurting and destitute of society—sought to minister. It was not a clerical or some other position involving routine, nondiscretionary tasks. Instead, it involved numerous contacts with clients, working with and counseling them and as such serving as the voice and arm of the Salvation Army, an organization that is a Protestant church within the more conservative or evangelical tradition of Protestantism.[11] On her application, Dodge had indicated that she was Catholic.

After working for about a year it was discovered that Dodge was in fact not a Catholic or a Christian of any type, but a witch—a devotee of the ancient, pagan religion of Wicca. Upon the discovery of her non-Christian religious beliefs, the Salvation Army fired her, holding that being a believer in Wicca was inconsistent with working as a councilor in a Christian organization. Dodge filed a complaint with the Equal Employment Opportunities Commission (EEOC) and later brought suit in Federal District Court. Federal civil rights laws—as seen earlier—explicitly provide for an exemption for religious organizations from the law's general prohibitions against religious discrimination: "This subchapter [Title VII of the Civil Rights Act of 1964, 42 U.S.C. § 2000e et seq.] shall not apply . . . to a religious corporation, association, educational institution, or society with respect to the employment of individuals of a particular religion to perform work connected with the carrying on by such corporation, association, educational institution, or society of activities."[12] Earlier decisions had held that the Salvation Army is a church and, as just seen in the *Amos* case, that the religious exemption language of the Civil Rights Act even applies to a custodial position in a church-owned recreation center. The Salvation Army would seem to be on firm grounds in dismissing Dodge.

The District Court, however, ruled that since the Salvation Army was receiving substantial public funds in support of Dodge's position and its Domestic Violence Center, it had no legal right to dismiss her. The Court held that due to the public money involved the provision of the Civil Rights Act assuring religious organizations the right to discriminate on the basis of religion in their hiring practices was an unconstitutional violation of the establishment clause. Judge Dan M. Russell Jr. ruled:

> Based on the facts in the present case, the effect of the government substantially, if not exclusively, funding a position such as the Victims' Assistance Coordinator and then allowing the Salvation Army to choose the person to fill or maintain the position based on religious preference clearly has the effect of advancing religion and is unconstitutional.[13]

Later Judge Russell reemphasized the fact that it was the Salvation Army's receipt of public money that he saw as being controlling in this case:

> The benefits received by the Salvation Army were not indirect or incidental. The grants constituted direct financial support in the form of a substantial subsidy, and therefore to allow the Salvation Army to discriminate on the basis of religion, concerning the employment of the Victims' Assistance Coordinator, would violate the Establishment Clause of the First Amendment.[14]

The District Court thereby held that because of its receipt of public money, the Salvation Army, in seeking to dismiss a witch who was actively engaged in pagan rituals, violated the second and third prongs of the three-pronged *Lemon* test, discussed earlier in Chapter 2. Doing so advanced religion and ran the danger of excessive government entanglement with religion. In short, the Salvation Army gave up its religious autonomy when it accepted public money to help fund one of its programs.

The Salvation Army did not appeal this decision to a higher court, but settled the case with Dodge without further legal proceedings. Thus this decision ought not to be interpreted as established law, but it surely stands as a warning sign of the sort of mindset and perspectives that are abroad in American society. The assumption underlying the court's ruling is that if a religious nonprofit receives public money, it to all intents and purposes loses its religious autonomy and becomes indistinguishable from a government agency. It rejects the concept of a religious autonomy guarded by legal and constitutional bulwarks. When a religious organization such as the Salvation Army runs into a lower-court judge such as the one in this case, it does not have religious autonomy protections clearly articulated by the Supreme Court with which to defend itself.

Beyond this basic observation on this case two more need to be made. One is that the judge largely relied on *Lemon v. Kurtzman* and other decisions dealing with the constitutionality of aid to elementary and secondary schools in reaching his conclusion. For example, at one point he quoted from a footnote in *Mueller v. Allen* (in which the Supreme Court had upheld a Minnesota tax deduction program for expenses parents incur in sending their children to public or nonpublic schools). There the Supreme Court had distinguished that case from the *Lemon* case (which had held school aid laws in Rhode Island and Pennsylvania unconstitutional) on the basis that the public funds in the *Lemon* case went directly to the nonpublic schools, while in *Mueller* a tax credit program was at issue. This was used by the judge in the *Dodge* case, since there too the funds went directly to a nonprofit, religious organization. The point here is that language used by the Supreme Court in cases dealing with public funds going to religious K–12 schools was now being used to severely restrict the religious autonomy of a religious nonprofit receiving public funds for a social welfare program. There are many more instances out there of language and reasoning used by the Supreme Court to rule against aid to K–12 schools that could be used to rule against or restrict the freedom of religious nonprofits operating in other areas.

A second observation deals with statements made by the mother of Dodge, Faye Milton, as quoted in a news story. She said, in objecting to her daughter's dismissal by the Salvation Army: "I had always preached tolerance of the beliefs of others. I told my kids not to judge others on the basis of the color of their skin or their religion." And later she was quoted as saying: "If the Salvation Army is going to be a church, that's fine, but if they are going to engage in secular activities and use public tax dollars, they have to forego religious discrimination."[15] These statements would be of no special significance, except that they reflect an attitude or mindset prevalent in American society. At their root is the sacred-secular distinction. Milton was assuming that counseling and assisting frightened, hurt, confused victims of domestic violence is a purely secular activity. This assumption is false. When churches such as the Salvation Army engage in such activities they are seeking to live out their sense of Christian compassion, and for any sincere Christian believer, healing the hurts suffered by a victim of domestic violence has physical, emotional, and spiritual dimensions. But legally the Salvation Army—and countless other religious nonprofit agencies—can only receive public money on the subterfuge that that money is going to fund secular activities. Implicitly, they are in agreement with Milton. If counseling and helping victims of domestic violence is a purely secular activity, there is no rational reason why preference should be given in hiring counselors to persons in religious agreement with the agency, and the practice of religious preference is pure discrimination in the same league as racial discrimination.

But if counseling and helping victims of domestic violence has emotional and spiritual dimensions, then a particular religious orientation is a reasonable, bona fide job qualification. The awful dilemma into which religious organizations such as the Salvation Army in this case have been forced is that no doubt they sincerely believe as a Christian organization having only Christians counsel their clients is defensible and even essential; yet in receiving government funds they have to pretend the persons they hire are engaging in purely secular tasks, and they thereby give up the rationale for hiring only Christians.

A second example of the difficulties in which a religiously based nonprofit can find itself has been related by Carl Esbeck. It concerns the experiences of a Catholic home for girls that had—in keeping with Catholic moral teaching—refused two teenage girls contraceptives. The District Court ruled that the agency had to provide contraceptives in direct violation of its collective religious conscience. Esbeck has noted that "because the Mission was substantially financed with public funds, the court thereby reasoned that 'the Mission is engaged in state action under the [F]ourteenth [A]mendment and thus controlled by the said [E]stablishment [C]lause.' "[16] If this was really the case, the religious autonomy of this Catholic home for girls would have been destroyed. Esbeck was right when he commented, "If everything the Mission does is state action because of public funding, then the home cannot operate in any way other than to be devoid of religious teaching and practice. Accordingly, under the court's view, the foster home would have to be secular in all its operations or the Establishment Clause is violated."[17]

A third example involves the action of a state agency. The New York constitution prohibits aid to religiously affiliated K–12 schools and colleges and universities. In 1968 the legislature enacted the Bundy program of state grants to independent colleges and universities that are "constitutionally eligible."[18] By not defining the term, "constitutionally eligible," the legislature passed the task of determining what religious colleges and universities were or were not eligible to receive public funds to the state's Education Department. Maureen Manion has reported the New York Education Department has engaged in a series of intrusive inquiries into religious colleges and universities applying for funds to make sure they are not too religious. If they are, they do not get the money; if they are not, they do. The pressures on institutions to reduce or play down their religious practices are all too evident. Wagner College, a Lutheran college, was initially turned down for being too religious, but after making some changes and "after the on-site visit in October, it was concluded that Wagner was 'not engaged in the teaching of denominational doctrines and tenets . . . and was not seeking to promote Lutheranism or uphold that particular heritage through the classroom . . .

academic program, or even in informal programs.' "[19] If this report is accurate, the college essentially gave up its Lutheran character. Manion also reports there are one Catholic university and two conservative Protestant colleges that have not pursued state funds, since they are unwilling to give up the religiously motivated practices they would need to drop to gain such funds.[20] In response to my questionnaire study the president of a conservative Protestant college in New York also indicated his or her institution has not pursued Bundy aid because qualifying for such funds would have required them to change certain of their religiously based hiring practices. That institution and the ones Manion cited had to choose between receiving financial aid all other institutions in the state were receiving or giving up a part of their religious autonomy. By choosing to protect their religious autonomy, they have been put at a state-created financial disadvantage. That is a choice no organization should have to make.

That these are not isolated instances is documented by Stephen Sweeny, who has reported that 21 percent of the Catholic colleges he surveyed had to drop the use of the phrase "Catholic" in legal and published materials before being able to receive direct government grants (some in order to qualify for New York Bundy funds).[21] This was also a requirement one of the colleges responding to my questionnaire indicated it had to fulfill. Many more examples could be added from published reports that demonstrate the problematic situation in which religious nonprofit organizations that receive public money sometimes find themselves.

Another factor that adds to the vulnerability of religious nonprofits receiving public funds concerns civil rights laws and expectations. In the 1984 case of *Grove City College v. Bell,* as described earlier in Chapter 2, the Supreme Court held that even federal funds the college received indirectly via student financial aid were sufficient to trigger the federal civil rights act anti-sex discrimination provisions. Thus nonprofit institutions and agencies can face anti-discrimination provisions of one type or another both as legal entities and as recipients of public money, even when that money reaches them indirectly via grants to students or clients that make use of their services.

Recognizing that religiously based nonprofits may have a legitimate basis to discriminate based on religion, if they are to maintain their religious autonomy and freedom, many civil rights laws allow religious organizations to engage in certain types of discrimination based on religion that other, nonreligious organizations are not allowed to practice. Earlier we saw that federal civil rights law allows for such an exemption. Many states have made similar provisions. Michigan, for example, provides in its basic civil rights law: "The provisions of section 402 related to religion shall not apply to a religious educational institution or an educational institution operated, supervised, or controlled by a religious institution or organization which limits admission or give preference to an applicant of the same religion."[22]

Nevertheless, questions remain. One such question concerns the definition of a "religious corporation, association, educational institution, or society." The more clearly a nonprofit organization can demonstrate its religious nature by its ownership and control and by the number and significance of its religious activities, the better the chance it has of demonstrating its religious nature and thereby obtaining an exemption from civil rights laws that might otherwise interfere with its religious autonomy. But as seen earlier in *Equal Employment Opportunity Commission v. Kamehameha Schools* there is a catch-22 situation here. If a school or other nonprofit is not religious enough (is not "pervasively sectarian") it might not qualify for the religious exemption provided by many civil rights laws—as was the case with the Kamehameha schools in Hawaii. If it is highly religious (is "pervasively sectarian") its chances of attaining exemption from certain civil rights laws is increased, but it runs the risk of losing all public funds since the courts have ruled pervasively sectarian nonprofits may not receive public funds. The president of one conservative Protestant college has expressed the dilemma clearly:

> So evangelical colleges find themselves in a strange position. In order to maintain their students' eligibility for government financial assistance they may be forced to minimize the extent of their Christian activities. Yet in order to maintain the right to exercise religious preference in hiring they need to appear as religious as possible.[23]

And the president of another conservative Protestant college reported in his or her questionnaire that his or her college has purposely engaged in all its religious practices "openly on the assumption that if challenged, we will have a better case for being pervasively religious." This is a good strategy for obtaining exemption from civil rights laws that would interfere with the college's religious autonomy, but it puts the college in danger of being challenged in terms of public funds. Significantly, the same president reports: "We did have a state agency conclude we were ineligible for a low interest loan for construction because we were 'too religious.' " It is already paying a price for its strategy aimed at assuring its exemption from civil rights laws that would interfere with its religious autonomy.

In a circuit court case, it was decided Mississippi College, a Southern Baptist institution, could discriminate in employment on the basis of religion since it was "readily apparent that the character and purposes of the College are pervasively sectarian."[24] Its religious autonomy—its ability to define itself religiously—was thereby protected, but if some litigant were to challenge its receipt of public funds (assuming it or its students receive such funds), it would take some fast footwork to justify its receipt of such funds under current Supreme Court doctrine.

At the end of a long consideration of the vulnerability of nonprofits that receive public funds it is clear that religious nonprofits that receive public dollars have few constitutional protections for their religious autonomy and the religious freedoms they possess under such autonomy. Their protections are political; not legal. The free exercise clause has not been used by the Court to protect the autonomy of religious nonprofits receiving public funds. As a result their religious autonomy has been placed in a legally precarious position.

Subtle Pressures to Compromise Religious Practices

The legally uncertain position in which the Supreme Court's legal principles have placed religious nonprofits receiving public money gives rise to another potential force that could compromise their religious autonomy. It is a more subtle, indirect force than the overt, direct pressures considered in the previous section, but its very nature may make it an even greater danger at the present time to nonprofits' religious autonomy than the more concrete, legal vulnerability just discussed. This danger consists of societal attitudes and expectations that both exert pressures on religious nonprofits and mold the minds of those in positions of leadership in them.

These subtle pressures—to the extent they exist—would presumably be made more powerful by the legal uncertainties and vulnerabilities already discussed. For example, the director of a child service agency, facing some indirect, subtle pressures or expectations from United Way officials and his professional colleagues in other, less overtly religious agencies, would be in a stronger position—not only legally, but also psychologically—if he was convinced the law and courts were clearly in support of his agency's right to engage in certain distinctive religious practices. But as a result of feeling vulnerable in a legal sense and needing to defend his agency and its budget by maintaining good relations with influential persons in the community, with his professional colleagues, and with government agency officials, the pressures not to look too different—to conform to professional and community expectations—will be real. If, on the other hand, he felt the law was clearly supportive of his agency's right to live out the beliefs of its religious tradition in distinctive religious practices, he would be strengthened in his resolve to do so.

Several scholars have taken note of societal, cultural forces as having a major impact on religiously based organizations. Michael McConnell has written about the secularized nature of American culture: "America's secularized Protestant culture presses about us from all sides with subtle nudges to conform. It invites us, it tempts us, to become full insiders even when we are not."[25] In reference to the mainline Protestant colleges and universities that in the first half of the twentieth century almost uniformly abandoned any distinctive Christian features, historian George Marsden has written:

> Why is it that Protestants have voluntarily abandoned their vast educational enterprise and are even embarrassed to acknowledge that they ever ran such a thing? The answer is that, on the one hand, they were confronted with vast cultural trends, such as technological advance, professionalization, and secularism, which they could not control; but, on the other hand, the combination of the pressures of cultural pluralism and Christian ethical principles made it awkward if not impossible to take any decisive stand against the secularizing trends.[26]

In a study of the impact of public funds on the religious missions of 104 Catholic colleges, Sweeny concluded that "there is no compelling evidence linking reception of state aid with changes in elements determining religious character."[27] He did, however, note the colleges were changing in ways that moved them away from a distinctively Catholic nature. He reported that the presidents of the colleges cited

> a number of issues to explain the changes: growing emphasis on freedom including religious freedom; basic changes in the understanding of what religiously oriented institutions should be; changing clientele expectations; the ecumenical movement; general permissiveness in society and declining resources of the sponsoring religious body, to name but a few.[28]

Sociologists Paul DiMaggio and Walter Powell, in an essay that has received wide recognition and acceptance, suggest there are three factors that promote homogenization among organizations that start out being quite different from each other.[29] One factor is coercive in nature, resulting "from both formal and informal pressures exerted on organizations by other organizations upon which they are dependent and by cultural expectations in the society within which organizations function."[30] A second factor they present that leads organizations to become more like each other is a mimetic, or imitative, process that is especially strong in the face of uncertainty. When faced with an uncertain environment the natural tendency of an organization is to model itself after already existing organizations that are perceived "to be more legitimate or successful."[31] The third factor leading organizations to become more homogenous is what DiMaggio and Powell term normative processes, which are processes stemming primarily from the professionalization of an organization. As an organization professionalizes, common expectations are placed on it and its employees tend to come from similar educational and experiential backgrounds.

Much of what DiMaggio and Powell have written is highly relevant to a consideration of subtle, indirect pressures on the religious autonomy of nonprofits. Cultural expectations may have a coercive effect, raising standards of professionalization may lead to subtle pressures, and—most important— the uncertain environment created by uncertain legal standards may lead religiously based nonprofits to model themselves after already existing organizations that are less religious and whose receipt of public funds is more clearly legitimate. The tendency may be for religiously based nonprofits receiving public money to drop or tone down their distinctive religious characteristics, thereby making themselves more like their secular or nominally religious counterparts who are successfully receiving public funds.

The issue here is whether or not the receipt of public money works to heighten the power of these societal, cultural factors. Does public money have the effect of strengthening the ability of these factors to squeeze religiously based nonprofits into their mold? To answer this question I first examine these cultural forces more closely and then attempt a tentative answer.

There are three characteristics of American culture that could make it act as a seductive force, undermining the distinctive religious character of religious nonprofits: a spirit of relativism, a strong sense of individuality and the importance of individual choice, and a view of religion in its public manifestations as a generalized moral force. Allan Bloom began his best-selling 1987 book, *The Closing of the American Mind*, by noting the relativism with which almost all his students approach moral issues.[32] "I believe such-and-such is wrong, but, of course, I would not want to impose my beliefs onto you," is the prevailing spirit. Closely allied to this sense of moral relativism is Americans' fierce sense of individualism: the right of each individual to choose for one's self what she or he is to believe, do, or think. Combining these two characteristics, religious truth is typically seen as being relative to the individual and a matter of individual choice or preference, not a commitment rooted in communities of faith. As stressed in Chapter 1, religion is often seen as being a private, personal affair.

This leads to the third aspect of American culture that is relevant to the subtle pressures on religious nonprofits. This aspect sees religion in the public sphere as properly limited to broad, consensual themes of good citizenship, respect for others, and acts of charity. Thus the head of a religiously based social welfare agency is welcomed into community groups and is respected by the local new media as long as she does not critique the moral-religious views of others or appeal to church authority or biblical standards to support a controversial position, but if in a public forum she, for example, speaks out against abortion or questions certain widely accepted beliefs or practices, there is an embarrassed silence and countless clues will inform her she has transgressed certain unwritten rules of the game. Similarly, her agency will be recognized and honored in the community as long as its distinctive religious goals or activities are played down, and its commitment to a "nonjudgmental," generic moral ethos cut loose from its particularistic religious tradition is played up. The subtle pressures are there. One soon learns what will lead to being accepted by one's peers and to being respected in the public square of one's community.

Subtle pressures and signals of this nature can come from many sources. One consists of accrediting and licensing agencies. If one wishes easy accreditation visits or quick renewals of state licenses it may be best to play down particularistic religious beliefs and practices. Similarly, agencies that receive United Way money undergo periodic reviews of their practices. Ellen Netting relates various pressures United Way requirements have put on religious social welfare agencies with a secularizing impact.[33] Foundations and large individual donors may be more likely to give to what they perceive as "mainstream" organizations in distinction from what they would see as "narrowly sectarian" organizations, with what is mainstream and what is narrowly sectarian gauged by societal values and expectations such as those outlined above. Professional associations and the news media can play a similar role. Marsden reports: "Phi Beta Kappa, the nation's premier honor society, openly discriminates against institutions that have religious tests for faculty members."[34] With regard to the news media, *Money* magazine refuses to list in its annual *Money Guide: Best College Buys* colleges "that require an affirmation of faith from students, colleges that aspire to graduate students with a particular world theological view, . . . and colleges where religious study of any nature, even though it may not be restricted to one faith, is a significant academic requirement."[35]

None of these, of course, has anything to do directly with the receipt of public funds. Even organizations receiving no public funds at all are still subject to these societal, cultural forces; and organizations receiving public funds are free to resist them. As DiMaggio and Powell have theorized, however, the temptation for organizations to model themselves after ones clearly respected by society as legitimate and successful would tend to be strengthened by the situation of legal uncertainty and vulnerability current in which Supreme Court jurisprudence has placed religious nonprofits receiving public funds.

A factor adding to these tendencies is the very natural human desire to avoid controversy. Controversies take time and energy away from other activities, create dissonance—feelings of unease and uncertainty—and can threaten sources of support. Thus if controversy can be avoided and uncertainties reduced by making one's institution or agency more like respected, successful ones of the same types—thereby living up to the expectations of respected professionals in one's field, community and media leaders, and others of significance to one's organization—the pressures to do so, while subtle, will be real. Clearly articulated and widely understood legal standards defending the religious autonomy of religiously based organizations could very well work to strengthen their managers' resolve to maintain their religious distinctiveness.

The questionnaire results reported in Chapter 3 offer some insight into the existence of subtle pressures. The heads of all three types of nonprofit organizations studied reported some pressures and criticisms arising from groups and persons outside of government itself. Sixteen percent of the religiously based child service agencies receiving public dollars did so, as did 4 percent of the religious international aid agencies and 14 percent of the colleges and universities. Also, some religious nonprofits reported doing certain religious practices subtly and indirectly rather than openly and directly, and some indicated there were religious practices they did not engage in, not because they had no desire to do them, but because they either felt they ought not to do them or legally could not do them. This was the case with upwards of one-fourth of the child service agencies. Such findings suggest that there is a basis to believe that a minority of religious organizations receiving public funds may indeed be subject to the sort of subtle pressures under consideration here.

Findings such as these, however, really do not tap the probably more powerful but more subtle role played by a network of expectations. For example, the extent to which organizations unconsciously position themselves to receive public funds by slowly toning down or giving up some of their distinctive religious practices is unknown. They may even rationalize their doing so under the cause of raising their professional or academic standards, embracing greater diversity, or better serving a diverse constituency. In interviews with leaders in religiously based nonprofits, I probed for the existence of such tendencies. Two conclusions stand out. One is that leaders of clearly and distinctively religious organizations usually reported having felt such pressures. Second, they differed on whether or not the receipt of public funds exacerbated these pressures, but generally they indicated most religious organizations are able to resist them, *if* they have a clear vision of their religious nature and goals. It appears most likely that subtle societal or cultural pressures largely affect those organizations that do not have a clearly articulated and self-consciously held religious mission. In such cases especially, the existence of public funds can work to increase these pressures.

K–12 Schools are Left Out of the Public-Nonprofit Partnership

The current legal doctrines put forward by the Supreme Court—as well as the attitudes of the public and societal elites—leave religiously based elementary and secondary schools out of the public-nonprofit partnership. Excluding a large segment of the nonprofit sector that is effectively working in an area of increasing, nationwide concern from the public-nonprofit partnership unnecessarily narrows the options available to public policy makers. This is a topic on which others have written at length and thus I will deal with it only briefly by way of three observations. One is that many of the religiously based K–12 schools are doing a superb job of educating children, including children that often are considered hard to educate. Both journalistic observations and more rigorous studies support this conclusion. Among the latter, best known are several studies James Coleman of Harvard University and his associates have conducted comparing educational achievements of children in public schools with those in nonprofit, largely Catholic schools. They have concluded that Catholic schools are more effective in reducing the gap in the educational achievements of children coming from dissimilar backgrounds than are the public schools.

> [T]he performance of children from parents with differing educational levels is more similar in Catholic schools than in public schools (as well as being, in general, higher). . . . Thus we have the paradoxical result that the Catholic schools come closer to the American ideal of the "common school," educating all alike than do the public schools. Furthermore, . . . a similar result holds for race and ethnicity. The achievements of blacks is closer to that of whites, and the achievement of Hispanics is closer to that of non-Hispanics in Catholic schools than in public schools.[36]

Another study by Coleman and Thomas Hoffer led them to conclude: "The achievement growth benefits of Catholic school attendance are especially strong for students who are in one way or another disadvantaged: lower socioeconomic status, black or Hispanic."[37] Similarly, political scientists John Chubb and Terry Moe, based on a study of 25,000 students in 1,000 schools that followed them from grades eight to ten, concluded, "The upshot of all of this, we think, is that private schools do a better job than public schools of providing equal educational outcomes. . . . [P]rivate schools accomplish this by helping students at the bottom of the achievement distribution without hurting students at the top of the distribution."[38]

In addition, journalistic reports frequently take note of the effective work that Catholic schools in particular are doing in educating children from high-poverty areas. The differences are often not minor or marginal, but substantial. The mayor of Jersey City, New Jersey, has testified:

> At one high school [in Jersey City] only 28 percent of the students passed this year's basic skills tests. Despite the school's evident failings, poor students who live near it must attend it—even though there are readily available nonpublic schools that graduate more than 90 percent of their students while spending far less.[39]

A *Newsday* reporter has written of a Catholic school located in the Bronx, "in one of the nation's poorest urban communities":

> Despite the surrounding threats of violence and their own humble beginnings, students at St. Angela's—like many of the archdiocese's inner-city schools—do remarkably well. Test scores for St. Angela's 489 students show a pattern of exceeding state standards for reading, writing and especially math.[40]

It is in this area of K–12 education that the evidence documenting the excellent job being done by religious nonprofits is most complete, and, ironically, it is in this very area the Supreme Court has largely foreclosed the normal public-nonprofit partnership as a public policy option.

A second observation concerns the position, adopted by many, that a key way to improve the public schools is by creating greater competition in the school system, with one means of achieving this being public-nonprofit school competition. This has been one of the key cases being made by the choice-in-education movement. Chubb and Moe have made this point in an especially thorough and compelling fashion. They have argued, "Choice is a self-contained reform with its own rationale and justification. It has the capacity *all by itself* to bring about the kind of transformation that, for years, reformers have been seeking to engineer in myriad other ways."[41] But when it comes to the issue of religiously based K–12 schools and whether or not they should be included among the schools parents could choose, Chubb and Moe waver. They indicate they would prefer them to be included, but imply it would not be necessary.[42] Yet the stubborn fact is that "well over 80 percent of the students in private elementary and secondary schools are . . .

enrolled in schools with an explicit religious affiliation."[43] If religiously based K–12 schools would be left out of a choice-in-education policy, that policy would be severely handicapped from the outset in its primary public policy objective of improving all of education—public and private—by introducing market forces into elementary and secondary education.

A third observation rests on the point I developed earlier in Chapter 4, namely, that there are no significant differences in the religiously motivated practices of approximately one-third of the nonprofit organizations included in my study and the practices found in most religiously based K–12 schools. The legal principles developed by the Supreme Court to distinguish K–12 religious schools from religious colleges and universities and other religiously based nonprofits are simply not rooted in actual practice. It is hard to find a justification to select out one type of nonprofit and exclude it while all the others are included. As I argued earlier, doing so presumably has more to do with nineteenth-century common school ideals and anti-Catholic prejudices of thirty years ago than present-day realities.

Conclusions

The terms under which religious nonprofits are included in the public-nonprofit partnership are deeply troubling. The general public, the policy elites, and the nonprofits all desire a certain outcome, so things are arranged to achieve it; but the legal foundation for doing so is shot full of contradictions, subterfuges, evasions, and confusions. J. Bruce Nichols has written in reference to international aid and relief agencies, but his comments are equally applicable to other types of religiously based nonprofit agencies and institutions: "Undergirding the government's cooperative attitude toward religious welfare institutions is the public perception that the institutions are not primarily religious and that they serve broad secular purposes. This political fact . . . has in a sense bought time for the existing arrangements."[44] But time may be running out. The vulnerability of religious nonprofits is great and the societal pressures real. In addition, religious K–12 schools—one of the most vital type of nonprofit in the religious nonprofit sector—are almost totally left out of the public-nonprofit partnership.

This situation poses problems for religious nonprofit organizations, but it may pose even greater problems for the broader society and for public policy attempts to meet societal needs. Religious nonprofits today need the public funds they receive, but society may need the educational and social services religious nonprofits are providing even more. And in the area of K–12 education, one can easily envision the fresh energy and new ideas religiously based K–12 schools could bring to this area that is marked by great needs and many failed reforms.

If religious nonprofits should face increasing, more insistent pressures on their religious missions, they can react in two ways. Both have equally negative public policy consequences for the United States. They could drop out of the public funding schemes and struggle on as best they can at a reduced level of activity. The director of a child service agency told me that his agency had received some pressure from state officials due to their requirement that youth in their residential facility attend Sunday morning worship services. He went on to state that thus far they have been permitted to maintain that requirement, but that his board has already decided if the state should ever forbid this requirement, they would drop out of the state funding scheme. If large numbers of religiously based nonprofit organizations would follow this pattern, society would suffer as it would be deprived of many of the services now provided by religious nonprofits, and religious nonprofits would be put at a government-created disadvantage as long as government would continue to fund similar programs of its own and of secular nonprofits. A second option would be for religious nonprofits gradu- ally to secularize, giving up the distinctive practices that would be causing them problems in achieving public funds. This would mean religious nonprofits' religious autonomy would be violated as they are forced to give up their religious practices and the beliefs in which they are rooted. But society itself would also be hurt. Much of what religious nonprofits have to offer society they can only offer because of their religious nature. Their religious nature and the religious communities in which they are rooted are their strength. The compassion, caring, and dedication that are vital to their successful meeting of societal needs and the financial and volunteer resources they can elicit are rooted in their religious nature. Sociologist Peter Berger once put his finger on a basic paradox—the truth of which American society needs to face—when he took note of the temporal, this-world services rendered by religious organizations and then observed that the "worldly contribution of religion is possible only if religion itself remains other- worldly."[45] To offer effective secular benefits to society, religious nonprofits themselves must avoid becoming secular.

A stronger, more defensible legal theory justifying and setting the condi- tions and limitations of public funding for religiously based nonprofit organi- zations is clearly needed. It is needed in order to help protect the religious autonomy of religiously based nonprofits. But it is also needed in order to maintain and strengthen the contributions nonprofits can make in responding to the mounting educational and social needs the United States polity is seeking to meet at home and abroad. The next chapter seeks to develop one possible approach.

Notes

1. Letter from Amy L. Sherman to the Center for Public Justice (May 24, 1995).
2. *Corporation of Presiding Bishop v. Amos*, 483 U.S. at 339 (1987).
3. *Corporation of Presiding Bishop v. Amos*, at 343.
4. *Lemon v. Kurtzman*, 403 U.S. at 652 (1971).
5. *Bowen v. Kendrick*, 487 U.S. at 612 (1988). Italics added.
6. *Bowen v. Kendrick,*, at 613.
7. *Bowen v. Kendrick*, at 640. The quotation from Simmons is from the plaintiffs' brief in this case.
8. *Bowen v. Kendrick*, at 639–40.
9. The quotations are from *Roemer v. Maryland Public Works Board*, at 764.
10. The following information on this case is from *Dodge v. Salvation Army*, 1989 WL 53857 (S. D. Miss.), and Joseph L. Conn, "Bewitched," *Church and State*, 42 (June, 1989): 124–26.
11. In an earlier case the courts had ruled that legally the Salvation Army is a church. See *McClure v. Salvation Army*, 353 F. Supp. 1100 (N.D. Ga. 1971). Affirmed 460 F.2d 553 (5th Cir. 1972).
12. *Dodge v. Salvation Army*, at 6.
13. *Dodge v. Salvation Army*, at 3.
14. *Dodge v. Salvation Army*, at 4.
15. Quoted by Conn, "Bewitched," 125.
16. Carl H. Esbeck, "Government Regulation of Religiously Based Social Services: The First Amendment Considerations," *Hastings Constitutional Law Quarterly*, 19 (1992): 405.
17. Esbeck, "Government Regulation."
18. See Maureen Manion, "The Impact of State Aid on Sectarian Higher Education: The Case of New York State," *Review of Politics*, 48 (1986): 264–88.
19. Manion, "The Impact of State Aid," 278. The quotation is from the report of a team of outside experts that made an on-site visit to determine whether or not the religious nature of the college excluded it from eligibility to receive state funds.
20. Manion, "The Impact of State Aid," 277–78.
21. See Stephen J. Sweeny, *State Financial Assistance and Selected Elements Influencing Religious Character in Catholic Colleges Sponsored by Women Religious* (Ph.D. dissertation, School of Education, Health, Nursing, and Arts Professions, New York University, 1991), 140.
22. *Michigan Compiled Laws*, 1979, 37.2403.
23. David K. Winter, "Rendering unto Caesar: The Dilemma of College-Government Relations," in Joel A. Carpenter and Kenneth W. Shipps, eds., *Making Higher*

Education Christian: The History and Mission of Evangelical Colleges in America (St. Paul, MN: Christian University Press, 1987), 250.

24. *EEOC v. Mississippi College*, 626 F.2d at 487 (1980).

25. Michael W. McConnell, "Taking Religious Freedom Seriously," in *Religious Liberty in the Supreme Court*, Terry Eastland, ed. (Washington, DC: Ethics and Public Policy Center, 1993), 503.

26. George M. Marsden, "The Soul of the American University: A Historical Overview," in *The Secularization of the Academy*, George M. Marsden and Bradley J. Longfield, eds., (New York: Oxford University Press, 1992), 28.

27. Sweeny, *State Financial Assistance*, 157.

28. Sweeny, *State Financial Assistance*, 157.

29. Paul J. DiMaggio and Walter W. Powell, "The Iron Cage Revisited: Institutional Isomorphism and Collective Rationality in Organizational Fields," *American Sociological Review*, 48 (1983): 147–60.

30. DiMaggio and Powell, "The Iron Cage Revisited," 150.

31. DiMaggio and Powell, "The Iron Cage Revisited," 152.

32. Allan Bloom, *The Closing of the American Mind* (New York: Simon and Schuster, 1987), 25–43.

33. See F. Ellen Netting, "Secular and Religious Funding of Church-Related Agencies," *Social Service Review*, 56 (1982): 593–94.

34. George M. Marsden, "Church, State and Campus," *New York Times*, 26 April 1994, A21.

35. *Money Guide: Best College Buys*, 1996 edition (New York: Time, 1995), 23.

36. James S. Coleman, Thomas Hoffer, and Sally Kilgore, *High School Achievement: Public, Catholic, and Private Schools Compared* (New York: Basic Books, 1982), 144.

37. James S. Coleman and Thomas Hoffer, *Public and Private High Schools* (New York: Basic Books, 1987), 213.

38. John E. Chubb and Terry M. Moe, "Politics, Markets, and Equality in Schools," (paper delivered at the annual meeting of the American Political Science Association, September 3–6, 1992), 19. Also see Thomas Vitullo-Martin, *Catholic Inner-City Schools: The Future* (Washington, DC: United States Catholic Conference, 1979).

39. Bret Schundler, "The Simple Logic of School Choice," *New York Times*, 28 October 1993, A15.

40. Thomas Maier, "Learning in Fortress Bronx," *Newsday*, 17 May 1993, 17. Also see Jean Merl, "Inner-City Students Find Success at Catholic Schools," *Los Angeles Times*, 31 March 1992, A12, A18-A19.

41. John E. Chubb and Terry M. Moe, *Politics, Markets, and America's Schools* (Washington, DC: Brookings Institution, 1990), 217. Emphasis present in original.

42. See Chubb and Moe, *Politics, Markets and America's Schools*, 219.

43. Lester M. Salamon, *America's Nonprofit Sector* (Baltimore, MD: The Foundation Center, 1992), 76.

44. J. Bruce Nichols, *The Uneasy Alliance*, (New York: Oxford University Press, 1988), 232–33.

45. Peter L. Berger, "The Serendipity of Liberties," in Richard John Neuhaus, ed., *The Structure of Freedom: Correlations, Causes and Cautions* (Grand Rapids, MI: Eerdmans, 1991), 16. Emphasis removed.

Chapter Six

Positive Neutrality

A new standard that both supports and circumscribes the use of public money by religiously based nonprofit organizations is needed. If the government-nonprofit partnership is to flourish and to fulfill its potential in the public policy realm, and if it is to include religiously based nonprofits as full members without putting their religious autonomy at risk, a more realistic, more defensible basis for that partnership is needed. Such a standard needs to be rooted in an accurate understanding of the nature of religion and an openness to religiously based nonprofit organizations playing a fulsome, active role in the public realm, *as religious organizations*. But that standard must not compromise the ideal of governmental neutrality towards all religions and between those with a deep religious faith and those with none. No organization should be either advantaged or disadvantaged because of its religious orientation—or lack of religious orientation.

Law professor Frederick Gedicks expressed the desired ideal in these words: "The critical issue will always be how to protect important governmental interests and individual rights while still permitting a meaningful plurality of groups."[1] An approach is needed that will deal with both the religiously based and the secularly based nonprofits in an evenhanded manner, and at the same time enable the government to live up to its responsibility to protect the rights of persons of all faiths and of none. Such an approach would strike a balance among the appropriate interests of the government, individual citizens, and society's many associations and communities—religious and nonreligious alike.

This chapter suggests a basic standard I am convinced would bring greater direction and clarity to this area of policy formation and church-state jurisprudence, while assuring both deeply religious and secular nonprofits a new measure of freedom. The chapter's first section suggests five basic ideals or principles any new standard for public money flowing to nonprofits should

173

seek to meet. The next section introduces the standard I advocate—what I have termed positive neutrality—and then I apply that standard to a number of the tensions and problems documented earlier in this study. The last section of the chapter seeks to spell out several key public policy advantages that basing government-nonprofit cooperation in positive neutrality would have for the American polity.

Principles to Be Attained

In thinking through the basics of an appropriate approach or standard for guiding the American polity as it struggles with issues raised by the shifting religious and public policy landscapes, I would suggest five principles or ideals that should be kept in mind. All five grow out of the conceptual framework based on structural pluralism, as presented in Chapter 1.

The first principle is that the religious autonomy of religiously based nonprofit organizations must be protected. The religious autonomy of nonprofits, as seen at many points in this study, is sometimes being violated or undermined and—more frequently—is being left in a legally vulnerable, precarious position. Yet, as Chapter 1's conceptual framework made clear, if the American polity is to be marked by full freedom of religion, it is crucial that the religious autonomy of the many religious communities and associations be recognized and respected. Associations and communities—including religiously based ones—are vital, indispensable features of society. It is through them that persons meet many of their physical and emotional needs, receive a sense of purpose and meaning, and learn a basic sense of morality. Individual religious conscience makes little sense outside the context of the religious group. It is within that context that individuals' religious consciences are shaped, affirmed, and expressed. To seek to protect freedom of religion for the individual without protecting the freedom or the autonomy of the religious group makes no sense. As Gedicks has written: "Just as autonomy and society in general are inconceivable in the United States without familial autonomy, procreational choice, and (hetero)sexual privacy, so also one cannot conceive of meaningful individual religious freedom unless religious *institutions* are protected from government encroachments."[2] Thus the new approach or standard that is needed must somehow do a better job than current approaches of protecting the autonomy of religious groups.

Underlying or empowering this first principle of protecting the religious autonomy of religious groups is a mindset or orientation. Without a change in American society at this level, it is unlikely the judicial and policy elites will fully understand the nature of religious autonomy. This new mindset is one that sees religion as a vital, contributing force in society, not as a marginal force extraneous to the mainstream cultural world of the arts, business, technology, science, and politics. The concept deeply rooted among American public policy and societal elites is the view of what Stephen Carter has called "religion as a hobby."[3] If the concept of religious group autonomy is to be fully understood and acted upon, American society needs to gain a new respect for religion as a major cultural force that has significance and relevance for society and the issues and problems with which it is struggling. It needs to understand and appreciate—even without necessarily agreeing with—the perspective expressed by the president of one of the leading conservative Protestant seminaries in the United States when he wrote: "Since religion has to do with our relationship to the ultimate meaning and value found in every aspect of human existence, and since public life is ineluctably drawn to matters of ultimate concern, religion is bound to reassert itself in the public sphere."[4]

A second fundamental principle grows out of the first: any new approach needs to be rooted in both the free exercise and establishment clauses taken together, as a unity. The Supreme Court has often interpreted the First Amendment to consist of two separate, distinct clauses, doing two separate, distinct things, and then taken a limited view of the protections offered by the free exercise clause and an expansive view of the no-establishment burdens of the establishment clause. But both clauses need to be read together as having as a single end: the protection of full and complete religious freedom. On a visceral level Justice Potter Stewart strikes a positive chord in almost all Americans with his eloquent words, from which I quoted earlier:

> What our Constitution indispensably protects is the freedom of each of us, be he Jew or Agnostic, Christian or Atheist, Buddhist or Freethinker, to believe or disbelieve, to worship or not worship, to pray or keep silent, according to his own conscience, uncoerced and unrestrained by government.[5]

What needs to be more fully recognized and appreciated is that both free exercise and no-establishment provisions contribute to this ideal of religious freedom set forth by Stewart. If, in violation of free exercise protections, certain religious beliefs or practices would be directly proscribed by government, religious liberty would clearly be violated. Similarly, if in violation of no-establishment provisions, government should officially endorse or use tax dollars to support any one religion to the exclusion of all others or to support either religion or nonbelief in general to the exclusion of the opposite, religious liberty would also be violated. Government would—through its endorsement and support—be advantaging one particular religion or either religion generally or secularism generally to the disadvantage of the alternatives. But in both cases it is full and complete religious freedom that is the end. Whether or not it is being compromised is what should be controlling. This a point Justice Arthur Goldberg once made clearly:

> The First Amendment's guarantees . . . foreclose not only laws "respecting an establishment of religion" but also those "prohibiting the free exercise thereof." These two proscriptions are to be read together, and in light of the single end which they are designed to serve. The basic purpose of the religion clause of the First Amendment is to promote and assure the fullest possible scope of religious liberty and tolerance for all and to nurture the conditions which secure the best hope of attainment of that end.[6]

This conclusion may appear unremarkable, but in fact it has often been ignored by the Supreme Court and policy elites as they have put forward Jefferson's "wall of separation" metaphor or no-aid-to-religion as ends in themselves, even when doing so has compromised full religious freedom by putting religious organizations or practices at a comparative disadvantage.

A third principle that any standard of interpretation should seek to uphold is that of government neutrality in regard to all religious beliefs—and between belief and nonbelief. This is what religious liberty demands. If persons and groups are to be free—are to possess religious autonomy—then government must adopt a position of neutrality in relationship to them, neither endorsing nor disparaging, advantaging nor disadvantaging them because of who they are, the beliefs they profess, or the practices they follow. Neutrality means to safeguard an appropriate autonomy for all of society's communities and associations, religious and nonreligious alike.

The fourth principle is that any standard of interpretation should be framed in such a way that, while conforming to the first three principles, it also allows as much as possible for and encourages public policies that are practical, efficient, and in keeping with American history and existing practices. The long American tradition of achieving public policy goals via a cooperative relationship between government and nonprofits should be allowed and even further protected and enhanced, if it can be done without violating either the religious autonomy of the religious nonprofits or the free exercise protections of the First Amendment.

A final, fifth principle may sometimes be in tension with some of the foregoing principles. It is that government must be free to protect the public interest of, or promote a just order in, society as a whole. Pluralism by its very nature emphasizes the plurality of communities and associations in a polity and seeks to affirm and enhance the roles they play. As such it has a certain centrifugal aspect to it. This must be balanced in a successful society by unifying, centripetal forces, and therefore must be balanced in public polices by a concern with the unity of society. The plurality of communities and associations must be affirmed and enhanced; the forces that unite and create common ground must also be affirmed and enhanced. This is a large part of the "governmental interests" Gedicks mentions in the sentence quoted earlier. Government has an obligation to protect the interests of society at large—the public interest, the common good, a just order—while also protecting the autonomy of the plurality of communities and associations found within the national society. The warring ethnic-religious groups of the former Yugoslavia stand as end-of-the-twentieth-century testimonies to the awesome, tragic consequences that can flow from a breakdown of the ties of history, respect, civility, justice, and beliefs that bind a society together.

Positive Neutrality

The equal-treatment strain present in current Supreme Court reasoning, as described earlier in Chapter 2, offers the kernel of a hopeful, new approach to church-state issues in general and to public funding for religious nonprofit organizations in particular. This line of reasoning resolves the clash between granting some benefits to religious groups that all other secular groups are receiving and the strict no-aid-to-religion principle in favor of the former. Equal treatment says religious groups should have public benefits available to them on the same terms as all other groups. Being a religious group ought not to put it at a disadvantage, so that it cannot use school facilities to which all other groups have access, cannot rent a hall other groups are allowed to rent, cannot put up a display on public property where other groups are allowed to put up displays, or cannot receive subsidies that all other groups are receiving.[7] Neutrality or evenhandedness of government policy is at the heart of the equal-treatment concept. In a passage quoted earlier, Justice Kennedy makes this clear:

> A central lesson of our decisions is that a significant factor in upholding governmental programs in the face of Establishment Clause attack is their *neutrality* towards religion. . . . We have held that the guarantee of neutrality is respected, not offended, when the government, *following neutral criteria and evenhanded policies*, extends benefits to recipients whose ideologies and viewpoints, including religious ones, are broad and diverse.[8]

Governmental benefits, in other words, may go to religious groups as long as they are doing so in a neutral, evenhanded manner. When that occurs, religion is not being singled out for favored treatment, nor would there be a "realistic danger that the community would think that the . . . [government] was endorsing religion."[9]

This equal-treatment line of reasoning—as promising as what it is—is not yet fully developed, is being contested by the older, no-aid-to-religion line of reasoning, and has been applied primarily in settings involving the private free expression of religion. In this section, therefore, I present a standard that is rooted in the equal treatment strain, but seeks to develop it more fully and broaden its application. This standard is based in a pluralist view of society, government, and religious freedom and is in keeping with the five principles articulated in the prior section. I have termed it positive neutrality.

Positive neutrality holds that the First Amendment religious freedom language should be interpreted so as to assure the neutrality of government towards persons and groups of all faiths and those of none.[10] This means government should neither advantage nor disadvantage any particular religion, nor should its actions either advantage or disadvantage religion in general or secularism in general. I refer to this standard as *positive* neutrality because it recognizes that if a true neutrality is to be achieved government will sometimes have to take certain positive steps that recognize, accommodate, or support religion. It also has a positive aspect in that it represents the positive effort of government to fulfill the norm of public justice. By adopting a position of neutrality towards persons and groups of all religious faiths and of none, government is promoting a just order in society. It is protecting the freedom and autonomy of all persons and groups, religious and secular alike. The key to governmental neutrality is that government does not recognize, accommodate, or support any one particular religion over any other nor either religious or secular worldviews and groups over one another.

Under positive neutrality the no-aid-to-religion doctrine would be replaced with the principle that public money could go to fund the programs and activities of religiously based nonprofits that are of a temporal, this-world benefit to society, as long as public funds are supporting similar or parallel programs of all religious traditions without favoritism and of similar or parallel programs of a secular nature, whether sponsored by secularly based nonprofits or by government itself. In this manner governmental neutrality would be upheld within the framework of certain positive steps. Programs of certain religious traditions would not be favored over any others, nor would either secularly based or religiously based programs be favored.

For example, if parents have three children and twelve pieces of candy and wish not to favor one child over the others, they could give none of their

children candy or they could give each child four pieces of candy. What they could not do is to give candy to one of their children and none to the others. If one thinks of child A as religion A, child B as religion B, and child C as secular belief system C, what are usually called strict separationists would give candy to C, but not A and B, and what are usually called accommodationists or nonpreferentialists would give candy to A and B, but not C.[11] In either case neutrality is being violated. Things will become more complex shortly, but this concept of neutrality is the starting point.

Two of the developments discussed in Chapter 2 that deeply affect the realities of the church-state situation found in the United States today are, first, the rise of the comprehensive administrative state and, second, the chief religious division in American society being the one that divides religiously rooted belief systems of various types and traditions from secularly rooted belief systems. Because of these two developments, the concept of positive neutrality has become crucial if First Amendment interpretations are to be truly protective of religious freedom. If it were not for the comprehensive administrative state, with its corresponding high rates of taxation, the government could simply not be involved in health care, education, and other social service programs. It would be like the parents in the example maintaining neutrality by not giving candy to any of their children. Religiously based groups and secularly based groups would alike be free to engage in deeds of caring, helping, and education, using their own resources and guided by their own visions. But that day was abandoned long ago—if it ever really marked American society—and we are not going back to it. The government is deeply involved—directly and indirectly—in a host of social service programs in which a host of religious and secular nonprofits are also involved. The candy—so to speak—is being passed out; the only question left is how to pass it out in an evenhanded manner. Justice Anthony Kennedy recognized the significance of this situation in a 1989 concurring opinion:

> In this century, as the modern administrative state expands to touch the lives of its citizens in such diverse ways and redirects their financial choices through programs of its own, it is difficult to maintain the fiction that requiring government to avoid all assistance to religion can in fairness be viewed as serving the goal of neutrality.[12]

In judging neutrality or evenhandedness, one must also take into account a second societal development discussed in Chapter 2, namely, the "culture war" between the orthodox and the progressives, religion and secularism. It is because of it that both the strict separationist approach of giving candy only to the "secular child" and the nonpreferentialist approach of giving candy only to the two "religious children" will not do. At an earlier time most public agencies and institutions and most private, "nonsectarian" ones were marked by a generalized, consensual religion. Under those circumstances the nonpreferentialist approach of giving candy to all "religious children" might be justified on the basis that in practice doing so included all the children. But powerful secularizing currents in society and strict separationist victories in the courts have removed even consensual religious exercises and accommodations from most public agencies. Thus many of society's agencies and institutions are thoroughly secular. Either aiding only them or aiding all but them would violate neutrality.

Some details need to be added to what thus far is a rather general concept. In the process it will be changed from a general concept into a standard capable of guiding public policy in the area of public money and religious nonprofits. Positive neutrality would allow public money to flow to programs whether or not they have religious aspects woven into them. There are only three basic conditions the programs and activities of religious nonprofits would have to meet in order to be eligible for public funds: they would have to be of temporal, this-world benefit to society for which there are similar or parallel programs that are secularly based, they could not be teaching hatred or intolerance or in other ways attack the fabric of society, and they would have to submit to minimal, non-intrusive accountability standards.

Under the first of these three conditions, public money could not go to activities and programs that are primarily other-worldly in nature, that is, those that are oriented towards religious worship or teaching, affirming, and celebrating core religious beliefs. The benefits of such programs and activities are primarily other-worldly, in the sense of relating either to life after death or the inner religious self. They would, of course, also have no similar or parallel programs and activities sponsored by secularly based organizations or operated by government itself. Thus there would be a double safeguard against public funds going to support programs or activities of a purely other-worldly, core religious nature. Such activities as worship services, the construction of chapels, or classes in religious doctrine could not be funded under positive neutrality. Yet when it comes to religious nonprofit organizations and their programs with temporal benefits for society, they would be free to integrate religious concepts and themes into those programs and to take steps needed to do so, such as the freedom to hire persons in agreement with their religious orientation. This condition is clearly distinguishable from the current sacred-secular bifurcation that says only activities and programs of religious nonprofits of a secular nature can be funded. Under positive neutrality, programs that have strong religious aspects integrated into them would still be eligible for public funds. It would be the temporal benefits for society of the activity or program that would be controlling, not some supposed secular-sacred distinction.

A second limitation on the use of public funds by religious nonprofits is that public funds could not go to nonprofits that teach hatred or intolerance or in other ways work to destroy the social fabric fundamental to civil society. Religious groups would not be singled out for special limitations or conditions, but all nonprofit organizations—secular and religious alike— would have an obligation to be supportive of the basic norms and rules of the game that unite the American people as a nation. Some careful distinctions are important here in order that this limitation not be misused. Yet it is a necessary limitation and one that must not be slighted.

All societies—and certainly all free, democratic societies—are held together by a common commitment to certain ideals and to certain rules of the game. In free, democratic societies these revolve around such concepts as the worth and dignity of all persons ("All men are created equal and are endowed by their Creator with certain inalienable rights. . . ."), the rule of law, the right to privacy, and freedom of expression. Along with rights such as these go certain social obligations, such as refraining from engaging in and refraining from urging others to engage in unlawful acts (except in certain extreme situations when the law itself seems to be violating other fundamental norms and then civil disobedience becomes an acceptable option). Also, a sense of civility and tolerance is important. Tolerance and civility do not mean persons cannot disagree with and strenuously argue against others and their opinions and actions; they do mean one does not read others out of society or out of the human race.[13] Within Christianity there is the old adage, "Hate the sin but love the sinner." Something of this nature is relevant in the social realm more broadly, as all have the right to "hate" the opinions and practices of others—we are free to speak, argue, and demonstrate against them—but we are to "love" the persons and groups that are seeking to advance the opinions and practices we "hate." We are to give them space, not purposely seek to provoke or antagonize them, or oppose them by unlawful or violent means. This is civility and tolerance.

The nonprofit groups—whether religiously or secularly based—that under positive neutrality would be excluded from receiving government funds are those that reject the rule of law, teach religious or racial hatred and bigotry, or in other ways go against the basic norms that make possible a free society. Under its terms groups such as the Ku Klux Klan or various neo-Nazi groups would not be eligible for aid. There will be some hard cases here. Among religious groups, for example, some would probably argue the Nation of Islam, given the anti-Semitic, anti-white rhetoric of some of its leaders, should not be eligible to participate in government funding.[14] Others would argue it should be eligible. With any standard, however, there will always be borderline cases, and their existence does not mean the standard itself is inadequate or inappropriate.

A third limitation on the nonprofit organizations that may receive government funds is that they must be willing to submit to certain limited reviews and licensing standards, as long as they are directed at assuring the this-world services or programming for which they are receiving public funds are in fact being provided. Again, religious and secular nonprofits would be treated in the same manner. Neutrality, therefore, would be maintained.

The suggested standard of positive neutrality would constitute a sharp break with the no-aid-to-religion principle, the sacred-secular distinction, and the pervasively sectarian standard. All three are rooted in the assumption that strictly separating church and state—and especially separating public money from religion—leads to governmental neutrality towards religion. As I have argued throughout the book, this assumption is clearly, demonstrably false in today's world. Positive neutrality is based on the belief that it is when government is neutral towards all religions and their competing secular belief systems that the ideal of full religious freedom is assured. Then the thumb of government is not weighing the scales in favor of any religion or in favor of either religion or secularism.

The Supreme Court has time and again professed its strong commitment to a religious neutrality of this exact type. Nowhere was this done more clearly than when Justice Abe Fortas in a 1968 case, speaking for a unanimous Court, declared the following to be "fundamental to freedom":

> Government in our democracy, state and national, must be neutral in matters of religious theory, doctrine, and practice. It may not be hostile to any religion or to the advocacy of no-religion; and it may not aid, foster, or promote one religion or religious theory against another or even against the militant opposite. The First Amendment mandates governmental neutrality between religion and religion, and between religion and nonreligion. [15]

This is the neutrality for which positive neutrality calls.

Where the Supreme Court's no-aid-to-religion line of reasoning and many policy elites go wrong is in their assumption that neutrality is maintained by a "wall of separation" between church and state, a wall that stops public money from flowing to some religious nonprofits all together and assures its flow only to supposedly secular aspects of other religious nonprofits. Thus on numerous occasions—and especially when K–12 education is at issue—the Supreme Court, as well as the nation's editorial writers and other policy leaders, will fall back on the wall of separation metaphor to condemn various forms of public moneys going to some nonprofits, and to legitimize restrictions of one sort or another on the religiously motivated practices of other nonprofits that are receiving public money. This does not lead to neutrality. Either blocking public funds from going to religious nonprofit organizations that similar nonprofits of a secular nature are receiving, or requiring religious nonprofits to give up certain of their religious practices as a condition of receiving public funds violates the norm of neutrality. In either case religion is being disadvantaged by government policies.

Positive Neutrality, Religious Nonprofits, and Public Money

Even though positive neutrality is compatible with the equal-treatment strain within Supreme Court jurisprudence and the neutrality that is at the heart of that strain, it would nonetheless—if fully adopted and implemented—result in sharp breaks with current practice. In this section I consider six issues or problem areas that this study has shown to exist under current interpretations and attitudes, and how they would be handled under positive neutrality.

One issue is the anomaly of religiously based secondary and elementary schools being denied almost all forms of public money, while almost all other religiously based nonprofit organizations receive significant amounts of public money. Under positive neutrality—with the no-aid-to-religion doctrine and the sacred-secular and pervasively sectarian distinctions no longer serving as guidelines—K–12 schools would be eligible for aid under the same conditions as other religiously based nonprofits. The legal doctrines and principles that have been used for the past thirty years to block aid to religious K–12 schools would no longer be in force.

The question to be considered and weighed in deciding whether or not a particular elementary or secondary school would be eligible to receive public funds would be fourfold. First, one would need to determine if the school is educating and training children in knowledge, skills, and attitudes that will equip them to function in and contribute to society. In other words, is the education the children are receiving one that has this-world benefits for the children and therefore for the broader society as well? Schools that are training children only in religious rituals, prayers, meditation or other such other-worldly skills would be excluded from receiving public funds. To receive public money schools would have to be educating children in such a way that there would be this-world benefits for them and society. This is different from saying they would have to be receiving a purely secular education, for an education with this-world benefits could have religious themes and perspectives interwoven into it. The old sacred-secular distinction would no longer be relevant.

Second, it would have to be clear that any school receiving public funds—secular or religious, public or private—could not be teaching hatred or fomenting violence, lawlessness, and hatred for other societal groups. This is a basic provision of positive neutrality, since pluralism properly gives space for the diversity of society, but also believes in the importance of the building of community, civility, and procedures for living together in a cooperative, peaceful manner.

Third, to be eligible for public funding, the government would have to be itself sponsoring or helping to fund similar schools that reflect a secular perspective, and would have to be helping to fund the schools sponsored by all of the religious traditions present in society. The schools of any particular religious tradition could not be singled out for public support nor could either religious schools as a whole or secular schools as a whole be favored over the other. Thereby governmental neutrality would be maintained and government could not be construed as endorsing religion.

Fourth, any school receiving public funds would have to be willing to submit to basic regulations and to submit reports to the government that assure the above conditions are being met and that the public funds being received are going toward the purposes for which they are intended. There would need to be accountability.

As long as these four conditions are met, religiously based K–12 schools would be free to receive public funds. Thereby the current artificial distinctions between K–12 schools and all other nonprofits would be removed. I am not necessarily arguing here that such funds should be made available, nor am I advocating any certain form of aid. These are decisions the normal public policy-making process—fought out in state legislatures, governors' offices, Congress, the White House, and countless interest group and election struggles—will have to make. What positive neutrality says is that whether or not public funds go to religious K–12 schools should be decided by the normal policy-making process. The option of going in that direction ought not to be foreclosed by First Amendment interpretations that have more to do with nineteenth-century holdovers of a common school ideal and anti-Catholic prejudices than the current public policy needs of American society.

A second issue that has come up at many points in this study is the issue of the hiring policies of nonprofit organizations that receive public money. Whether or not religious nonprofit organizations that receive public money may discriminate in favor of co-religionists is a question that has divided the courts, observers, and the religious nonprofits themselves. It is clear that religious nonprofits may, under federal civil rights laws, discriminate in hiring on the basis of religion, but it is less clear what impact the receipt of public money has on this. Part of the problem is the very legal basis on which religious nonprofits can now receive public money for certain of their programs—that such money is funding only secular programs—makes it difficult to insist only their fellow religionists are able to run those programs.

Positive neutrality insists that the autonomy of religious nonprofit organizations clearly allows them to favor persons from their own religious tradition in their hiring practices. Justice William Brennan, in a 1987 concurring opinion, wrote:

> For many individuals, religious activity derives meaning in large measure from participation in a larger religious community. Such a community represents an ongoing tradition of shared beliefs, an organic entity not reducible to a mere aggregation of individuals. Determining that certain activities are in furtherance of an organization's religious mission, *and that only those committed to that mission should conduct them*, is thus a means by which a religious community defines itself.[16]

Brennan here clearly gave expression to the twin ideas of the importance of a religious community to the individual religious believer and the importance of that religious community being able to define itself by controlling who is to run the mission of the community.

To hold that the receipt of public funds changes all this can only mean that the receipt of public funds means a religious nonprofit organization surrenders its religious autonomy. A nonprofit should not have to surrender its legal-Constitutional rights as the price for receiving public funds. Often it is the religious character of the religiously based nonprofit that helps enable it to play a valuable, effective public policy role. To force such a nonprofit to give up its religious distinctiveness as the price of receiving public funds, thereby forcing it into the same mold as its secular and governmental counterparts, would therefore not only be a violation of its free-exercise rights, but would also be counterproductive in terms of achieving public policy goals.

A third area where questions have sometimes arisen in regard to what is permitted in religiously based nonprofit organizations that are receiving public funds is whether or not they may have close, formal ties to a church or other formal religious body. In the Supreme Court cases dealing with aid to religiously based college and universities, for example, an indication that college and universities were not pervasively sectarian and K–12 schools were was the fact that K–12 schools were more likely to have close ties to a church than were the colleges and universities. Positive neutrality, however, would say this is immaterial. The key factor is whether or not the religious nonprofit organization is providing services with a temporal benefit to society, not the presence or absence of formal ties to a church and the pervasively sectarian character of the nonprofit supposedly revealed by those ties.

A fourth area where questions have arisen is in regard to whether or not required religious exercises are permitted in religious nonprofits receiving government funding. Chapter 3 revealed that many child service agencies have run into challenges and pressures when they have required the children in their care to attend Sunday worship services. Similarly, questions have sometimes arisen in regard to colleges and universities requiring student attendance at chapel services and other nonprofit organizations requiring or encouraging involvement in other types of religious exercises or activities, some of which may have a proselytizing motivation.

Positive neutrality approaches this issue by looking at the overall mission or program of the nonprofit organization and at the degree of choice possessed by those taking part in its programs. Taking these in order, if the overall mission or programs of the religious nonprofit has this-world benefits to society and if its programs and activities are not dominated by and built around required religious exercises or efforts at proselytizing, their existence does not pose a problem. One needs to go back to the concept of the programs of religious nonprofits having to have a temporal benefit for society. As long as this is the case, requiring religious exercises would not be a problem. It is only if the religious exercises or proselytizing efforts would become so prominent a feature of the overall programming that they would be interfering with the nonprofit's ability to achieve results with temporal benefits to society that they would become a barrier to the receipt of public funds. If a drug treatment center, for example, is really no more than a center for religious meditation or worship or a recruiting ground for new converts and not a genuine drug treatment and counseling center, then it should not receive public funding.

A second question to be asked is whether or not those taking part in the nonprofit's programs are there by choice. If one chooses to join one's self to a religious nonprofit, then one should be prepared to be required to take part in certain religious exercises that it may judge to be important to maintaining its religious character. If one has chosen to join a certain religious organization one has no basis to object to its compulsory religious activities. Here positive neutrality's concept of pluralism and diversity comes into play. One should be free, for example, to decide whether to attend a college that is Catholic, conservative Protestant, mainline Protestant, Jewish, Mormon, nominally religious, secular, or whatever. The religious diversity of the American people is reflected in the pluralism of the colleges and universities that are available. Persons are free to choose the type of college education they desire. Choice enters in at the point the institution or agency is selected; it is not necessarily guaranteed for all those in a religious institution or agency once they have chosen to affiliate themselves with it. To force all nonprofit organizations to forego requiring those who have chosen to affiliate with them to take part in certain religious practices is to move in the direction of forcing a gray sameness onto them, instead of allowing for a colorful diversity.

A problem only emerges when a person is assigned to a certain religiously based institution or agency, as might happen to youths who have gotten in trouble with school or juvenile justice authorities. They might be assigned without being consulted and against their will to a religiously based youth and family service agency. Positive neutrality suggests, first, that the system should seek wherever possible to avoid such assignments. If possible, a choice of agencies should be preserved, with their religious character, or lack thereof, being made clear. When a choice cannot be given, any normally compulsory religious exercises should be voluntary in nature. But this is an anomalous situation that usually does not arise. In most cases persons who are part of a religiously based organization are there by choice.

A fifth issue that repeatedly came up in this study is whether public funds should go to nonprofit organizations whose religious identity is indicated by way of their names or logos, mission statements, or use of religious pictures or symbols in their facilities. All these are what I would call symbolic indications of a nonprofit's religious orientation, giving evidence of that orientation in written or visual form. Under existing church-state practice they are suspect because they have sometimes been taken as indications of a pervasively sectarian character. Even when they are more symbol than substance, their high visibility make them especially convenient targets for government regulators or outside groups concerned with violations of the no-aid-to-religion doctrine.

Since positive neutrality would no longer engage in the futile task of trying to separate out pervasively from nonpervasively sectarian nonprofits, or secular from sacred aspects of their programs, these sorts of symbolic indications of a religious orientation would no longer be of any real concern. The focus of attention would be on the evenhandedness with which government is supporting all types of religious nonprofits and religious and secular nonprofits alike; and it would be on the this-world benefits of the programs on which public funds were being expended.

The sixth and final problem area to be considered is that of the ability of religious nonprofits receiving public funds to take religion into account in selecting those who use their services or their staff members on the basis of religion, race, ethnicity, gender, or sexual orientation. Clearly related, in the case of adoption and foster care agencies, is the freedom to make adoption and foster care placements on the basis of religion. I have already discussed the ability to make hiring decisions on the basis of religion. Here we are faced with a broader issue that includes not only the religious background, but also the race, ethnicity, gender and sexual orientation of staff members and all of these characteristics for those who use the nonprofits' services. Some important distinctions need to be made, for there is the potential in this area for the protection of the religious autonomy of nonprofits to clash with the protection of the interests of society as a whole.

One basic distinction is between a situation where a nonprofit organization and those it serves constitute a community or where other on-going group relationships are at stake, and a situation where the nonprofit is providing a service to persons in a situation where the contacts are temporary or episodic. Examples of the first situation are that of a college and its students or foster or adoptive parents and children. Examples of the second situation would be a homeless shelter providing overnight sleeping quarters or an international aid agency providing famine relief overseas.

I make this distinction due to the concept of religious autonomy and the importance of its not being compromised, even when a group receives public dollars. Thus I would argue that under positive neutrality a religiously based college receiving public funds should be able to favor in its admission policies students from its own religious tradition. A long term, on-going relationship is involved and who is or is not included in that relationship will deeply affect the nature of that group. Similarly, placing foster or adoptive children with parents of the same religious background as their biological parents or, as a second choice, of the same religious tradition as the placing agency shows respect for the religion of the biological parents or the placing agency. Similarly, to require religious nonprofit organizations for whom homosexual practices are a direct violation of their deeply held beliefs to accept and condone homosexual behavior would do violence to their religious autonomy.

In such instances I would favor protecting the religious autonomy of the group even at the expense of some individuals' freedom of choice. Forcing nonbelievers or practicing homosexuals into a particular institution or agency, contrary to its deeply held religious beliefs, would tend severely to compromise and even destroy that organization as a closely-knit religious organization. But doing so will have a much less significant impact on the individuals affected, since they have many other institutions or agencies to which they can turn. As Gedicks has pointed out, this is an issue of religious pluralism or diversity. If society allows, and even encourages, differing religious groups with differing beliefs and standards to exist and to live out their differences, their religious autonomy is protected, but so is individual choice:

> Individual autonomy is adequately protected by religious pluralism. The remedy for religious group infringement upon individual autonomy by discriminatory membership decisions is not government intervention, but withdrawal from the discriminatory group and subsequent association with other groups or individuals whose beliefs and behavior are more congenial. Thus, the external harm imposed by discriminatory membership decisions is typically marginal.[17]

But things—at least in my thinking—become more difficult when it comes to discrimination based on gender, race, or ethnicity. Here both the history of widespread discrimination in the United States and the current consensus on the wrongness of that discrimination are both so strong it becomes difficult to justify sending public money to nonprofits—whether religious or secular in nature—that are discriminating in hiring or membership on these bases. Especially in the case of discrimination based on race or ethnicity I believe the public interest in societal unity outweighs the right any religious group might claim to discriminate. Some gender discrimination should be allowed in the case of nonprofits from religious traditions with long-standing and sincerely held beliefs that make gender-based role distinctions, and when there are practical reasons for gender distinctions, such as in the case of an all boys' or all girls' home for troubled youths. But these should be exceptions to the normal requirement of equal treatment of men and women by nonprofits that receive public funds. The need to promote and protect societal unity and a sense of respect and civility on which that unity depends means government should not be in the business of supporting discrimination by nonprofits based on race, ethnicity, and—with some exceptions—gender.

The issues become easier when one considers nonprofit organizations that are offering services to clients in situations that do not involve inducting them into the community or group. Here, if government funds are involved, no discrimination based on religion, race, ethnicity, gender, or sexual orientation should be allowed. For a government-funded nonprofit agency providing relief to victims of a flood to do so only to certain religious, racial, or ethnic groups or only to heterosexuals would be wholly wrong and would violate any concept of societal unity and the public interest. A similar point can be made with regard to other service programs. Since these service relationships do not involve inducting the persons being served into the group, the religious autonomy of the group is not threatened by the requirement they not discriminate on these bases. Thus there would be no case to be made in favor of allowing them to discriminate on these bases.

Positive Neutrality and Public Policy

Positive neutrality is first of all not a principle or standard of constitutional interpretation designed to resolve certain legal-theoretical questions. I am not an attorney nor a constitutional law specialist, nor am I trying to make the law more tidy and internally consistent as an end in itself. Doing so may be a worthy goal, but it is not mine. Instead, I engaged in the study reported in this book and have developed the concept of positive neutrality out of a concern for the state of religious freedom and a desire to broaden the public policy options available in the United States. Certain church-state interpretations and assumptions currently ascendant in the courts and among the policy elites are severely constricting the ability of the United States to deal flexibly and creatively with persistent domestic problems, and are putting religion in a government-created disadvantaged position. Positive neutrality, if fully embraced and followed, would unleash new forces to deal with many current policy needs and would level the playing field among all religions and between religion and secularism generally. In this final section of the book, I organize the public policy advantages positive neutrality carries with it under three basic headings.

The first set of advantages revolve around new opportunities to privatize the delivery of public services, thereby increasing competition in the delivery of those services and, many are convinced, saving money and improving efficiency.[18] As noted in the previous chapter, John Chubb and Terry Moe have written persuasively and in detail concerning the need to reintroduce greater competition into the delivery of elementary and secondary education.[19] They, along with almost all the policy elites in the United States, deplore the state of education in the United States, especially for the poor living in urban central city areas. Chubb and Moe have made a powerful case for the proposition that top-heavy educational bureaucracies are the prime cause of the too frequent shortcomings of American public education. Their solution is not to legislate certain reforms in the public school system—this has been tried untold times to almost uniformly disappointing results—but to introduce a strong element of competition into the school system. If schools would have to compete for students, with parents choosing the schools—public or private—to which they would send their children, the ineffective schools would change or go out of business and the effective schools would flourish and be copied by others. But for this proposal to work there would have to be genuine competition in the sense that parents would have the opportunity to choose from a number of schools that offer genuinely different approaches to education with differing results. If a poor family living in a central city area has only three schools from which to select, since they are the only schools for which transportation is available, and all three are traditional public schools with top-heavy bureaucracies, the same education philosophy, dispirited teachers, the constant threat of violence, and high dropout rates, Chubb and Moe's scheme of improving educational opportunities for all by injecting competition into the system is not going to work.

As noted before, 80 percent of all children attending nonpublic schools attend one of the 25,000 religiously based nonpublic schools. If those schools are excluded from the voucher system suggested by Chubb and Moe, the amount of competition, and therefore the beneficial effects projected to result from this competition, will be severely restricted. In this area, as in countless other social service areas, the nonprofit sector is dominated by religiously based nonprofits. Especially in the central areas of large cities often the only alternative to failing public schools are Catholic schools. If they would be excluded from a voucher program, much of the competition a voucher system promises would be a cruel mirage for low-income, central-city families. In addition, if one wishes to increase competition one surely wants to include those competitors that are now doing the best job. It is they that will push those that are less effective and challenge them to improve themselves and reach similar levels of accomplishment. With this in mind, it is highly significant that numerous studies have shown it is the religious nonprofit K–12 schools that are the most effective.[20] If privatization is to move ahead in a full, well-rounded fashion, religiously based nonprofit agencies and institutions must be included.

It is equally important that religious nonprofit organizations—whether K–12 schools, colleges and universities, or nonprofits of other types—be able to participate in publicly funded programs without having to compromise their religious beliefs. Even Chubb and Moe, in an otherwise excellent study, reveal a misconception with a potential to interfere with the religious autonomy of schools that would be eligible to receive vouchers. They write, "Our own preference would be to include religious schools as well, as long as their sectarian functions can be kept clearly separate from their educational functions."[21] The assumption here is that the "sectarian functions" of a religiously based school play no educational role and are separate and distinct from the "educational functions." But for many religious schools their religious components are intertwined with their educational components. As noted in the prior chapter, to keep to the Supreme Court's old no-aid-to-religion formula, and its sacred-secular and pervasively sectarian standards—all implicitly present in Chubb and Moe's statement—puts the religious autonomy of most religiously based K–12 schools in a legally vulnerable position.

In turn, this vulnerability could have a negative effect on privatization policies if it results in many religious nonprofits choosing not to participate in public funding programs. Protecting the religious autonomy of nonprofits would encourage more of them to participate in public funding programs, thereby increasing the privatization options and gaining its public policy advantages. Chapter 3 revealed that 30 percent of the religious international aid agencies and 16 percent of the religious child service agencies surveyed have failed to participate in public funding programs. If public funds continue to be offered only on the condition that the religious elements of the nonprofit organization be segregated out and, perhaps, downplayed, many may choose to get along without such funds. The public policy advantages of a privatization of public services that increases competition, saves money, and increases efficiencies would be correspondingly reduced.

The introduction of competition that is at the heart of the case for privatization could also be hurt by policies that encourage the marginalization of their religious practices. As noted a couple of times earlier in the book, one of the advantages religiously based nonprofit organizations bring to the public policy table is their religious nature. For many that is what binds constituencies to them in support of their programs, serves as a motivating and inspiring force for their staffs, and forms an integral part of their frequent successes with clients or students. To put the religious practices of religiously based nonprofits into a precarious position—where the pressure is either to abandon them altogether or to de-emphasize them and place them outside the mainstream of the organizations' educational or service programs—is to weaken their religious natures. When that occurs, their ability to provide effective services that differ from those any governmental or secular agency could provide just as well is put at risk.

In short, privatization and its goal of increased competition are served by having more nonprofit organizations and more effective nonprofit organizations being encouraged to take part in the public-nonprofit partnership. Positive neutrality allows for this. Policy makers may still decide that in certain areas privatization is not appropriate. But positive neutrality—by opening the door for religiously based nonprofit organizations to take part in the partnership as religious nonprofits true to their faith commitments—works to make a broader array of policy options available to policy makers than is currently the case.

A second advantage of positive neutrality from a public policy point of view is that following it would protect and enhance diversity in the United States. There are two ways to view diversity. One is to expect that all associations or institutions should exhibit a similar type of diversity. Under this approach all colleges and universities, for example, would be expected to have diversity in terms of gender, religion, race, sexual orientation, and other population characteristics. This is an appropriate form of diversity and carries with it certain clear advantages. But it also carries with it a danger in it that can, paradoxically, work against diversity. The danger is that instead of differences being openly discussed and appreciated for what they are, a unity built around a lowest common denominator emerges. No institution can, of course, exist simply on the basis of diversity; there must also be common elements. There must be what unites as well as what divides. This can lead to efforts at playing down diversity to the point it is not fully explored or discussed. Instead, differences are papered over and ignored—as in the old saying of avoiding discussions of religion and politics if a friendship is to prosper, because the differences are so great and explosive that their discussion might break up an otherwise pleasant friendship.

This suggests that under some circumstances a different type of diversity may have something to offer—a diversity of institutions, each of which by itself is homogeneous in some important respects. Thus predominately African American colleges and universities continue to exist and even prosper and all female prep-schools and colleges do so as well. Some African American students and some women report they are freer to explore their feelings and beliefs as African Americans or as women, and to explore the history of racism or gender discrimination and racial and gender politics in a setting of fellow African Americans or women. Similarly, an institution or agency rooted in a particular religious tradition, respectful of that tradition and its beliefs and committed to learning—and other human activities— within the context of that tradition, can have certain practical advantages. In the process a diversity on a societal level is still preserved and honored, in some ways even more fully and deeply than if every institution or agency sought to incorporate a similar degree of diversity within it, often at the price of having to play down or ignore those very differences.

A third public policy advantage of positive neutrality is probably a more powerful factor than the first two I mentioned, but it is also harder to describe and document. It is that positive neutrality would help make possible the honoring and encouraging of a sense of public morality or virtue that is essential to a free, peaceful society. Forty years ago the famous historian Clinton Rossiter made the key point that sets the stage for what I am getting at:

> It takes more than a perfect plan of government to preserve ordered liberty. Something else is needed, some moral principle diffused among the people to strengthen the urge to peaceful obedience and hold the community on an even keel. . . . [Free] government rests on a definite moral basis: a virtuous people. Men who are virtuous may aspire to liberty, prosperity, and happiness; men who are corrupt may expect slavery, adversity, and sorrow. In addition to such

recognized virtues as wisdom, justice, temperance, courage, honesty, and sincerity, these may be singled out as attitudes or traits of special consequence for a free republic: the willingness to act morally without compulsion, love of liberty, public spirit and patriotism, official incorruptibility, and industry and frugality. Men who display these qualities are the raw material of free government. Without such men [and women], in low places as well as high, free government cannot possibly exist.[22]

Two types of problems emerge whenever a people are marked by a weakened, distorted civic virtue or public moral sense. One is that leaders and citizens alike will see politics as no more than a game of ripping off others in society for as much as they can. The public official weighs each vote on the basis of its effect on campaign contributions or the perks and financial rewards he or she will enjoy, and the citizen casts his or her vote purely on the basis of his or her perceived economic self-interest. ("Will *my* taxes go up or down?" or similar self-interested considerations are all that are weighed.) No free, democratic system can long survive—and surely cannot flourish—under a widespread absence of public morality.

A second type of problem that emerges when a society lacks a public moral sense consists of a whole series of social dislocations and their consequences. Government is asked but is clearly powerless to solve them. Rising levels of crime and children born out of wedlock are two of the clearest examples of what I have in mind. No government can prevent crime in the sense of stationing sufficient police officers in enough locations to stop crime, if most or even a significant minority of the population feels no moral compunction about engaging in crime. A society where crime does not pose a serious threat to social peace and safety must come from within the citizens and their sense of morality, obligation, self-restraint, and respect for others. Rising levels of children not born into stable, two-parent families is a situation no government can alter, yet the effects—low achievement levels and juvenile delinquency for starters—must be dealt with by government.[23] Clearly Rossiter was right. A strong sense of public morality is essential if a free, democratic government is to flourish.

The difficulty is that this sense of public morality cannot be created by government fiat. Governmental attempts to do so necessarily involve violations of individual and group rights. Political scientist Jerold Waltman has accurately observed that "the government's directly undertaking the promotion of virtue . . . would lead to a deadening uniformity, as well as opening the door to totalitarianism. Numerous historical examples of dogmatic attempts to enforce virtue leap to mind, such as the Spain of the Inquisition or the Soviet Union of the Stalinist purges."[24] If public morality is essential and if government itself cannot create it, from where does it emerge? Political scientists Richard Vetterli and Gary Bryner have answered this question:

> [T]he American founders . . . clearly believed that a republic also depended upon the quantity and quality of moral virtue in the people, which owes its origins to sources that are prior to and apart from the political system, and which have traditionally been nurtured at the breast, the hearth, the pulpit, the classroom and in private associations for public ends.[25]

It is within families, religious communities, and a host of other religious, educational, and neighborhood associations that we learn—or fail to learn—such civic virtues as respect for others, a sense of forbearance and civility, putting off immediate desires and urges, loyalty to the larger society, and a concern for the nation.

When public policies end up favoring a secular cultural ethos, and disadvantaging religion and religiously rooted family structures and their wishes for their children—as I have argued is happening in the United States today—the consequences are usually not immediate or obvious, but they are real and nonetheless severe. Harvard law professor Mary Ann Glendon put it well when she wrote in reference to certain Supreme Court Justices:

> In their zeal to protect certain preferred individual liberties, they seem in retrospect—like the French revolutionaries—to have given little thought to the structures that ultimately sustain a regime of rights. Where, one wonders, did they expect Americans to acquire that ingrained respect for the dignity and worth of others that we now demand from our citizens to a higher degree than ever before? How were citizens of our increasingly diverse country supposed to internalize a sense of concern for their fellow human beings in need that would be strong enough to support the expanded welfare activities of government? To pin so many of their hopes in this regard on the public schools, as some of the judges seem to have done, was to underestimate seriously the extent to which the public schools themselves depended, and still depend, on the support of, and interaction with, families and their surrounding communities.[26]

Perhaps an illustration will help make the needed point. In July, 1993, Congressman Paul Henry from Michigan's third congressional district died from a brain tumor while in office. Congressman Henry was praised by the local newspaper as a person of integrity, honesty, and commitment to the broad public interest. He was a personal friend of mine and I had always known him as a person who exemplified the ideal of a public official with a strong sense of public morality (that is why I have dedicated this book to his memory). I also knew where that sense of public morality had come from: It was rooted in a strong religious faith that in turn had been nurtured in a deeply religious family, a religiously based college in the conservative Protestant tradition that he had attended, and the church with which he was affiliated as an adult. Thus it struck me as the height of irony when the same local newspaper that praised Henry for his sense of civic virtue ran an editorial at about the same time praising the city government's decision to bar religious exercises from ethnic festivals held on city property. "[T]he city's legal staff correctly reversed the long-standing policy allowing the Masses. . . . Such a service on public property during a city-sponsored event would make it look as if the city is endorsing or promoting that religion. . . . City officials have the Constitution and the U.S. Supreme Court on their side."[27] As I wrote in a response to the newspaper's editorial,

> All of us rejoice and the entire community gains when a public official of decency and integrity is elected to office, and we all grieve when the public career of such an official is cut short. But among the reasons we sometimes are fortunate enough to have persons such as Paul Henry are the communities of faith and remembrance within which faith, integrity, and a commitment to a greater good beyond narrow self-interest can develop and flourish. . . . Yet a few days before Paul Henry's death, the faith communities we necessarily depend upon to inspire and nurture public officials of his caliber were spurned and disparaged by the city's decision and the *Press's* endorsement of that decision.[28]

That one conjunction of events is all too representative of what has been occurring in the United States. Every time a religiously based nonprofit organization must get along without public funds while similar secular agencies are receiving them, and every time a religiously based nonprofit puts its religious practices at risk because it receives public funds, those communities of faith that are probably the most significant source of the civic virtue crucial to free, democratic governance are weakened. Thus far only K–12 schools have been denied funds, and the limitations and restraints put on other religious nonprofits have been muted, but the threat is there. The atmosphere is one of religious limitations and restrictions even when most religious nonprofits have learned how to finesse and live with those limitations and restrictions.

Positive neutrality's basic aim is to give freer rein for religion to play a positive role in the public realm, and for the public realm to recognize, accommodate, and support religion without violating the norm of governmental neutrality on matters of religion. Positive neutrality's basic concern is how we as a people are to live together with "our deepest differences,"[29] while building a stronger society with more effective public policies. To do so we need to acknowledge and honor our differences and not try to squeeze them onto the sidelines. When "our deepest differences" are squeezed onto the sidelines, distrust and division are the result; when they are acknowledged and honored, powerful forces for dealing with persistent social ills are unleashed. The public-nonprofit partnership has accomplished much in the past; it can do so again today. But to do so *all* nonprofits must be empowered to take part in that partnership as full partners without having to deny or jettison their most deeply held beliefs.

Notes

1. Frederick Mark Gedicks, "Toward a Constitutional Jurisprudence of Religious Group Rights," *Wisconsin Law Review*, 1989 (1989): 118–19.
2. Gedicks, "Religious Group Rights," 158–59. Emphasis added.
3. Stephen L. Carter, *The Culture of Disbelief* (New York: Basic Books, 1993), 115.
4. Richard Mouw and Sander Griffioen, *Pluralisms and Horizons: An Essay in Christian Public Philosophy* (Grand Rapids, MI: Eerdmans, 1993), 51. Richard Mouw is president of Fuller Theological Seminary in Pasadena, California.
5. From Justice Stewart's dissenting opinion in *Abington v. Schempp*, 374 U.S. at 319–20 (1963).
6. From Justice Goldberg's concurring opinion in *Abington v. Schempp*, 374 U.S. at 305 (1963). It is significant to note the Goldberg even referred to "the religion clause" (singular), rather than to the religion clauses (plural). Several commentators, most notably Richard John Neuhaus, have made this same point. See Richard John Neuhaus, "A New Order of Religious Freedom," *First Things*, 20 (February, 1992): 15. Also see William A. Carroll, "The Constitution, the Supreme Court, and Religion," *The American Political Science Review*, 61 (1967): 657–74; and Arlin M. Adams and Charles J. Emmerich, *A Nation Dedicated to Religious Liberty* (Philadelphia: University of Pennsylvania Press, 1990), 37–42.
7. These examples are based on the cases discussed in Chapter 2. See *Widmar v. Vincent*, 454 U.S. 263 (1981); *Lamb's Chapel v. Center Moriches School District*, 1993 WL 187864; *Capitol Square Review Board v. Pinette*, 1995 WL 382063; and *Rosenberger v. Rector*, 1995 WL 382046. On student use of school facilities also see *Westside Community Schools v. Mergens*, 58 LW 4720 (1990).
8. *Rosenberger v. Rector*, at 10–11. Emphasis added.
9. *Lamb's Chapel v. Center Moriches Union School District*, at 5–6 .
10. I originally developed the concept of positive neutrality in my book *Positive Neutrality: Letting Religious Freedom Ring* (Westport, CT: Greenwood, 1993), especially chap. 5. Positive neutrality is very similar to what Douglas Laycock has termed substantive neutrality, which he has defined in these terms: "the religion clauses require government to minimize the extent to which it either encourages or

discourages religious belief, practice or nonpractice, observance or nonobservance."
See Douglas Laycock, "Formal, Substantive, and Disaggregated Neutrality Toward
Religion," *DePaul Law Review*, 39 (1990): 1001.

11. Strict separationists believe government may support secular activities, programs, and organizations, since they see them (falsely, I believe) as being religiously
neutral, but may not support any religiously based activities, programs, or organizations. Accommodationists or nonpreferentialists believe government may favor religious activities, programs, or organizations over secular ones as long as it treats all
religious traditions without favoritism. On these distinctions, see Carl H. Esbeck, "A
Typology of Church-State Relations in Current American Thought," in *Religion,
Public Life, and the American Polity*, Luis E. Lugo, ed. (Knoxville, TN: University
of Tennessee Press, 1994), 3–34.

12. From Justice Anthony Kennedy's concurring opinion in *Allegheny v. American
Civil Liberties Union*, 109 St.Ct. at 3135 (1989).

13. On tolerance and civility, see Richard J. Mouw, *Uncommon Decency: Christian Civility in an Uncivil World* (Downers Grove, IL: InterVarsity Press, 1992), and
James Q. Wilson, *The Moral Sense* (New York: Free Press, 1993).

14. See the series of articles on the Nation of Islam published by *New York Times*
(March, 3, 4, and 5, 1994).

15. *Epperson v. Arkansas*, 393 U.S. at 103–104 (1968).

16. *Corporation of the Presiding Bishop v. Amos*, 483 U.S. at 342 (1987). Emphasis
added. In this case the question of the impact of the receipt of public funds was not
at issue, since the religious organization whose hiring practices were under challenge
had received no public funds.

17. Gedicks, "Religious Group Rights," 153.

18. On privatization, see President's Commission on Privatization, David F.
Linowes, Chairman, *Privatization: Toward More Effective Government* (Urbana, IL:
University of Illinois Press, 1988); David Osborne and Ted Gaebler, *Reinventing
Government* (New York: Penguin Books, 1993); and E. S. Savas, *Privatization: The
Key to Better Government* (Chatham, NJ: Chatham House, 1987).

19. See John E. Chubb and Terry M. Moe, *Politics, Markets, and America's
Schools* (Washington, DC: Brookings, 1990).

20. See, for example, James S. Coleman, Thomas Hoffer, and Sally Kilgore, *High
School Achievement: Public, Catholic, and Private Schools Compared* (New York:
Basic Books, 1982), John E. Chubb and Terry M. Moe, "Politics, Markets, and
Equality in Schools" (a paper prepared for delivery at the annual meeting of the
American Political Science Association, September, 1992), and other references
given in Chapter 5.

21. Chubb and Moe., *Politics, Markets, and America's Schools*, 219.

22. Clinton Rossiter, *Seedtime of the Republic* (New York: Harcourt, Brace, 1953),
447. The English language has changed since Rossiter wrote in 1953. Forty years ago
it was understood that *man* and *men* were gender inclusive terms. They no longer are
so. I added *and women* at only one point, but Rossiter would have (hopefully)
intended their inclusion where ever he uses *man* or *men*.

23. On the negative consequences of children being raised in single-parent families see Barbara D. Whitehead, "Dan Quayle Was Right," *The Atlantic*, 271 (April, 1993): 47–84. Also see news reports of President Clinton's 1994 speech to the National Baptist Convention. *New York Times*, 10 September 1994, A1 and A10.

24. Jerold L. Waltman, *American Government: Politics and Citizenship* (Minneapolis, MN: West, 1993), 9.

25. Richard Vetterli and Gary Bryner, *In Search of the Republic: Public Virtue and the Roots of American Government* (Totowa, NJ: Rowman and Littlefield, 1987), 247.

26. Mary Ann Glendon, "Law, Communities, and the Religious Freedom Language of the Constitution," *George Washington Law Review*, 60 (1992): 677.

27. "City Says, 'No Mass,' " *Grand Rapids Press*, 30 July 1993, A10.

28. Stephen V. Monsma, "Dissent," *Grand Rapids Press*, 7 September 1993, A11.

29. The phrase is from Os Guinness, "Introduction," in Os Guinness and James Davison Hunter, eds., *Articles of Faith, Articles of Peace* (Washington, DC: Brookings, 1990), 2.

Appendix A

The Questionnaires

Following are the three questionnaires used for the three types of nonprofit organizations. I sought to keep them as similar as possible to each other in order to facilitate comparisons. To save space some changes have been made in the layout of the questionnaires as they appear here.

Questionnaire on Independent Higher Education and Government Funds

Part I: First, I would like some information about your college or university—

Q1. Which of the following programs are provided by your institution? (Please circle all that apply.)
  1. Baccalaureate degree programs
  2. Master's degree programs in a few, select fields
  3. Master's degree programs in a wide variety of fields
  4. PhD or other doctoral programs in a few, select fields
  5. PhD or other doctoral programs in a wide variety of fields
  6. Other programs not listed. Please specify.

Q2. In what year was your college or university founded?

Q3. Please give me some indication of the size of your institution:
  a. The approximate number of full-time students (or their equivalent)?
  The approximate number of baccalaureate degrees awarded annually?
  The approximate number of master's degrees awarded annually?

The approximate number of doctorates awarded annually?
The approximate number of full-time faculty members (or their equivalent)?
b. What percentage of full-time faculty have their doctorates (or equivalent)?
c. Your estimated total annual budget? (Circle one.)
   1. Under $10 million
   2. $10 to $15 million
   3. $25 to $50 million
   4. $50 to $100 million
   5. Over $100 million

Q4. Which statement best describes your institution? (Circle one.)
   1. A private, secular institution with no religious base or history
   2. A private institution that at one time had a religious orientation, but today has evolved into an institution that is largely secularly based
   3. A private institution that continues to have a clear religious base and orientation

Q5. If your institution one time had or continues to have a religious orientation, would you describe that orientation as: (Circle one.)
   1. Orthodox Jewish
   2. Reform Jewish
   3. Conservative Jewish
   4. Catholic
   5. Protestant denominational. Which denomination?
   6. Protestant interdenominational: evangelical
   7. Protestant interdenominational: mainstream protestant or liberal protestant
   8. Mormon
   9. Other. Please specify.

Q6. If your institution has a continuing religious orientation (if it one time had a religious orientation but no longer does, go to Q7), please indicate which of the following characterize your college or university. (Circle as many as apply.)
   1. A chapel or other center for worship on your campus
   2. Religious symbols (such as crosses or religious pictures) on your campus
   3. Voluntary chapel services
   4. Compulsory chapel services

5. Other voluntary religious exercises (such as bible studies or prayer meetings) organized by the college or university
6. Other compulsory religious exercises organized by the college or university
7. Encouraging faculty to integrate religious concepts and ideals into their courses and research
8. Taking your religious beliefs into account in establishing policies for student behavior
9. A spirit of service/concern/love among your faculty and staff
10. Mandatory religion or theology courses
11. Only hiring faculty in agreement with your religious orientation
12. Giving preference in hiring faculty to those in agreement with your religious orientation
13. Admitting only students in agreement with your religious orientation
14. Giving preference in admitting students to those in agreement with your religious orientation
15. Efforts to encourage students to make personal religious commitments
16. Other practices your institution engages in that are motivated by your religious orientation. Please specify.

Q7. Which of the following government funds (national, state or local) does your institution receive? (Circle as many as apply.)

1. We receive no government funds of any kind (including no government-funded student aid)
2. Grants for the construction of buildings
3. Low interest loans or loan guarantees
4. Grants of in-kind materials (food, supplies, etc.)
5. Direct grants on a per student or per graduate basis
6. Scholarship grants going to some of your students
7. Loans or loan guarantees going to some of your students
8. Work-study funds for students
9. Research grants to individual faculty members
10. Research grants to the college or university (or schools or departments)
11. Other types of government funds. Please specify.

Q7a. If you receive no government funds, is this due to a self-conscious policy of not accepting them, or is this just the way things have worked out?

      1. A policy

      2. The way things have worked out

Q8. What percentage of your total annual budget would you estimate can be attributed to government funds, including government-funded student aid?

Q9. Which of the following have occurred in your college or university because you receive government funds? (Circle as many as apply.)
1. Expanded your services and programs
2. Raised your level of academic excellence
3. Expanded your student body and campus
4. Put more time and effort into paperwork than should be necessary
5. Improved the quality of your faculty
6. Increased the research and publication done by your faculty
7. Avoided having to close down
8. Became more "bureaucratic" and less flexible and creative
9. Changed your building or development priorities to meet government desires or priorities
10. Changed your research programs or priorities to meet government desires or priorities
11. Became involved in "lobbying" legislators and government agencies
12. Received fewer private gifts than you otherwise would have
13. Other. Please specify.

Part II. If your institution receives government funds and has a continuing religious orientation, go to Q10. (If not, skip this section and go right to Q16.)

Q10. In light of government funds you receive, indicate whether your institution does each of the following practices from Q6 (1) openly and directly; (2) do it, but feel you must do it subtly or indirectly; (3) would like to do it, but feel you ought not to do it; (4) would like to do it, but feel you legally cannot do it; or (5) have no desire to do it.
1. A chapel on campus
2. Religious symbols on campus
3. Voluntary chapel services
4. Compulsory chapel services
5. Other voluntary religious exercises
6. Other compulsory religious exercises

    7. Encouraging faculty to integrate religious concepts and ideals into their courses and research

    8. Taking religious beliefs into account in establishing policies for student behavior

    9. A spirit of service/concern/love among faculty and staff

   10. Mandatory religion or theology courses

   11. Only hiring faculty in agreement with your religious orientation

   12. Giving preference in hiring faculty to those in agreement with your religious orientation

   13. Admitting only students in agreement with your religious orientation

   14. Giving preference in admitting students to those in agreement with your religious orientation

   15. Efforts to encourage students to make personal religious commitments

Q11. Are there any other religious practices you feel you have had to curtail or eliminate because you receive government funds? Please specify.

Q12. Have you ever had any disputes with government officials over what constitutes proper use of campus facilities constructed with government financial assistance? Please explain.

Q13. What reporting requirements or other checks, if any, have governmental agencies put on you to make sure you do not improperly use government funds in support of religion?

Q14. Have any government officials ever questioned any of your religiously-based practices or brought pressure to bear on you to change any of them? Please explain.

Q15. Have you received any other criticism or pressure, or law suits or threats of law suits, due to any of your religiously-based practices? Please explain.

Part III. Finally, I'd like to ask you about some of your own personal attitudes towards some church-state questions.

Q16. Many grade schools and high schools around the country are run by various churches and religious groups. Do you think the government should provide financial help to these schools?
    1. Yes

  2. No
  3. Undecided

Q17. Which of the following statements comes closest to your opinion? (Circle only one.)
  1. The government should take special steps to protect the Judeo-Christian heritage
  2. There should be a high wall of separation between church and state

Q18. For each of the following statements please indicate whether you (1) agree strongly with it, (2) agree somewhat, (3) are undecided, (4) disagree somewhat, or (5) disagree strongly.
  a. It's good for Congress to start sessions with a public prayer
  b. It's OK for a city government to put up a manger scene on government property at Christmas
  c. A religiously-based, private college or university has as much right to receive government funds as does a similar, secularly-based private college or university.

Questionnaire on Homes and Services for Children and Government Funds

Part I: First, I would like some information about your agency—

  Q1. Which of the following services are provided by your agency? (Please circle all that apply.)
  1. Residential care
  2. Out-patient counseling services for troubled children and youth
  3. Out-patient counseling services for families of troubled children and youth
  4. Out-patient mental health services
  5. Emergency shelter for children
  6. Foster care services
  7. Adoption services
  8. Pregnancy counseling and services
  9. Other services not listed. Please specify.

  Q2. In what year was your agency founded?

  Q3. Please give me some indication of the size of your agency:
  a. The approximate number of full-time, paid employees (or their equivalent)?

The approximate number of part-time volunteers?

The approximate number of volunteer hours per week you receive?

b. If you provide residential or foster care, the approximate number of clients in residential care at any one time?

The approximate number in foster care?

c. The approximate total number of clients being served at any one time?

d. The number of sites you have for the delivery of services?

c. Your estimated total annual budget? (Circle one)

    1. Under $500,000

    2. $500,000 to $1 million

    3. $1 to $5 million

    4. $5 to $10 million

    5. Over $10 million

Q4. Which statement best describes your agency? (Circle one)

    1. A private, secular agency with no religious base or history

    2. A private agency that at one time had a religious orientation, but today has evolved into an agency that is largely secularly based

    3. A private agency that continues to have a clear religious base and orientation

Q5. If your agency one time had or continues to have a religious orientation, would you describe that orientation as: (Circle one.)

    1. Orthodox Jewish

    2. Reform Jewish

    3. Conservative Jewish

    4. Catholic

    5. Protestant denominational. Which denomination?

    6. Protestant interdenominational: evangelical

    7. Protestant interdenominational: mainstream protestant or liberal protestant

    8. Mormon

    9. Other. Please specify.

Q6. If your agency has a continuing religious orientation (if it one time had a religious orientation but no longer does, go to Q7), please indicate which of the following characterize your agency. (Circle as many as apply.)

    1. A paid chaplain on staff (full or part time)

    2. A volunteer chaplain on staff (full or part time)

3. Religious symbols or pictures in your facilities
4. Voluntary religious activities
5. Required religious activities
6. Spoken prayers at meals
7. Informal references to religious ideas by staff in contacts with clients
8. A generalized spirit or atmosphere of service/concern/love among your staff
9. Only hiring staff in agreement with your religious orientation
10. Giving preference in hiring staff to those in agreement with your religious orientation
11. Efforts to encourage clients to make personal religious commitments
12. Taking religion into account in making foster care or adoption placements
13. Giving preference in accepting clients to those in agreement with your religious orientation.
14. Other practices your agency engages in that are motivated by your religious orientation. Please specify.

Q7. Which of the following government funds (national, state or local) do you receive? (Circle as many as apply.)
1. We receive no government funds of any kind
2. Purchase of service contracts
3. Construction grants
4. Grants for equipment
5. Grants of in-kind materials (food, supplies, etc.)
6. Loans or loan guarantees
7. Other types of government funds. Please specify.

Q7a. If you receive no government funds, is this due to a self-conscious policy of not accepting them, or is this just the way things have worked out? (Circle one.)
1. A policy
2. The way things have worked out

Q8. Approximately what percentage of your agency's total annual budget can be attributed to government funds (including funds from purchase of service contracts)?

Q9. Which of the following have occurred in your agency because you receive government funds? (Circle as many as apply.)
1. Expanded your services

2. Hired staff with higher levels of education
3. Used more professional staff instead of volunteers
4. Put more time and effort into paperwork than should be necessary
5. Provided more effective services
6. Avoided having to close down
7. Became more "bureaucratic" and less flexible and creative
8. Had to deal with clients with more severe emotional and behavioral problems
9. Had to become involved in "lobbying" legislators and government agencies
10. Received fewer private gifts and volunteer hours than we otherwise would
11. Other. Please specify.

Part II. If your institution receives government funds and has a continuing religious orientation, go to Q10. (If not, skip this section and go right to Q15.)

Q10. In light of government funds you receive, indicate whether your agency does each of the following practices from Q6 (1) openly and directly; (2) do it, but feel you must do it subtly or indirectly; (3) would like to do it, but feel you ought not to do it; (4) would like to do it, but feel you legally cannot do it; or (5) have no desire to do it.
  1. A chaplain on staff
  2. Religious symbols/pictures in facilities
  3. Voluntary religious exercises
  4. Required religious exercises
  5. Spoken prayers at meals
  7. Informal references to religious ideas by staff in contacts with clients
  8. A generalized spirit or atmosphere of service/concern/love among your staff
  9. Only hiring staff in agreement with your religious orientation
  10. Giving preference in hiring staff to those in agreement with your religious orientation
  11. Efforts to encourage clients to make personal religious commitments
  12. Taking religion into account in making foster care or adoption placements
  13. Giving preference in accepting clients to those in agreement with your religious orientation

Q11. Are there any other religious practices you feel you have had to curtail or eliminate because you receive government funds? Please specify.

Q12. What reporting requirements or other checks, if any, have governmental agencies put on you to make sure you do not improperly use government funds in support of religion?

Q13. Have any government officials ever questioned any of your religiously-based practices or brought pressure to bear on you to change any of them? Please explain.

Q14. Have you received any other criticism or pressure, or law suits or threats of law suits, due to any of your religiously-based practices? Please explain.

Part III. Finally, I'd like to ask you about some of your own personal attitudes towards some church-state questions.

Q15. Many grade schools and high schools around the country are run by various churches and religious groups. Do you think the government should provide financial help to these schools?
   1. Yes
   2. No
   3. Undecided

Q16. Which of the following statements comes closest to your opinion? (Circle only one.)
   1. The government should take special steps to protect the Judeo-Christian heritage
   2. There should be a high wall of separation between church and state

Q17. For each of the following statements please indicate whether you (1) agree strongly with it, (2) agree somewhat, (3) are undecided, (4) disagree somewhat, or (5) disagree strongly.
   a. It's good for Congress to start sessions with a public prayer
   b. It's OK for a city government to put up a manger scene on government property at Christmas
   c. A religiously-based, private social service agency has as much right to receive government funds as does a similar, secularly-based private agency.

Questionnaire on Private Voluntary International Aid Agencies and Government Funds

Part I: First, I would like some information about your agency—

Q1. Which of the following services are provided by your agency? (Please circle all that apply.)
1. Overseas emergency disaster relief
2. Overseas long-term relief
3. Overseas large-scale development
4. Overseas refugee relief and resettlement
5. Human rights monitoring
6. Domestic emergency disaster relief
7. Domestic long-term relief
8. Domestic large-scale development
9. Domestic refugee and immigration resettlement
10. Other services not listed. Please specify.

Q2. In what year was your agency founded?

Q3. Please give me some indication of the size of your agency:
a. The approximate number of full-time, paid employees (or their equivalent)?
The approximate number of these employees overseas?
The approximate number of these employees in the Untied States?
b. The approximate number of volunteers, if any?
The approximate number of volunteer hours per week you receive?
c. In how many countries do you have programs?
d. How many field offices do you have?
c. Your estimated total annual budget? (Circle one)
1. Under $5 million
2. $5 to $50 million
3. $50 to $100 million
4. $100 to $300 million
5. Over $300 million

Q4. Which statement best describes your agency? (Circle one)
1. A private, secular agency with no religious base or history.
2. A private agency that at one time had a religious orientation, but today has evolved into an agency that is largely secularly based.

3. A private agency that continues to have a clear religious base and orientation.

Q5. If your agency one time had or continues to have a religious orientation, would you describe that orientation as: (Circle one.)
1. Orthodox Jewish
2. Reform Jewish
3. Conservative Jewish
4. Catholic
5. Protestant denominational. Which denomination?
6. Protestant interdenominational: evangelical
7. Protestant interdenominational: mainstream protestant or liberal protestant
8. Mormon
9. Other. Please specify.

Q6. If your agency has a continuing religious orientation (if it one time had a religious orientation but no longer does, go to Q7), please indicate which of the following characterize your agency. (Circle as many as apply.)
1. A religious affiliation or mission clearly reflected in your name or logo
2. Voluntary worship services or other religious activities integrated into your relief and/or development programs
3. Informal references to religious ideas by staff in contacts with persons being served
4. A spirit of service/concern/love among your staff
5. Only hiring staff in agreement with your religious orientation
6. Giving preference in hiring staff to those in agreement with your religious orientation
7. Making efforts to encourage persons being served to make personal religious commitments
8. Overt religious activities sponsored by an associated organization that parallels you relief and development efforts
9. Helping in the construction of centers for worship or religiously based education
10. Other practices your agency engages in that are motivated by your religious orientation. Please specify.

Q7. Which of the following government funds (national, state or local) do you receive? (Circle as many as apply.)
1. We receive no government funds of any kind

2. Direct program grants
3. Institutional support grants
4. Grants of in-kind materials (food, supplies, etc.)
5. Grants for transportation or free transportation of material
6. Other types of government funds. Please specify.

Q7a. If you receive no government funds, is this due to a self-conscious policy of not accepting them, or is this just the way things have worked out? (Circle one.)
   1. A policy
   2. The way things have worked out

Q8. Approximately what percentage of your agency's total annual budget can be attributed to government funds (including funds from purchase of service contracts)?

Q9. Which of the following have occurred in your agency because you receive government funds? (Circle as many as apply.)
   1. Expanded your services and programs
   2. Hired staff with higher levels of education
   3. Used fewer volunteers and more professional staff
   4. Put more time and effort into paperwork than should be necessary
   5. Provided more effective services
   6. Avoided having to close down
   7. Became more "bureaucratic" and less flexible and creative
   8. Changed your relief or development priorities to meet government desires or priorities
   9. Became involved in "lobbying" legislators and government agencies
   10. Received fewer private gifts and volunteer hours
   11. Other. Please specify.

Part II. If your institution receives government funds and has a continuing religious orientation, go to Q10. (If not, skip this section and go right to Q15.)

Q10. In light of government funds you receive, indicate whether your agency does each of the following practices from Q6 (1) openly and directly; (2) do it, but feel you must do it subtly or indirectly; (3) would like to do it, but feel you ought not to do it; (4) would like to do it, but feel you legally cannot do it; or (5) have no desire to do it.
   1. A religious affiliation or mission reflected in your name or logo

      2. Voluntary worship services or other religious activities integrated into relief/development activities

      3. Informal references to religious ideas by staff in contacts with persons being served

      4. A spirit of service/concern/love among your staff

      5. Only hiring staff in agreement with your religious orientation

      6. Giving preference in hiring staff to those in agreement with your religious orientation

      7. Making efforts to encourage persons being served to make personal religious commitments

      8. Overt religious activities sponsored by an associated organization that parallels you relief/development efforts

      9. Helping in the construction of centers for worship or religiously based education

Q11. Are there any other religious practices you feel you have had to curtail or eliminate because you receive government funds? Please specify.

Q12. What reporting requirements or other checks, if any, have governmental agencies put on you to make sure you do not improperly use government funds in support of religion?

Q13. Have any government officials ever questioned any of your religiously-based practices or brought pressure to bear on you to change any of them? Please explain.

Q14. Have you received any other criticism or pressure, or law suits or threats of law suits, due to any of your religiously-based practices? Please explain.

Part III. Finally, I'd like to ask you about some of your own personal attitudes towards some church-state questions.

Q15. Many grade schools and high schools around the country are run by various churches and religious groups. Do you think the government should provide financial help to these schools?
1. Yes
2. No
3. Undecided

Q16. Which of the following statements comes closest to your opinion? (Circle only one.)

1. The government should take special steps to protect the Judeo-Christian heritage
2. There should be a high wall of separation between church and state

Q17. For each of the following statements please indicate whether you (1) agree strongly with it, (2) agree somewhat, (3) are undecided, (4) disagree somewhat, or (5) disagree strongly.

   a. It's good for Congress to start sessions with a public prayer
   b. It's OK for a city government to put up a manger scene on government property at Christmas
   c. A religiously-based, private international aid agency has as much right to receive government funds as does a similar, secularly-based private international aid agency.

Appendix B

The Study

The study focused on three types of nonprofit organizations, not on nonprofits more generally. I selected the three types of nonprofits that I did because preliminary investigation indicated most of the organizations of all three types receive at least some government funds and many of them are religiously based. Also, comprehensive lists of agencies and institutions of all three types were available.

In the case of agencies serving children and youth, the goal was to survey multiservice child and family service agencies with a strong emphasis on agencies with residential and foster care programs. Some 579 questionnaires were mailed out and 286 were received back, for a return rate of 49 percent. A combination of four membership lists were used: those of the National Association of Homes and Services for Children (NAHSC), the California Association of Services for Children, the Association of Jewish Family and Child Agencies, and the Catholic members of the Michigan Federation of Private Child and Family Agencies. The NAHSC list, with 331 agencies nationwide, was the basic list. Most of its member agencies started out providing and most still provide residential care to children and youths. For historical reasons, however, it does not have many members in California (only three members as of 1993), a limited number of Catholic agencies, and very few Jewish agencies (none were evident by the names of the listed agencies). Thus I supplemented the NAHSC membership list with the California, Michigan, and Jewish lists. The California list added 90 agencies, the Jewish one 145 agencies, and the Michigan one 13 agencies.

For the international aid and relief agencies I used the membership directory of InterAction, an umbrella association of 146 private, voluntary organizations involved in "disaster relief, refugee protection, assistance and resettlement, long-term sustainable development, educating the American public about the developing world, and public policy and advocacy."[1] In order to increase the pool of religiously based agencies, I also mailed questionnaires to the heads of 28 religiously based agencies that are registered with the State Department's Registry of U.S. Voluntary Agencies and are not members of InterAction.[2] Questionnaires were thereby sent to the heads of a total of 174 agencies. Ninety responded with completed questionnaires for a return rate of 52 percent.

For the private, independent colleges and universities I used the list of independent colleges and universities compiled by Higher Education Planning Services.[3] The questionnaire was mailed to the presidents of the 853 private, independent colleges and universities throughout the United States. Two-year colleges, proprietary institutions, seminaries or theological colleges, and Bible colleges were excluded. Thus the institutions surveyed were all the nonprofit, private colleges and universities offering either four-year baccalaureate programs or baccalaureate and graduate programs. Of the 853 questionnaires mailed out, 390 completed ones were returned, for a return rate of 46 percent.

The questionnaires were mailed out in November 1993 and followed up with a second mailing four to five weeks later to those agencies and institutions that had not responded. However, due to certain logistical limitations I made only one mailing in the case of the members of the Association of Jewish Family and Child Agencies, the thirteen[1] Catholic members of the Michigan Federation of Private Child and Family Agencies, and the twenty-eight religious agencies registered with the State Department's Registry of U.S. Voluntary Agencies. The mailing to the last two groups was made in early 1994. In an attempt to increase the response rate among the heads of the Catholic child service agencies in NAHSC I made a third mailing in February 1994 to the Catholic agencies that had not responded to the first two mailings.

Due to the sensitive nature of many of the questions and some nonprofits' possible fears of law suits or other legal challenges, the survey was an anonymous one. There is no way anyone can identify a returned questionnaire with a specific agency or institution. I kept track of who had responded by having the respondents mail in a postcard, indicating they had filed out the questionnaire and were returning it in a separate envelope.

Given the fairly lengthy questionnaire and the busyness of heads of agencies and colleges and universities—plus the flood of questionnaires I was often informed confront them—the return rate, which hovered around the 50 percent level for all three types of nonprofits, was good.[4]

In order to obtain a clearer idea of whether or not the agencies or institutions whose heads returned completed questionnaires differed significantly from the organizations whose heads did not do so, I made several comparisons between the nonprofit organizations that completed the questionnaires and those that did not do so. In doing so I sought comparisons likely to be as revealing as possible, within the limits of the available data.

First, I compared the geographic regions in which the responding organizations were located with those of all the organizations receiving the questionnaires. The results are given in Table B1. It shows that in the case of all three types of organizations, those whose heads completed the questionnaires were distributed geographically in roughly the same proportions as were all of the organizations receiving the questionnaires.

For the independent colleges and universities I also compared the responding institutions with the nonresponding institutions in terms of their classification according to the Carnegie Classification of Institutions of Higher Education. This widely used scheme classifies colleges and universities "into categories on the basis of the level of degree offered—ranging from prebaccalaureate to the doctorate—and the comprehensiveness of their missions."[5] From Table B2 it is clear that the institutions whose presidents sent in completed questionnaires did not differ greatly in terms of their Carnegie

TABLE B1
Responding Organizations, by Region*

Region***	Child Services**		College/University		Internat'l Aid	
	All agencies	Responding agencies	All colleges	Responding colleges	All agencies	Responding agencies
Northeast	15%	12%	31%	27%	66%	62%
Border	5%	4%	6%	7%	1%	1%
Southeast	15%	17%	16%	15%	9%	7%
Great Lakes	20%	25%	17%	17%	4%	4%
Midwest	11%	11%	13%	17%	3%	6%
West	11%	12%	8%	8%	4%	5%
Pacific	24%	19%	9%	10%	13%	15%
TOTAL	101%	100%	100%	101%	100%	100%
	(N=434)	(N=222)	(N=853)	(N=357)	(N=174)	(N=82)

*Those organizations for which I did not know the region in which they are located have been eliminated from this table.

**The Association of Jewish Family and Child Agencies mailed out the questionnaire to their own member agencies in order to keep their membership list confidential. Thus they could not be included in this table.

***Northeast equals the states of ME, VT, NH, MA, RI, CT, NY, NJ, PA, DE, and MD, and Washington, DC; Border equals the states of WV, KY, TN, and AR; Southeast equals the states of VA, NC, SC, GA, FL, AL, MS, and LA; Great Lakes equals the states of OH, IN, MI, IL, and WI; Midwest equals the states of MN, ND, SD, NE, IA, MO, OK, and KS; West equals the states of MT, ID, WY, CO, UT, NV, TX, NM, and AZ; and Pacific equals the states of CA, OR, WA, AK, and HI.

TABLE B2

Responding and Nonresponding Colleges and Universities by the Carnegie Classification of Institutions of Higher Education*

Classification**	Responded	Did Not Respond
Research Universities I	1%	4%
Research Universities II	1%	1%
Doctorate-Granting Universities I	1%	2%
Doctorate-Granting Universities II	2%	4%
Comprehensive Universities and Colleges I	14%	15%
Comprehensive Universities and Colleges II	22%	18%
Liberal Arts Colleges I	17%	20%
Liberal Arts Colleges II	42%	36%
Total	100%	100%
	(N=335)	(N=526)

*Since the questionnaires were returned anonymously, in determining who had and had not responded I had to depend upon the postcards the respondents mailed in indicating they had sent in the completed questionnaires separately. Some sent in completed questionnaires but not the postcard. I received 386 completed questionnaires back but only 333 postcards. That is why the total give in this table of responding institutions does not match the total given for completed questionnaires. This gap of 53 institutions of course also affects the accuracy of this table.

**The classification scheme used is the Carnegie Classification of Institutions of Higher Education. See The Carnegie Commission, *A Classification of Institutions of Higher Education, 1987 Edition* (Princeton, NJ: Carnegie Foundation for the Advancement of Teaching, 1987).

Classification from the institutions whose presidents did not do so. Among the responding institutions there were somewhat fewer major research and doctoral granting institutions and somewhat greater numbers in the less selective Liberal Arts Colleges II category than was the case for the nonresponding institutions, but the differences were not great. The general picture that emerges from Table B2 gives added confidence in the representativeness of the institutions whose presidents completed the questionnaire.

In regard to the international aid and relief agencies, I had information on the 1992 (and for a few agencies the 1991) budgets of almost all the agencies that received the questionnaire. Thus I could compare the agencies whose heads filled out the questionnaire with all the agencies receiving the questionnaire based on the size of their budgets, a good indication of the overall size and scope of the agencies. Table B3 gives the results of this comparison. The agencies whose heads completed and returned the questionnaires tended to be somewhat larger (as measured by their annual budgets) than all the agencies that received the questionnaire. But the overall differences were not

TABLE B3

Responding and Nonresponding International Aid Agencies
by the Size of Their Annual Budgets

Budget size	All Agencies*	Responding Agencies**
Under $4 million	56%	45%
$5 to $50 million	32%	39%
$50 to $100 million	7%	8%
$100 to $300 million	3%	6%
Over $300 million	2%	2%
Total	100%	100%
	(N=167)	(N=89)

*Data for the agencies receiving the questionnaire were obtained from *InterAction Member Profiles, 1993* (Washington, DC: American Council for Voluntary International Action, 1993) and Agency for International Development, *Voluntary Foreign Aid Programs, 1993* (Washington, DC: Agency for International Development, Office of Private and Voluntary Cooperation, 1993). Six agencies that received the questionnaire were not included in this table because budget figures were not given for them in the above references.

**The data for the agencies that responded were taken from the completed questionnaires. One agency did not respond to the budget question and thus is not included in this table.

great. Table B3 gives added confidence that the responding agencies did not differ greatly from those that did not respond.

Comparing the responding and nonresponding child services agencies on characteristics other than region posed some difficulties. I did not have any information other than the names and addresses of the member agencies and their directors for three of the four lists I used: the California Association of Services for Children, the Association of Jewish Family and Child Agencies, and the Michigan Federation of Private Child and Family Agencies. Thus their members could not be included in any comparisons. However, I did have some additional information on the members of the third and largest of the three lists that were used: that of the National Association of Homes and Services for Children (NAHSC). Thus Table B4 shows the size of the agencies as measured by the number of full-time equivalent employees for the agencies whose heads responded and those of all the members of NAHSC. (Unfortunately, this comparison is further weakened by 17 percent of the NAHSC members not reporting on the number of their full-time

TABLE B4
Responding Child Service Agencies and All NAHSC Members
by the Number of Full-Time Equivalent Employees

Full-Time Equivalent Employees	All NAHSC Members*	All Responding Child Service Agencies**
Less than 14	11%	16%
15 to 49	34%	28%
50 to 99	28%	25%
100 to 199	18%	19%
More than 200	9%	12%
Total	100%	100%
	(N=275)	(N=285)

*The information concerning the members of the National Association of Homes and Services for Children (NAHSC) was obtained from National Association of Homes and Services for Children, *Who's Who in NAHSC, 1993-94* (Washington, DC: National Association of Homes and Services for Children, 1993). Fifty-six of the 331 listed member agencies did not give the number of their full-time equivalent employees and were not included in this table.

**The data for the agencies that responded were taken from the completed questionnaires. One agency did not respond to the question on the number of full-time equivalent employees and is not included in this table.

equivalent employees in the source I used.) Keeping the above limitations in mind, Table B4 reveals the responding child service agencies were very close to all NAHSC members for whom information was available on their numbers of employees. A few more responding agencies fell into the smallest category of fourteen or fewer employees, but overall the size of the NAHSC agencies (as measured by full-time employees) was very similar to those of the agencies that responded to the questionnaire. If one combines the "Less than 14" and the "15 to 49" employee categories, one finds in them 45 percent of all NAHSC members and 44 percent of all responding agencies. These findings must be taken with caution, but it is of some note that what comparative measure it was able to develop points in the direction of the responding agencies being representative of all the agencies receiving the questionnaire.

It is important to note, however, that only in the case of colleges and universities did the pool to which the questionnaires were sent include all the organizations of that type. In the case of both the child service agencies and the international aid agencies membership lists of several umbrella associations constituted my initial pool of agencies. This method assured diverse, national pools of agencies, but ones that clearly left out many agencies that are not members of the associations whose lists I used. My basic goal—and one that seems to have been achieved—was to obtain broad, diverse, national samplings of nonprofit organizations of the three targeted types, not necessarily to obtain samplings precisely representative of all nonprofit organizations of the three types. Measured by region, size, age, types of programs, religious-secular nature, and a number of other characteristics, many of which are not reported here, the study was largely successful in this goal. Even though I often cannot with confidence project the exact proportion of all nonprofits of a certain type with a certain characteristic or experience from the nonprofits of that type that returned the questionnaire, yet it is clear the organizations completing the questionnaires do not represent only a narrow slice of the nonprofit organizations of the three types surveyed. One finds among them the wide diversity of organizational characteristics that one finds in the broader American society.

Notes

1. *InterAction Member Profiles, 1993* (Washington, DC: American Council for Voluntary International Action, 1993), vii.

2. See Agency for International Development, *Voluntary Foreign Aid Programs, 1993* (Washington, DC: Agency for International Development, Office of Private and Voluntary Cooperation, 1993), 11–58.

3. Higher Education Planning Services of Lake Forest, Illinois, ought not to be confused with Higher Education Publications in Falls Church, Virginia. Higher Education Planning services is largely a venture by Dr. Robert T. Sandin, who periodically publishes "HEPS Profiles of Independent Higher Education" and has developed a comprehensive database on independent colleges and universities in the United States, with special attention paid to ones with a religious base or history. Due to the comprehensive nature of his database and information Sandin has developed in regard to the religious nature of institutions of higher education, I judged his list the best for my purposes. Since his list was several years old as of the fall of 1993, the names of the college and university presidents were checked and updated by the names given in Mary Pat Rodenhouse, ed., *1994 Higher Education Directory* (Falls Church, VA: Higher Education Publications, 1993).

4. For comparison purposes, the 1978 Notre Dame Study of religiously affiliated colleges and universities had a questionnaire return rate of 28.2 percent, Stephen

Sweeny's more targeted 1991 study of Catholic colleges sponsored by women religious had a return rate of 78 percent, and Bernard Couglin's early 1960s study of religiously based social service agencies had a 37.5 percent return rate. See Edward McGlynn Gaffney Jr. and Philip R. Moots, *Government and Campus: Federal Regulation of Religiously Affiliated Higher Education* (Notre Dame, IN: University of Notre Dame Press, 1982), 9; Stephen J. Sweeny, *State Financial Assistance and Selected Elements Influencing Religious Character in Catholic Colleges Sponsored by Women Religious* (Ph.D. dissertation, School of Education, Health, Nursing, and Arts Professions, New York University, 1991), 56; and Bernard J. Coughlin, *Church and State in Social Welfare* (New York: Columbia University Press, 1965), 151.

5. See the Carnegie Commission, *A Classification of Institutions of Higher Education, 1987 Edition* (Princeton, NJ: Carnegie Foundation for the Advancement of Teaching, 1987), 7.

Appendix C

The Religious Practices Scale

The heads of each of the three types of nonprofit organizations that had indicated their organizations had a continuing religious orientation were asked whether or not their organizations engage in a number of practices in which their organizations' religious orientations could lead them to engage. The questionnaire for child service agencies listed fourteen practices such agencies potentially could engage in because of their religious orientation, the questionnaire for the colleges and universities listed sixteen, and the one for international aid agencies listed nine. In addition, the head of each organization was given the opportunity to list any other practices not included in the list with which they were presented. From out of the responses to these items I placed each respondent on a "Religious Practices Scale."

The scale was designed to measure the degree to which the religious orientation of an organization—as perceived and reported by its chief executive officer—permeated or was diffused throughout it and its various activities and programs, in distinction from a religious orientation that essentially was something added onto and separate or distinct from the other activities and programs of the organization. Thus I did not want to weigh positive responses to the various religious practices equally, since they clearly were not of equal weight in terms of the degree to which the religious orientation pervaded or permeated the organization. For example, I weighed only hiring staff in keeping with an organization's religious orientation the highest, since if religion is truly to permeate an organization an essential precondition is to have staff members of that religious orientation. In contrast, I weighed such practices as having religious symbols or pictures in one's facilities or making informal references to religious ideas at a lower level, since they could exist in a situation where religion was essentially a separate, distinct "add-on" to essentially secular programs or activities. I also weighed practices with a compulsory nature more heavily than ones of a voluntary nature, since the more voluntary practices can be ignored at will whereas compulsory activities would necessarily permeate the organization.

I gave one to five points for each religious practice in which an organization head indicated his or her organization engaged. I then totaled up the points for each organization and divided the organizations into three groups (or, in the case of international aid agencies due to the small number of agencies, two groups), based on their total scores. Following are—for each of the three types of organizations—the religious practices from which their heads could choose, the number of agency heads who chose that practice, the points assigned each practice, and the scores that resulted in an organization being ranked high, medium or low on the resulting scales (or either high or low in the case of international aid agencies).

CHILD SERVICE AGENCIES

Religiously motivated practices	No. citing	Points assigned
• A paid chaplain on staff	48	2
• A volunteer chaplain on staff	22	1
• Religious symbols or pictures in your facilities	103	1
• Voluntary religious activities	109	1
• Required religious activities	51	2
• Spoken prayer at meals	93	2
• Informal references to religious ideas by staff in contacts with clients	100	1
• A generalized spirit or atmosphere of service/concern/love among your staff	131	1
• Only hiring staff in agreement with your religious orientation	25	5
• Giving preference in hiring staff to persons in agreement with your religious orientation	41	4
• Efforts to encourage clients to make personal religious commitments	48	3
• Taking religion into account in making foster care or adoption placements	44	2
• Giving preference in accepting clients to those in agreement with your religious orientation	12	2
• Other practices your agency engages in that are motivated by your religious orientation. Please specify.	28	1
TOTAL		26

Religious practices scale for child service agencies:
    Low   0 to 5 points (37 agencies)
    Medium   6 to 12 points (68 agencies)
    High   13 to 26 points (41 agencies)

COLLEGES AND UNIVERSITIES

Religiously motivated practices	No. citing	Points assigned
• A chapel or other center for worship on your campus	255	1
• Religious symbols (such as crosses or religious pictures) on your campus	217	1
• Voluntary chapel services	205	1
• Compulsory chapel services	79	2
• Other voluntary religious exercises (such as Bible studies or prayer meetings) organized by the college or university	243	1
• Other compulsory religious exercises organized by the college or university	23	2
• Encouraging faculty to integrate religious concepts and ideals into their courses and research	161	2
• Taking your religious beliefs into account in establishing policies for student behavior	229	1
• A spirit of service/concern/love among your faculty and staff	261	1
• Mandatory religion or theology courses	217	2
• Only hiring faculty in agreement with your religious orientation	79	5
• Giving preference in hiring faculty in agreement with your religious orientation	72	4
• Admitting only students in agreement with your religious orientation	9	3
• Giving preference in admitting students to those in agreement with your religious orientation	42	2
• Efforts to encourage students to make personal religious commitments	163	3
• Other practices your institution engages in that are Motivated by your religious orientation. Please specify.	61	1
TOTAL		32

Religious practices scale for colleges and universities:
    Low   0 to 7 points (46 institutions)
    Medium 8 to 15 points (126 institutions)
    High   16 to 32 points (102 institutions)

INTERNATIONAL AID AGENCIES

	No. citing	Points
• A religious affiliation or mission clearly reflected in your name or logo	26	1
• Voluntary worship services or other religious activities integrated into your relief and/or development programs	10	1
• Informal references to religious ideas by staff in contacts with persons being served	17	1
• A spirit of service/concern/love among your staff	28	1
• Only hiring staff in agreement with your religious orientation	7	5
• Giving preference in hiring staff to those in agreement with your religious orientation	8	4
• Making efforts to encourage persons being served to make personal religious commitments	7	3
• Overt religious activities sponsored by an associated organization that parallels your relief and development efforts	7	2
• Helping in the construction of centers for worship or religiously based education	5	2
• Other practices in which your agency engages that are motivated by your religious orientation. Please specify.	15	1
TOTAL		21

Religious practices scale for international aid agencies:
    Low   0 to 6 points (20 agencies)
    High   7 to 20 points (13 agencies)

Selected Bibliography

Books:

Adams, Arlin M., and Charles J. Emmerich. *A Nation Dedicated to Religious Liberty*. Philadelphia: University of Pennsylvania Press, 1990.

Beaver, R. Pierce. *Church and State, and the American Indians*. St. Louis, MO: Concordia, 1966.

Bellah, Robert N. *The Broken Covenant: American Civil Religion in Time of Trial*. New York: Seabury, 1975.

Bellah, Robert N. and Frederick E. Greenspahn, eds. *Uncivil Religion: Interreligious Hostility in America*. New York: Crossroads, 1987.

Berger, Peter L., and Richard John Neuhaus. *To Empower People: The Role of Mediating Structures in Public Policy*. Washington, DC: American Enterprise Institute, 1977.

Carlson-Thies, Stanley W., and James W. Skillen, eds. *Welfare in America: Christian Perspectives on a Policy in Crisis*. Grand Rapids, MI: Eerdmans, 1996.

Carter, Stephen L. *The Culture of Disbelief*. New York: Basic Books, 1993.

Coleman, James S., Thomas Hoffer, and Sally Kilgore. *High School Achievement: Public, Catholic, and Private Schools Compared*. New York: Basic Books, 1982.

Coleman, James S., and Thomas Hoffer. *Public and Private High Schools*. New York: Basic Books, 1987.

Coughlin, Bernard J. *Church and State in Social Welfare*. New York: Columbia University Press, 1965.

Chubb, John E., and Terry M. Moe. *Politics, Markets, and America's Schools*. Washington, DC: Brookings Institution, 1990.

Gaffney, Edward McGlynn, Jr., and Philip R. Moots, *Government and Campus: Federal Regulation of Religiously Affiliated Higher Education*. Notre Dame, IN: University of Notre Dame Press, 1982.

Garland, Diana S. Richmond. *Church Agencies: Caring for Children and Families in Crisis*. Washington, DC: Child Welfare League, 1994.

Gelen, Ted. G., and Clyde Wilcox. *Public Attitudes Toward Church and State*. Armonk, NY: M. E. Sharpe, 1995.

Glenn, Charles Leslie. *The Myth of the Common School*. Amherst, MA: University of Massachusetts Press, 1987.

Guinness, Os. *The American Hour*. New York: Free Press, 1993.

Hodgkinson, Virginia Ann, Murray S. Weitzman, Christopher M. Toppe, and Stephen M. Noga. *Nonprofit Almanac, 1992–93*. San Francisco: Jossey-Bass, 1992.

Hunter, James Davison, and Os Guinness, eds. *Articles of Faith, Articles of Peace*. Washington, DC: Brookings, 1990.

Hunter, James Davison. *Before the Shooting Begins: Searching for Democracy in America's Culture War*. New York: Free Press, 1994.

———. *Culture Wars: The Struggle to Define America*. New York: Basic Books, 1991.

Jeavons, Thomas H. *When the Bottom Line Is Faithfulness*. Bloomington, IN: Indiana University Press, 1994.

Kaestle, Carl F. *Pillars of the Republic: Common Schools and American Society, 1780–1860*. New York: Hill and Wang, 1983.

Kramer, Ralph. *Voluntary Agencies in the Welfare State*. Berkeley, CA: University of California Press, 1981.

Marsden, George M. *The Soul of the American University: From Protestant Establishment to Established Nonbelief*. New York: Oxford University Press, 1994.

Monsma, Stephen V. *Positive Neutrality*. Westport, CT: Greenwood, 1993 and Grand Rapids, MI: Bakers, 1995.

Mouw, Richard J., and Sander Griffioen. *Pluralisms and Horizons*. Grand Rapids, MI: Eerdmans, 1993.

Nichols, J. Bruce. *The Uneasy Alliance: Religion, Refugee Work, and U.S. Foreign Policy*. New York: Oxford University Press, 1988.

Olasky, Marvin. *The Tragedy of American Compassion*. Washington, DC: Regnery Gateway, 1992.

O'Neill, Michael, *The Third America: The Emergence of the Nonprofit Sector in the United States.* San Francisco: Jossey-Bass, 1989.

Osborne, David, and Ted Gaebler. *Reinventing Government.* New York: Penguin, 1992.

Powell, Walter W., ed. *The Nonprofit Sector.* New Haven, CT: Yale University Press, 1987.

Regan, Richard J. *The Moral Dimension of Politics.* New York: Oxford University Press, 1986.

Reichley, A. James. *Religion in American Public Life.* Washington, DC: Brookings Institution, 1985.

Salamon, Lester M. *America's Nonprofit Sector.* New York: The Foundation Center, 1992.

————. *Partners in Public Service.* Baltimore, MD: The Johns Hopkins University Press, 1995.

Sandin, Robert T. *The Search for Excellence: The Christian College in an Age of Education Competition.* Macon, GA: Mercer University Press, 1982.

Skillen, James W. *Recharging the American Experiment.* Grand Rapids, MI: Baker, 1994.

Smith, Steven Rathgeb, and Michael Lipsky. *Nonprofits for Hire: The Welfare State in the Age of Contracting.* Cambridge, MA: Harvard University Press, 1993.

Sweeny, Stephen J. *State Financial Assistance and Selected Elements Influencing Religious Character in Catholic Colleges Sponsored by Women Religious.* Ph.D. dissertation, School of Education, Health, Nursing, and Arts Professions, New York University, 1991.

Tocqueville, Alexis de. *Democracy in America.* Vol. 2. Ed. and trans., Phillips Bradley. New York: Vintage Books, 1990.

Tyack, David, and Elisabeth Hansot. *Managers of Virtue: Public School Leadership in America, 1820–1980.* New York: Basic Books, 1982.

Van Til, Jon. *Mapping the Third Sector: Voluntarism in a Changing Social Economy.* New York: The Foundation Center, 1988.

Wald, Kenneth D. *Religion and Politics in the United States.* 2nd ed. Washington, DC: Congressional Quarterly, 1992.

Weber, Paul J., and Dennis Gilbert. *Private Churches and Public Money: Church-Government Fiscal Relations.* Westport, CT: Greenwood, 1981.

White, Ronald C., and Albright G. Zimmerman, eds. *An Unsettled Arena: Religion and the Bill of Rights.* Grand Rapids, MI: Eerdmans, 1990.

Wuthnow, Robert, and Virginia A. Hodgkinson. *Faith and Philanthropy in America: Exploring the Role of Religion in America's Voluntary Sector.* San Francisco: Jossey-Bass, 1990.

Scholarly articles

Carroll, William A. "The Constitution, the Supreme Court, and Religion." *American Political Science Review* 61 (1967): 657–674.

Chopko, Mark E. "Don't Exclude the Churches." *The National Law Journal* (February 29, 1988): 13–14.

———. "Religious Access to Public Programs and Governmental Funding." *George Washington Law Review* 60 (1992): 645–71.

DiMaggio, Paul J., and Walter W. Powell. "The Iron Cage Revisited: Institutional Isomorphism and Collective Rationality in Organizational Fields." *American Sociological Review* 48 (1983): 147–60.

Esbeck, Carl H. "Government Regulation of Religiously Based Social Services: The First Amendment Considerations." *Hastings Constitutional Law Quarterly* 19 (1992): 343–412.

———. "A Restatement of the Supreme Court's Law of Religious Freedom: Coherence, Conflict, or Chaos?" *Notre Dame Law Review* 70 (1995): 581–650.

———. "A Typology of Church-State Relations in Current American Thought." In *Religion, Public Life, and the American Polity,* Luis E. Lugo, ed. Knoxville, TN: University of Tennessee Press, 1994.

Gedicks, Frederick Mark. "Toward a Constitutional Jurisprudence of Religious Group Rights." *Wisconsin Law Review* 1989 (1989): 99–167.

Glendon, Mary Ann. "Law, Communities, and the Religious Freedom Language of the Constitution." *George Washington University Law Review.* 72 (1992): 672–84.

Laycock, Douglas. "Formal, Substantive, and Disaggregated Neutrality Toward Religion." *DePaul Law Review* 39 (1990): 993–1018.

Manion, Maureen. "The Impact of State Aid on Sectarian Higher Education: The Case of New York State." *Review of Politics* 48 (1986): 264–88.

McConnell, Michael W. "Academic Freedom in Religious Colleges and Universities," *Law and Contemporary Problems* 53 (1990): 303–24.

———. "Taking Religious Freedom Seriously." *First Things* 1 (May 1990): 30–35.

Murray, John Courtney. "Law or Preposessions?" *Law and Contemporary Problems* 14 (1949): 23–43.

Netting, F. Ellen. "Secular and Religious Funding of Church-Related Agencies." *Social Service Review* 56 (1982): 586–604.

Pickrell, Thomas W., and Mitchell A. Horwich. " 'Religion as an Engine of Civil Policy': A Comment on the First Amendment Limitations on the Church-State Partnership in the Social Welfare Field," *Law and Contemporary Problems* 44 (1981): 111–42.

Salamon, Lester M. "Nonprofit Organizations: The Lost Opportunity." In *The Reagan Record*, John L. Palmer and Isabel V. Sawhill, eds. Cambridge, MA: Ballinger, 1984.

———. "Rethinking Public Management: Third-Party Government and the Changing Forms of Government Action." *Public Policy* 29 (1981): 255–75.

Tyack, David. "The Kingdom of God and the Common School," *Harvard Educational Review* 36 (1966): 447–69.

Index

About the Author

Stephen V. Monsma is professor of political science and chair of the social science division at Pepperdine University in Malibu, California. A widely published scholar in the area of religion and politics, his books include *Positive Neutrality: Letting Religious Freedom Ring* (Greenwood Press, 1993), *Pursuing Justice in a Sinful World* (Eerdmans, 1984), and forthcoming from Rowman & Littlefield, *The Challenge of Pluralism: Church and State in Five Democracies*, with J. Christopher Soper.